This publication was made possible by
a research education grant from
Ross Laboratories
Division of Abbott Laboratories

John Dobbing (Ed.)

Brain, Behaviour, and Iron in the Infant Diet

With 27 Figures

Springer-Verlag
London Berlin Heidelberg New York
Paris Tokyo Hong Kong

John Dobbing, DSc, FRCP, FRCPath
Emeritus Professor of Child Growth and Development,
Department of Child Health, University of Manchester,
Oxford Road, Manchester M13 9PT, UK

ISBN 3-540-19605-6 Springer-Verlag Berlin Heidelberg New York
ISBN 0-387-19605-6 Springer-Verlag New York Berlin Heidelberg

British Library Cataloguing in Publication Data
Dobbing, John, *1922–*
  Brain behaviour and iron in the infant diet.
  1. Man. Iron
  I. Title
  612.3924
  ISBN 3-540-19605-6

Library of Congress Cataloging-in-Publication Data
Brain, behaviour, and iron in the infant diet/John Dobbing (ed.),
p. cm.
Includes bibliographical references.
ISBN 0-387-19605-6 (U.S.:alk,   paper)
1. Iron deficiency diseases in infants.   2. Brain–Growth.   3. Infants–Development.
1. Dobbing, John.
[DNLM: 1. Brain–drug effects. 2. Child Behavior–drug effects. 3. Child
Nutrition.   4. Infant Nutrition.   5. Iron–deficiency.   WS 120 B8135]
  RJ399.I75B73 1990
  618.92'8–dc20
  DNLM/DLC
  for Library of Congress   90-9577
                                                                          CIP

Typeset by MJS Publications, Buntingford, Herts
Printed by R. R. Donnelley & Sons Company, Virginia, USA
2128/3916-543210 Printed on acid-free paper

Preface

This monograph is concerned with the important question whether a reduced supply of dietary iron in infancy may result in impaired or altered brain growth, or in temporary or permanent deficits in higher mental function. The evidence that this may be so is not complete, but it already seems to be sufficiently good to make preventive action desirable.

Iron deficiency is very widespread in the world, in both privileged and underprivileged societies, often independently of general nutritional status. The means of prevention are readily available and cheap. In such circumstances, which have many parallels in clinical practice, doctors will rightly decide not to wait for complete proof before acting in what they believe to be the best interests of their patients and their community.

It will be surprising for some that the proposition is so resistant to absolute proof, but in the laboratory, in experimental animals, and, much more importantly, in field investigations in human communities, it is exceptionally complex, multifactorial and multidisciplinary. As will be seen, it is in the nature of such subjects that there may never be total proof.

We have compiled the present monograph in a rather unusual way which is particularly suitable for such difficult questions. The result makes no attempt to arrive at a clear answer, since that quite simply is not available to us. Neither does it attempt a consensus, something which is still equally elusive. What we have done is to set out the available evidence, and to discuss it extensively with the help of experts from the many disciplines concerned, so that you, the reader, will be able to come to an informed, personal opinion.

Each Chapter was sent to each of the other eight authors as well as to four other participating scientists. All were given the task of writing considered Commentaries on every Chapter. These were then sent to everyone else taking part. We then met together for three days of open-ended, informal argument and discussion of the outstanding points.

As a result the authors of the Chapters made modifications to their manuscripts, sometimes quite extensively, but in such a way that the author remained the sole judge of what would eventually be published under his or her name. Thus is can be said that all the Chapters have been reviewed by no fewer than 12 peers: a trial which was far more testing than the normal procedure for judging contributions to the usual scientific journals, and infinitely more so than is applied to Chapters in the customary "books of meetings". The resulting Chapters have therefore been refined to an extent which is not revealed to the reader, although it will be readily acknowledged by the authors.

The Commentary sections after each Chapter are not mere transcripts of our discussions, which were unrecorded and private to us. Instead they are well-considered, written, referenced Commentaries, dealing mostly with aspects of the subject which remained open. These Commentaries are often as important as the Chapters they accompany.

The "physical" development of the human brain continues at considerable speed well beyond the sixth postnatal month, the time when it used to be thought it was reasonably mature. Some of its most important features, for example the astonishing increase in dendritic complexity and the achievement of synaptic connectivity, continue very rapidly at least until the second human birthday. Its most distinctively human functions, those concerned with intellect and personality, continue to develop for many childhood years beyond that. All these aspects of development, both physical and behavioural, are particularly vulnerable to environmental deprivation or hostility at that time; but, what is even more important, the periods during which such growth and development are taking place are times of immense *opportunity* for us to *promote* good brain growth and to lay sound intellectual foundations. This is a much more positive "take home" message than that of mere vulnerability; and, as will be seen in our book, promotion of continuous good iron nutritional status, by very cheap and simple means, as well as the ensuring of optimum general nutrition throughout these early months and years, may well be an important part of this policy of wanting to do the best for our children.

We would like to acknowledge the enormous help we have received from Ross Laboratories, without which our endeavour would not have been possible. The Editor would also like to express his profound gratitude to all those who have contributed to the book. They had to work much harder than for most other comparable ventures. They responded valiantly to the many, sometimes importunate, demands made on them, and I hope they are happy with the result. He also acknowledges the efforts and continuous support throughout of his wife, Dr Jean Sands.

St Julien de Cénac, November 1989   John Dobbing

Contents

Chapter 9. Prevention of Iron Deficiency Anemia:
Iron Fortification of Infant Foods
Howard A. Pearson 177

Contributors

Peter R. Dallman, MD
Professor of Pediatrics, Department of Pediatrics M–650, University
of California, School of Medicine, San Francisco, CA 94143, USA

John Dobbing, DSc, FRCP, FRCPath
Emeritus Professor of Child Growth and Development, Department
of Child Health, University of Manchester, The Medical School,
Oxford Road, Manchester M13 9PT, UK

Barbara Felt, MD
Fellow in Behavioral Pediatrics, Case Western Reserve University
School of Medicine and Rainbow Babies' and Children's Hospital,
2074 Abingdon Road, Cleveland, Ohio 44106, USA

Laurence Finberg, MD
Professor and Chairman, Department of Pediatrics, State University
of New York, Health Science Center at Brooklyn, 450 Clarkson
Avenue, Brooklyn, New York 11203, USA

Edward C. Larkin, MD
Professor of Medicine and Pathology, University of California,
School of Medicine, Davis, California; Chief, Hematopathology
Section, Martinez Veterans Administration Medical Center, 150
Muir Road, Martinez, CA 94553, USA

Betsy Lozoff, MD
Associate Professor of Pediatrics, Case Western Reserve University
School of Medicine and Rainbow Babies' and Children's Hospital,
2074 Abingdon Road, Cleveland, Ohio 44106, USA

Yvonne A. Parks, MB, ChB, MRCP
Senior Registrar, Community Health and Handicap Services, 41 Old
Dover Road, Canterbury, UK

Howard A. Pearson, MD
Professor of Pediatrics, Yale University School of Medicine, 333
Cedar Street, PO Box 3333, New Haven, CT 06510–8064, USA

G. Ananda Rao, PhD
Senior Investigator, Department of Pathology, 113 Veterans
Administration Medical Center, 150 Muir Road, Martinez, CA
94553, USA

Jean A. Sands, PhD
Departments of Child Health and Pathology, University of
Manchester, The Medical School, Oxford Road, Manchester M13
9PT, UK

James L. Smart, PhD, DSc
Senior Lecturer in Growth and Development, Department of Child
Health, University of Manchester, The Medical School, Oxford
Road, Manchester M13 9PT, UK

Tomas Walter, MD
Associate Professor and Head, Hematology Unit, Instituto de
Nutricion y Tecnologia de los Alimentos, Casilla 15138, Santiago 11,
Chile

Brian Wharton, MD, FRCP, FRCPE, DCH
Rank Professor of Human Nutrition, University of Glasgow,
Yorkhill Hospital, Glasgow G3 8SJ, UK

Schlomo Yehuda, PhD
Professor and Director, Psychopharmacology Laboratory,
Department of Psychology, Bar Ilan University, Ramat Gan 52 100,
Tel Aviv, Israel

Ray Yip, MD, MPH
Medical Epidemiologist, Division of Nutrition, Center for Chronic
Disease Prevention and Health Promotion, Centers for Disease
Control, Atlanta, GA 30333, USA

Moussa B. H. Youdim, PhD
Finkelstein Professor of Life Sciences, Department of
Pharmacology, The B. Rappaport Family Medical Sciences Building
Technion, Efron Street, PO Box 9697, Haifa 31 096, Israel

Chapter 1

Vulnerable Periods in Developing Brain

John Dobbing

It is now quite clear that the process of normal development of the brain is vulnerable to adverse environmental influences well beyond the teratological period of classical embryogenesis in the first trimester of human gestation [1]. This Chapter will contain a general and historical analysis of that concept. It will describe how even relatively minor adversity can sometimes affect the physical growth and development of the brain in the later part of human gestation and well into the first years of postnatal life. This is altogether apart from the better known developmental neuropathologies of damage, or lesions, which can be produced by such severely noxious events as hypoxia, hypoglycaemia and intraventricular haemorrhage.

From the outset it is important to spell out the corollary of this meaning of vulnerability, which is that it leads to a more positive conclusion: the need for the active promotion of optimal brain development, beyond the mere prevention of harm, i.e. the positive mobilization of factors in the environment throughout this whole period which are supportive of normal, optimal developmental processes in the brain. The most effective of such measures for the promotion of later psychological and intellectual well-being may well be environmental enrichment and stimulation, especially in the sense of a normal, caring mother–infant relationship, rather than any more physical influence on brain growth. A major non-behavioural influence is adequate nutrition; and, for reasons which will be explained, this means optimal nutrition throughout the whole complex series of developmental processes which unfold in the nervous system throughout gestation but, even more particularly, since they are more at risk, in the early and later postnatal period. It will be seen that infant feeding is important for the brain, not only in the immediate first few postnatal months, but also during the later processes of weaning and the gradual adaptation of the diet from that required by the neonate to the very different nutritional needs of the older child.

The other Chapters in this monograph will discuss the possible specific role of iron in this context, certainly an exciting speculation which we cannot ignore. It is now much less of a speculation than, for example, the older Woosterian doctrine of the contribution made by fish to intelligence, a superstition which has been much more widespread in the world, from western Europe to China, and for far longer than was probably appreciated by P. G. Wodehouse. Essential fatty acid lipid biochemists have much more recently promoted fish for the same purpose from an allegedly more scientific base [e.g. 2].

Paediatric interest in the brain, apart from the purely academic, stems either from its neurological or its supposed behavioural functions. These are described as "neurobehavioural" by those for whom the connection between the two is assumed or clear. Although such a link is likely, and although we know, pragmatically, many ways in which molecules can influence behaviour, and in which ablation or stimulation of specific brain regions can also do so, any really coherent and detailed link between brain structure and higher mental function is still largely speculative, in spite of an ardent and continuing search for it by neurobiologists. In paediatrics the brain's known neurological functions are involved in much physical handicap, but the physical basis in the brain of most mental handicap is virtually unknown. We know, for example, that Down's syndrome and other chromosomal anomalies, as well as most untreated inborn errors of metabolism, can be associated with profound mental retardation, and that true microcephaly [see 3] is invariably so; but we have no understanding whatever of the mechanism, probably because we have no idea what to look for. Still less can we describe those much smaller apparent deficits in intellect, on the scale usually associated with infant undernutrition [4], in cellular, structural or metabolic terms.

Similarly, the proposition that the brain is the organ of thought, although obviously acceptable, is still scientifically an almost unsupported belief. Just as far from reality, surprisingly, is any pretence that the features of developing behaviour can be convincingly related in any detail to the physical development of the nervous system.

A clearer account of the possible mechanisms responsible for behavioural changes following exposure to, or shortage of, dietary substances, is sometimes proposed by pharmacologists. The effects on behaviour of anaesthetic substances, alcohol or caffeine, for example, are unequivocal; and they lend themselves to physiological investigation at a molecular, cellular or subcellular level. At another level psychotherapeutic agents can be similarly investigated. The further enticing proposition that normal dietary molecules, and the degrees of shortage or excess commonly found in human communities, can influence behaviour and can be "explained" in similar pharmacological terms is irresistible for some; but the smaller and more subtle the scale of behavioural effects, and the inevitably speculative nature of their possible mechanisms, demand a much higher level of proof [5,6]. This is an area much less amenable to proof than that required for the very obvious effects of drugs. The literature, including this review, abounds with speculations that such-and-such a belief "may" be well founded: an incontrovertible statement, since almost anything "may" be so.

These seemingly nihilistic remarks are partly in order to counterbalance the current widespread assumption in neuroscience that simply because a change can be demonstrated, by laboratory experiment, in the detailed chemical composition or metabolism or histological structure of the brain, that it inevitably matters to higher mental function [7]. A direct behavioural effect is only likely if it, and no other, can be shown to be causally related to the environmental change. This is much more difficult than is commonly supposed. The mere hypothesis of mechanism, derived from a selective review of the neurobiological literature, is no substitute for the truth, however exciting or however necessary it may be for scientific progress. It has become fashionable, in "breakthrough" biomedical science, to work from laboratory-based hypotheses and postulates towards what *ought* to be the result in real life, when it is usually more illuminating to begin with the real life phenomenon and then use laboratory science to seek the mechanism. In a sense the mechanism is much less important (except for the laboratory technician) unless knowledge of it leads to useful intervention; but such is our fascination with our laboratory skills that findings on the bench have almost come to predict what *ought* to happen, rather than to explain what has. There are now so many research papers (see *Current Contents* every week) that there is no hypothesis that need go unsupported if the evidence is sought sufficiently selectively.

Thus the bridge between neuroscience and behavioural science is simply not yet there, or is very flimsy. To cross it in our arguments is therefore dangerous, and risks misleading our less well-instructed fellow citizens, as well as those with a vested interest, either in politics or commerce, who are not as interested as we are in the discussion itself and do not appreciate the hazards. The latter really want to know with certainty, and are disappointed in, and may well reject, our prevarication. This does not relieve us of our responsibilities.

Vulnerable periods in the development of the brain can be demonstrated convincingly, and are no longer in the realms of hypothesis, but they still cannot be assumed to have their direct correlates in behaviour, especially in the light of the very crude parameters which are so far amenable to measurement. A parallel endeavour by behavioural scientists to investigate the topic of vulnerability is justified [6], not because their observations can be causally correlated with the neurobiological findings, nor need they be, but because they are important, even more directly so than the biochemistry and the anatomy, and there may one day be discernible causal links.

Possible Effects of Undernutrition on the Developing Brain

Around the turn of the present century nutritionists and others were driven to investigate the possible effects of undernutrition on the developing brain, probably by being daily witness to starvation and poverty in sections of their own contemporary society. Many in the last few decades have been similarly driven by a greater awareness of similar grinding poverty in so-called developing countries (a falsely comforting expression, since so many of them are not). In the early decades of this century elegant large-scale experiments on the effects of undernutrition on the developing brain were performed, using growing rats, and the opportunity was occasionally taken to examine the brains of animals who had died of prolonged total inanition as adults. Surprisingly, in neither developmental nor in the most severe adult undernutrition, such as starvation unto death, were any significant changes found in the gross composition of the brain, in spite of very clear alterations in the weight, histology and chemical composition of virtually all the other organ systems.

These experiments led to the concept of "brain sparing", renamed more recently "relative brain sparing", more in line with the "relative" sparing of, for example, the fetus during maternal undernutrition. The reason behind this important change in attitude came from the realization in the late 1950s that the developing brain was indeed vulnerable to undernutrition during the period which became known as the brain growth spurt, even though it remained much less affected in crude, quantitative terms than other tissues. The vulnerability of the brain growth spurt was missed by the earlier experimenters because they found it technically much more convenient to manipulate the dietary intake of weanling and post-weanling rats than of suckling pups. In this way they missed the brain growth spurt which, in that species, occurs during the suckling period of the first three postnatal weeks (Fig. 1.1). Soon after weaning the rat brain rapidly reaches a high degree of maturity, and assumes the invulnerability of the mature organ, even though most of the bodily growth spurt has yet to occur. The invulnerability of the adult brain is nevertheless astonishing, just as is the remarkable phenomenon of "relative" brain sparing in development. Sparing, however, is not by any means total, and it may be that the extent to which the developing physical brain is affected might, after all, be of greater functional importance.

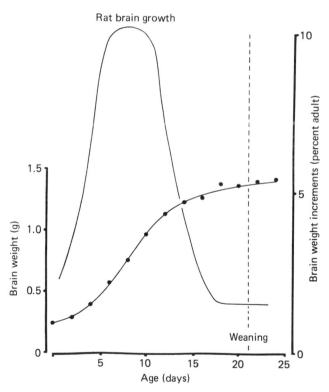

Fig. 1.1. The brain growth spurt illustrated as a characteristic sigmoid weight curve.

This is an area in which the pharmacologist is found in a different world from the developmental neurobiologist. It is, of course, easy to exaggerate the difference, since there is considerable overlap; but the clear and gross effects of many drugs on the maturing or adult brain are in marked contrast to its comparative immunity, structurally and in gross compositional terms, even to severe starvation.

For the experimentalist the finding of the special vulnerability of the developing brain during its growth spurt began with the classical experimental design of Widdowson and McCance [7], in which small and large litters were created at birth by random cross fostering, maintained until weaning, and then usually fed *ad libitum* until maturity. In this way the members of artificially large suckling litters were non-specifically restricted in their milk intake, and hence in their growth, throughout the important first three weeks. They could be compared at the time of weaning and throughout later life with their "controls" from small litters fed *ad libitum*. This classic experimental design is also important for the light it shed on the long-term effects of early undernutrition on bodily and other organ system growth, and there has still been no satisfactory explanation, nor indeed much investigation of these [8,9].

Since then several other experimental methods of varying the diet during the suckling period have been devised, the theoretically most important, from the point of view of brain and behaviour research being the artificial feeding of rat

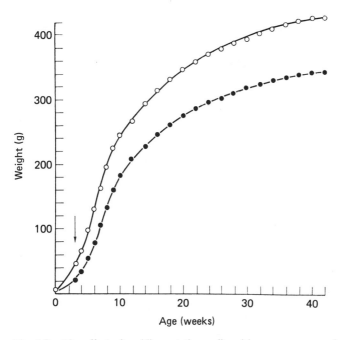

Fig. 1.2. The effect of suckling rats in small and large groups on subsequent growth in weight. *Arrow* shows weaning and commencement of *ad libitum* feeding. ○, suckled in small groups; ●, suckled in large groups [8].

pups without maternal contact in either experimental animals or controls [10]. In theory this eliminates the possibly confounding factor of the altered mother/ infant relationship of the small and large litter design, as well as allowing a more specific manipulation of the diet. In practice the method demands much more skill and effort from the experimenter, and it is still not used so extensively.

The remarkable finding from the original small and large litter experiments was that animals who are nutritionally growth-restricted throughout the suckling period, and then weaned to an *ad libitum* diet, fail to show any sign of true catch-up when liberated from the restriction. That is to say that, although the previously restricted weanlings continue to grow, their growth trajectories show no sign of converging on those of the "controls", and their ultimate growth achievement is for this reason reduced (Fig. 1.2). They are small as adults, not for genetic reasons, nor because of any concurrent restriction, but apparently as a result of an early period of undernutrition which has long been replaced by a continuous regime of nutritional bounty, well before the greater part of the bodily growth spurt of "childhood". Nutritionists have often found it difficult to come to terms with a nutritionally induced growth restriction occurring at a time of abundant nutrition. Many have still not done so, and this may be behind some of their reluctance to accept that the finding of permanent stunting in rats in these circumstances can almost certainly be extrapolated to human children and human growth. The validity of cross species extrapolation to humans will be discussed later, but human adult smallness can almost certainly be sometimes

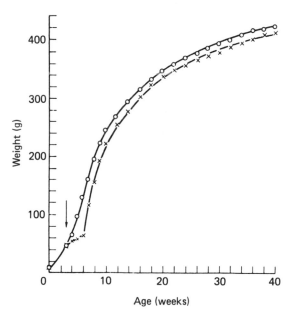

Fig. 1.3. The effect of undernutrition from the third to the sixth week of postnatal life on the growth of rats suckled in small groups. *Arrow* shows weaning. ○, unlimited food after weaning; X, unlimited food after the sixth week [8].

due to early infant undernutrition, and should be a valuable index of early nutritional history in those societies where a reliable history is not available. In most indigent society the stunted adults are probably not mainly genetically so.

In rats a comparable period of nutritional growth restriction shortly *after* weaning is followed by true catch-up (Figs. 1.3 and 1.4), just as it is in older children. The first three postnatal weeks or so in the rat are therefore a truly vulnerable period, during which it seems that the genetically ordained future growth trajectory can be permanently re-set downwards.

The relevance for the brain of this bodily growth vulnerability is two-fold: firstly it is not the period of the *bodily* growth spurt which is vulnerable for bodily growth, but that of the *brain* growth-spurt; and secondly, when bodily growth is restricted during the brain growth spurt, the brain itself suffers changes in its structure, as well as in its size, and possibly in aspects of its metabolism, some of which outlast the return to a normal diet. Conventional explanations for these effects on brain, such as the cell number/cell size hypothesis [11] can probably now be discarded [12].

The details of these alterations of brain structure, to be carefully distinguished from "damage", or lesions, are summarised in several reviews [e.g. 1], as are attempts to investigate possibly parallel changes in behaviour [6]. The physical changes in the brain represent a sort of teratology, that is a disorder of growth, rather than the destruction of, or damage to already existing structure; but, as has been said above, it is a teratology which relates to developmental events well

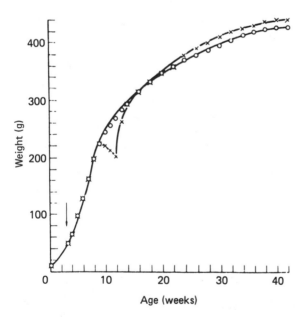

Fig. 1.4. The effect of undernutrition from the ninth to the 12th week of postnatal life on the growth of rats suckled in small groups. *Arrow* shows weaning. ○, unlimited food after weaning; X, unlimited food except from the ninth to the 12th week [8].

beyond the period of embryogenesis, probably extending into the second or third year of postnatal life, if not later, in our own species. It is this type of phenomenon which leads to the need for the active promotion of brain growth, by proper feeding amongst other things, throughout early infancy and childhood.

Much of what we have been discussing may be called a neuropathology of growth [1], quite different from neuropathology as usually understood by paediatricians and pathologists. It is a quantitative pathology, involving not only the size or number of brain components, but also their quantitative relationship to each other. As such it is outside the reach of the usual techniques of neuropathology, since its detection involves measuring, weighing, and, more particularly, the counting of histological components which is extremely laborious and rarely done. Pathology is more usually concerned with the relatively easy detection of lesions, or scars, or sometimes with biochemical changes. Perhaps it will soon also have to deal with enumeration.

An extremely important feature of the neuropathology of growth restriction is that the structures which are affected by it are those which are normally being constructed and assembled at the time of the restriction.

The growth and development of the brain takes place in a highly complex and orderly sequence, beginning in the earliest days following conception, and continuing at least until the second or third birthday [5]. Even after that there are structural developments, but these are on a much smaller and slower scale. Thus if nutritional growth restriction affects the developing brain it can be expected to interfere with whatever process should be happening at the time of the restriction, and there may be later changes secondary to these.

A second important feature of brain growth and development is that many of the developmental processes must be accomplished under good conditions at the proper chronological age, or be for ever restricted [13]. For example, the nerve cells of the brain, except for some microneurons in the cerebellum, hippocampus and olfactory bulbs [14] mainly multiply as neuroblast precursor cells between the 12th and 18th week of human gestation (Fig. 1.5) [15]. Differentiation of these cells into neurons around the 18th week is what signals the close of their proliferative period, and it seems that if the proper number is not achieved by that time a permanent shortage may result. Of course reality is a good deal more complex. Neuroblast multiplication is normally greatly in excess of the numbers required and many must perish before the model is complete, and any final description must take these complexities into account: but the model outlined may well be sufficiently valid as a general guide.

These two features: the effects of restriction being related to concurrent neurodevelopmental events and the "once-and-for-all" opportunity for these events to occur, again underlines the theoretical need for us to promote brain growth and to avoid restrictions throughout the whole period, although for different "structural" reasons at different ages.

On these somewhat simplistic assumptions it can be predicted that nutritional deprivation is unlikely ever to affect neuronal numbers in humans, except for the microneurons mentioned above, since adult numbers of neurons are achieved in our species at a time of gestation when the fetus is virtually immune to maternal undernutrition. However, the early second trimester is not so immune to such

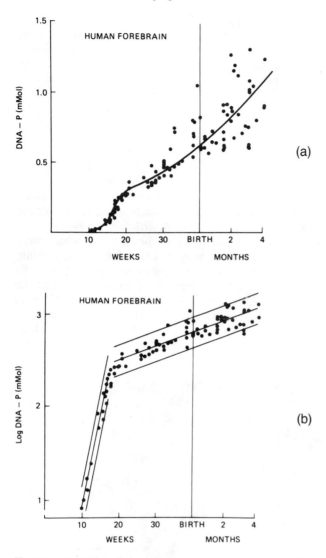

Fig. 1.5. Total DNA–P, equivalent to total cell number, in the human forebrain from 10 gestational weeks to 4 postnatal months, showing the two-phase characteristics of prenatal cell multiplication. **b** is a semi-log plot of the same data as appear in **a** [15].

noxious influences as viral infestation, biochemical anomalies, irradiation, drugs, etc., and any of these might well interfere at that time with the eventual number of neurons. Indeed the common occurrence of microcephaly with mental retardation in rubella embryopathy, maternal phenylketonuria and inadvertent radiotherapy as well as perhaps in drug abuse at this time may be related to an inhibition of neuroblast division. Even "unclassified" microcephaly, that which is so far without any explanation, and which mostly occurs in developed countries, may be similarly based [16]. General undernutrition is probably only important for fetal growth in the last one-third of gestation in any species. In the rat (being born much more immature than the human) the last "trimester" is its period of neuroblast multiplication, so that, unlike in the human, quite severe neuronal and behavioural deficits can be induced by undernutrition of the maternal rat during pregnancy.

Vulnerability of Particular Brain Structures

Since the vulnerability of particular brain structures is related to the normal time of their development there is a need to know the approximate timing of the major stages of brain growth [5]. Following the end of neuroblast proliferation, at about mid-gestation in humans, there follows the much greater proliferation of glial cells which continues until about the second birthday. These, together with the microneurons already mentioned, are the "brain cells" which were endlessly cited in the 1960s as those whose numbers were reduced by infant undernutrition. This was a very active era for laboratory research, and the relative timing of the neuroblast and glial phases of cell multiplication in the brain was not then understood. Of course glial cells multiply at different times in the different regions and tracts in an orderly sequence, as does the myelination which the oligodendroglia are responsible for, and which is accomplished, as would be expected, after the glia arrive. Nevertheless these major processes can

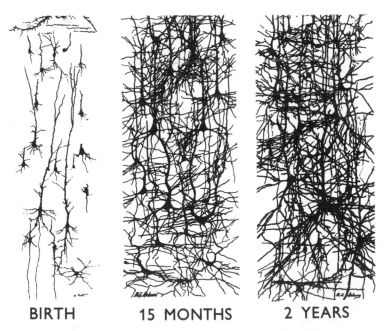

BIRTH   15 MONTHS   2 YEARS

Fig. 1.6. Qualitative illustration of the large extent of dendritic growth occurring postnatally in the human visual cortex [17].

be discerned by analysing large heterogeneous samples, such as the cerebrum or even the whole brain, even though to do so destroys the evidence for the regional sequence. Myelination "as a whole" begins a little before birth in man, to become a major process in infancy and the first two postnatal years. More important, it might be supposed, than myelination, the phase of dendritic growth and the appearance of by far the greatest number of synapses are also predominantly a postnatal phenomena in man, lasting throughout the first two or three years (Fig. 1.6) [17]. The number of synapses per neuron is known to be profoundly affected by nutritional growth restriction in experimental animals at the equivalent time, although it is thought that the substantial deficits which can be produced (up to 40%) [18] can be recovered later [19] when good nutritional conditions can be arranged.

The precise timing of the periods when particular brain regions or systems develop is not known in much detail. This applies, for example, to the auditory system, the various parts of the visual system, or to those regions where catecholamine metabolism is specially concentrated, so it is difficult to relate the principles of growth pathology to them specifically. As has been stressed, the pathology is quantitative, and the total number of a given structure in a region at different ages is difficult to determine when the region itself cannot be reliably and completely defined. One has to resort to realistic ratios between more than one component, as has been the case, for example, with the number of synapses per neuron [18,19].

Cross-Species Extrapolation

The rule repeatedly mentioned above, that it is the stage of brain growth which determines what structures will be affected in developmental undernutrition, together with the fact that different species are born at very different stages, leads logically to the proposition that the stage of maturity, for example at birth, must be seriously taken into account when comparing findings in one species with those in another [20]. Before this was realized in the 1960s there was a great deal of misunderstanding about cross-species extrapolation, a subject which is extremely important for those mainly interested in human children, since nearly all our knowledge has necessarily had to be determined in non-human animals.

First it was necessary [15] to confirm that the general shape of the various quantitative growth curves in human brain resembled those in other animals; but more important still was to outline the timing and approximate durations of the various phases of human brain growth. This involved collecting considerable numbers of human brains for analysis, and resulted in a confirmation that we, too, have a brain growth spurt, and that it is a long one, lasting from about mid-gestation until about the second birthday: much longer and later than had been thought hitherto. By analogy with the experimental data, this identified the period of human brain vulnerability, or, as we have preferred to call it, the period when human brain growth needs to be actively promoted as well as merely protected. It was confirmed that the predominantly postnatal timing of the human brain growth spurt more resembled that in the rat than that in the monkey, and a series of rough guidelines was elaborated for making more reasonable extrapolations from animal species to ourselves than had formerly been the case [20].

Extrapolation thus has to take into account a trilogy of parameters of developmental nutrition: its timing (in relation to developmental events), its severity and its duration, as well as the different stages of brain growth at which a species is born and their different "pace" of development.

For example it is suggested that the newborn rat, having just completed its phase of neuroblast multiplication, is at a stage of brain growth approximating to that of the human brain in mid-gestation; and that the full-term human neonate similarly resembles the rat of one postnatal week of age which is then about one-third of the way through its traditional suckling period. The end of the brain growth spurt in the rat is at about 20–25 postnatal days, and corresponds to that in a human child about 2–3 years old: a stage already reached by the guinea-pig at birth [21].

Once these simple rules are understood, the extrapolation of many developmental concepts and findings from the laboratory to the human nursery can be made with much greater confidence, and it will be seen that the inevitable choice of non-human animal species for various experimental models will often depend much less on an apparent resemblance to humans than on properly applying the principles of extrapolation. As can be seen in Fig. 1.7, the non-human primate is

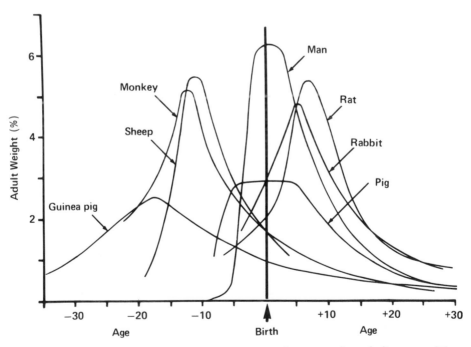

Fig. 1.7. The brain growth spurts of seven mammalian species expressed as velocity curves of the increase in weight with age. The units of time for each species are: guinea pig, days; rhesus monkey, 4 days; sheep, 5 days; pig, weeks; man, months; rabbit, 2 days; rat, days. Rates are expressed as weight gain as a percentage of adult weight for each unit of time [20].

further from being similar to the human in the timing of its brain growth spurt than might have been imagined.

The need to apply these principles of cross-species extrapolation is not, of course, confined to the developmental biology of the brain. In a sense the brain and its developing functions are indices of development generally, so that transferring the interesting phenomena of the later effects of early bodily growth restriction in the rat to humans also depends on them. Those who have sought to deny the relevance to humans of the Widdowson and McCance findings on the early nutritional predetermination of later bodily growth attainment, have often failed to apply the rules [8]. Thus the period of nutritional growth restriction in humans corresponding to that which permanently re-sets the growth trajectory downwards in rats, would be from about mid-gestation until about the second birthday. Much shorter periods of growth failure, either within that period or outside it, might be expected to be followed by catch-up on the return of favourable conditions, and that would be no argument against the general proposition.

In practice, because of virtually complete fetal "sparing" in the first two trimesters from the effects of maternal undernutrition, its effects on later bodily size, and, much more importantly on the developing brain, would be unlikely to be produced before the third trimester. This is not to say that adversity from which the pre-30 week fetus is not protected will not do harm: but the brain growth spurt, and the particular vulnerability to growth restriction it confers, effectively begins at about 30 weeks of human gestation, and is *relatively* immune until birth, being protected by the same mechanisms which tend to protect the fetus as a whole, as well as by its own "sparing" relative to other tissues. The greater vulnerability therefore begins at birth and lasts at least until the second birthday.

In indigent communities in developing countries, where widespread low birth weight is nearly always due to maternal energy imbalance (hard physical work and low nutritional intake), it will be especially important to feed infants adequately, for several reasons [22]. The nutritionally "small-for-dates" baby has a natural tendency to enter a catch-up growth trajectory, lasting many months, when released from the gestational restriction. This catch-up is possible, being within the vulnerable period, but only with adequate nutritional provision; the same dietary adequacy is also required for the post-catch-up period, to carry the child through at least until the brain growth spurt period is over. In the usual conditions of these underprivileged people the first few months of postnatal life are usually protected by breast-feeding, or, if not, by facing the difficulties of artificial feeding in such circumstances. Breast-feeding becomes inadequate on its own after a few months (the more deprived the mother the earlier this occurs), so that growth promotion with adequate dietary supplements, an ideal which is seldom reached, is essential [23].

Human Field Studies

The literature describing and discussing human field studies, which have sought to identify the possible role of early nutritional deprivation in the reduced achievement of individuals in malnourished communities around the world, is vast [e.g. 24–27]. It will only be briefly summarized here insofar as it is relevant to the present topic.

The failure of individuals in impoverished communities to reach their innate potential levels of achievement has long been recognized, and it was at first considered possible that this was largely due to the effects of malnutrition on the developing brain. The important political and social corollary was that food aid would correct the situation. It soon became clear, however, that infant malnutrition was almost invariably accompanied by a large number of other environmental adversities, principal amongst them being a host of factors conspiring to deprive children of normal, parental, emotional and educative care. The factors responsible for this were largely imposed by environmental circumstances on the parents, who were themselves ignorant and underfed, both of them having to work most of their waking hours to stay alive, and often without the knowledge or capacity to care for their children. In these circumstances nutritional deprivation is only one element restricting normal child development, and it may even be a small one in relation to the other deprivations to which they are subject, except where malnutrition leads to serious infective illness, as it often does. Several examples were found of nutritional relief on its own, without adequate attention to "stimulation" in the environment, being without effect. Indeed there were even examples of "stimulation" alone producing apparent restoration to bodily, if not intellectual normality [28], and, on the other hand, of undernutrition in an otherwise enriched environment not resulting in any detectable deficit at all [29].

The search to analyse the major environmental factors possibly responsible for the intellectual deficit, and to assign relative weightings to them, has been attempted in field studies, but has now largely been abandoned because of the overwhelming complexity of the environment itself and the great difficulties in measuring its features in any meaningful way. It is now even being questioned whether undernutrition *per se,* separately from the inevitable confounding factors, has any identifiable role at all.

Experimental animal behavioural scientists have also been aware of the large influence that enrichment or impoverishment of the environment has on behaviour, and some have even claimed specific physical changes in the brain in association with such intervention [see 30]. Interaction between the various features of the environment has also been studied, so that a mere algebraic sum of their scores is now also outdated.

Conclusions

Two main conclusions have occurred to the present author as a spectator of behavioural science in this area. One is a profound respect for the skills of the professional behavioural scientist, and the other is a parallel respect for the complexity of his subject, which is at least comparable to that of most non-behavioural disciplines. The non-behavioural scientist should tread very warily indeed in a field where he may be unaware or unskilled. It sometimes seems remarkably acceptable for the biochemist, for example, to "run his rats through the mazes", or to chase them from one side to the other of a shuttle box, forgetting that he would not pay much attention to work in his own subject in the hands of a psychologist. There sometimes seems to be little respect for the intricacies of behavioural science outside that field, so that dangerously erroneous "findings", involving "learning", "memory" and even "intelligence", profoundly influence the rest of us who are not behaviourally trained either. Perhaps we should develop the same attitudes towards behavioural science as we mostly have for statistics: which are that although we cannot, and should not, automatically trust the professional, we should at least recognize the complexities of a discipline which is not our own and seek help and criticism from those experts we think we can respect. The same strictures should apply to clinicians, who are not always immune from an apparent contempt for professionals in other fields. Measurements of "learning", "memory" and "intelligence" are merely assessments of performance in the various tests conventionally employed. They do not necessarily measure capacity to perform, since motivation, as well as capacity, can greatly influence the result.

Finally, does iron have a role in infant nutrition which is specific to brain growth and behavioural development? This monograph will address that question in some detail. The spectator may perhaps be permitted some last, general observations.

Iron deficiency may theoretically effect performance (let us not call it intelligence) either directly or indirectly, or not at all. The last seems unlikely. The effect may be indirect if, for example, its effects on the rest of the body lead to a poorer expression of behavioural capacity; or, in turn, to an altered mother/infant interaction. A mother will not interact with her offspring in the same way if she meets with a lethargic, unreactive response, any more than if she herself is similarly unresponsive. Most of these possibilities can be allowed for by devising adequate controls. Where iron deficiency acts similarly on performance at any age, the effect is unlikely to be one on brain development: it will be more in the nature of a "pharmacological" effect, such as, for example, an interference with catecholamine metabolism. In favour of a "pharmacological" effect, though not a precondition for it, will be a relatively short delay in response to deficiency, and reversability, again with a short delay.

Alternatively, iron deficiency may induce a growth pathology on the developing brain. In this case does it influence structural or metabolic development in any lasting way, or is the effect amenable to replacement therapy?

The range of possibilities is theoretically very wide. This monograph will examine some of them.

References

1. Dobbing J (1981a) Nutritional growth restriction and the nervous system. In: Thompson RHS, Davison AN (eds) The molecular basis of neuropathology. Edward Arnold, London, pp 221–232

2. Bourre J–M, Bonneil M, Dumont O et al. (1988) High dietary fish oil alters the brain polyunsaturated fatty acid composition. Biochim Biophys Acta 960:458–461
3. Dobbing J (1985a) Infant nutrition and later achievement. Amer J Clin Nutr 41:477–484
4. Dobbing J (ed) (1987) Early nutrition and later achievement. Academic Press, London
5. Dobbing J (1981c) The later development of the brain and its vulnerability. In: Davis JA, Dobbing J (eds) Scientific foundations of paediatrics, 2nd edn. Heinemann, London, pp 744–758
6. Smart JL (1987) The need for and the relevance of animal studies of early undernutrition. In: Dobbing J (ed) Early nutrition and later achievement. Academic Press, London, pp 50–85
7. Widdowson EM, McCance RA (1963) The effects of finite periods of undernutrition at different ages on the composition and subsequent development of the rat. Proc R Soc London Ser. B 158:329–342
8. Dobbing J (1981b) Vulnerable periods in somatic growth. In: Thomson AM, Bond J, Filer L et al. (eds) Infant and Child Feeding. Academic Press, New York, pp 399–411
9. Sands J, Dobbing J, Gratrix CA (1979) Cell number and cell size: organ growth and development and the control of catch-up growth in rats. Lancet ii:503–505
10. Smart JL, Massey RF, Nash SC, Tonkiss J (1987) Effects of early life undernutrition in artificially reared rats. Subsequent body and organ growth. Brit J Nutr 58:245–255
11. Winick M, Noble A (1966) Cellular response in rats during malnutrition at various ages. J Nutr 89:300–306
12. Dobbing J, Sands J (1981) Vulnerability of developing brain not explained by cell number/cell size hypothesis. Early Hum Dev 5:227–231
13. Dobbing J, Sands J (1971) Vulnerability of developing brain. IX. The effect of nutritional growth retardation on the timing of the brain growth spurt. Biol Neonat 19:363–378
14. Rodier PM (1980) Chronology of neuron development: animal studies and their clinical implications. Dev Med Child Neurol 22:525–545
15. Dobbing J, Sands J (1973) The quantitative growth and development of the human brain. Arch Dis Child 48:757–767
16. Dobbing J (1984) The pathogenesis of microcephaly with mental retardation. In: Streffner C, Patrick G (eds) Effects of prenatal irradiation with special emphasis on late effects. Commission of the European Communities, Radiation Protection, report no. EUR 8067EN
17. Conel JL (1939, 1955, 1959) Cited in: Thompson RHS, Davison AN (eds) The molecular basis of neuropathology. Edward Arnold, London.
18. Bedi KS, Thomas YM, Davis CA et al. (1980) Synapse-to-neuron ratios of the frontal and cerebellar cortex of 30-day-old and adult rats undernourished during early postnatal life. J Comp Neurol 193:49–56
19. Thomas YM, Peeling A, Bedi KS et al (1980) Deficits in synapse-to-neuron ratio due to early undernutrition show evidence of catch-up in later life. Experientia 36:556–557
20. Dobbing J, Sands J (1979) Comparative aspects of the brain growth spurt. Early Hum Dev 3:79–83
21. Dobbing J, Sands J (1970) Growth and development of the brain and spinal cord of the guinea pig. Brain Res 17:115–123
22. Dobbing J (1985b) Maternal nutrition in pregnancy and later achievement of offspring. Early Hum Dev 12:1–8
23. Dobbing J (1988) Medical and scientific commentary on charges made against the food industry. In: Dobbing J (ed) Infant feeding: anatomy of a controversy 1973–1984. Springer, Berlin Heidelberg New York, pp 9–27
24. Cravioto J, de Licardie ER, Birch HG (1966) Nutrition, growth and neurointegrative development: an experimental and ecologic study. Pediatrics 38:319–372
25. Galler JR (1987) The interaction of nutrition and environment in behavioural development. In: Dobbing J (ed) Early nutrition and later achievement. Academic Press, London, pp 175–207
26. Grantham-McGregor S (1987) Field studies in early nutrition and later achievement. In: Dobbing J (ed) Early nutrition and later achievement. Academic Press, London pp 128–174
27. Hertzig ME, Birch HG, Richardson SA et al. (1972) Intellectual levels of schoolchildren severely malnourished during the first two years of life. Pediatrics 49:814–824
28. Widdowson EM (1951) Mental contentment and physical growth. Lancet i:1316–1318
29. Lloyd-Still JD (1976) Clinical studies on the effects of malnutrition during infancy and subsequent physical and intellectual development. In: Lloyd-Still JD (ed) Malnutrition and intellectual development. MTP Press, Lancaster, pp 230–238

30. Katz HB, Davis CA (1983) The effects of early-life undernutrition and subsequent environment on morphological parameters of the rat brain. Behav Brain Res 5:53–64

Commentary

Smart: It is often interesting and illuminating to consider the pioneering studies in one's field of research. The early work on undernutrition and the brain conducted by Donaldson and his colleagues at the Wistar Institute [1,2,3] and by Jackson and Stewart at the University of Minnesota [4,5] gives some fascinating insights into the history of this topic and more generally into the faltering progress of science. That the concept of brain sparing came out of this considerable body of research but not that of the vulnerability of developing brain follows from their monolithic approach to the subject, which was dominated by a particular style of enquiry: "When increase in body weight is prevented by underfeeding, does growth cease in all parts or do some organs increase at the expense of others?" [5]. Associated with this was a marked tendency to compare undernourished animals only with well-fed controls of the same body weight (necessarily much younger) and not controls of the same age. This makes it difficult to arrive at the concept of vulnerability of developing brain. Nevertheless, almost certainly, these early researchers had available to them from their various experiments all the information on brain weight that was necessary for them to realize the especial vulnerability of the developing brain. By 1920, I feel that an elementary form of vulnerable period hypothesis could have been proposed without further experiment.

Indeed, Sugita's monumental study of the effect of early undernutrition on the development of the cerebral cortex [3] virtually assumes that the suckling period is a vulnerable period without quite talking in those terms. He appeared to know that cortical thickness and the number and size of cells in the cerebral cortex would normally attain near adult values by weaning, and reasoned that, to affect cortical development, undernutrition would have to be instituted prior to weaning. For whatever reason, these ideas lay dormant for 40 years, until the new wave of experimentation in the 1960s resulted in the formulation of the vulnerable period and other hypotheses of brain development.

There are, in fact, some large populations of microneurons in the cerebellum, hippocampus and olfactory bulbs which proliferate relatively late in development [6] and which are likely to be vulnerable to postnatal undernutrition in man. The brain cells cited in the 1960s as being reduced in number by early undernutrition would include such microneuronal cell populations.

Deficits in such populations coupled with the relative immunity of earlier formed neuronal populations can give rise to distortions of normal relationships, as, for instance, in the rat cerebellum where the ratio of granule cells to Purkinje cells is much reduced by undernutrition [7]. Interestingly, this may result in anatomical effects which arise *after* the period of undernutrition. Purkinje cells develop extensive dendritic trees, the extent of which is thought to depend on the local density of growing axons, which is a function of granule cell number. Dendritic networks have been found to be some 28% less extensive in rats recovered from undernutrition in early life [8].

References

1. Haiti S (1904) The effect of partial starvation on the brain of the white rat. Am J Physiol 12:116–127
2. Donaldson HH (1911) The effect of underfeeding on the percentage of water, on the ether-alcohol extract, and on medullation in the central nervous system of the albino rat. J Comp Neurol 21: 139–145
3. Sugita N (1918) Comparative studies on the growth of the cerebral cortex. VII. On the influence of starvation at an early age upon the development of the cerebral cortex in the albino rat. J Comp Neurol 29:177–239
4. Stewart CA (1919) Changes in the weights of the various parts, systems and organs in albino rats kept at birth weight by underfeeding for various periods. Am J Physiol 48:67–78
5. Jackson CM (1932) Structural changes when growth is suppressed by undernourishment in the albino rat. Am J Anat 51:347–379
6. Rodier PM (1980) Chronology of neuron development: animal studies and their clinical implications. Dev Med Child Neurol 22:525–545
7. Bedi KS, Hall R, Davies CA, Dobbing J (1980) A stereological analysis of the cerebellar granule and Purkinje cells of 30-day-old and adult rats undernourished during early postnatal life. J Comp Neurol 193:863–870
8. McConnell P, Berry M (1981) The effect of refeeding after neonatal starvation on Purkinje cell dendritic growth in the rat. J Comp Neurol 178:759–772

Yehuda: What kind of proof will satisfy the author that "the brain is an organ of thought"?

Author's reply: The answer is I do not know; and in any case I already believe the proposition is "obviously acceptable", as I have said. It is, nevertheless "scientifically an almost unsupported belief". Until we can identify the physical mechanism of thought the physical brain cannot be shown to be its site. I suppose I am only trying to emphasize how far we are from knowing that mechanism.

In addition to Yehuda's question, Walter says I am too dismissive of the link between neuroscience and behavioural science. My answer to Yehuda's question is that it is for those who claim one to produce the evidence! And to Walter's comment I would reply that I do not deny *some* link, but that I cannot accept the assumption that it is "total". By this I mean that the mere finding of a change in the structural or metabolic or constitutional make-up of the brain cannot automatically imply or predict a related change in behaviour.

Lozoff and Felt: This introductory chapter provides a number of thoughtful guides for researchers on the effects of iron deficiency on infant behavior, a much younger field. Among the sobering reminders are Dobbing's comments that any links between brain structure and higher mental function are still largely speculative. It is also helpful to remind us of the distinction between actual damage to the brain and a disorder of growth. Thus far, there is no reason to think that iron deficiency actually causes damage to the brain, unless alterations in the blood–brain barrier allow harmful or toxic proteins or other molecules to enter the brain that would not ordinarily do so.

Smart: Some of the problems of quantitative histology have been alluded to. A further problem, which is virtually intractable for the time being, is that of counting ultra-small structures which even in the rat brain, are present in vast numbers in a relatively large volume. The approaches that are used are to sample a tiny proportion of the whole volume and to use mathematical techniques to estimate total numbers of the structure in question (of dubious value), or (better) to calculate density per area or volume of tissue, or (best) to calculate the ratio of one structure to another [1].

I feel that the statement that " . . . some have claimed specific physical changes in the brain . . . " in association with enrichment or impoverishment of the environment, is over-cautious. There is now abundant evidence of such effects, including several papers from our laboratory in Manchester [e.g. 2].

References

1. Bedi KS (1987) Lasting neuroanatomical changes following undernutrition during early life. In: Dobbing J (ed) Early nutrition and later achievement. Academic Press, London, pp 1–36
2. Katz HB, Davies CA, Dobbing J (1982) Effects of undernutrition at different ages early in life and later environmental complexity on parameters of the cerebrum and hippocampus in rats. J Nutr 112: 1362–1368.

Author's reply: I am less sceptical than Smart about the mathematical techniques of stereology for estimating total numbers in quantitative histology. With proper interpretative caution I think they have been of value in a difficult field [see 1]. I am rather more sceptical than he, or than Yehuda (q.v.), about the physical effects on brain architecture of environmental diversity [1].

Reference

1. Bedi KS, Bhide PG (1988) Effects of environmental diversity on brain morphology. Early Hum Dev 17: 107–144

Yehuda: The importance of a proposed mechanism cannot be underestimated, as it so happens that in many cases it is the only logical way to look for an explanation. The relationships between pure and applied research are much too complex to deal with in a short commentary. However, it is only fair to indicate that vast numbers of results from the field of pure research are applied "all of a sudden" by other scientists. Most of the scientists investigating the biochemical pathway of dopamine before 1968 did not have treatment for Parkinson's disease in mind. Yet L-dopa is today a drug for sufferers of Parkinson's disease.

Author's reply: I do not deny that a mechanism is usually the way to an explanation. The point I was making could be expressed as that "a knowledge of the mechanism is, in a sense, much less important (than the observation)".

Of course I accept the occasional, accidental direct practical application of pure research. However, if you are mainly interested in human application, it could be more economical not to spray the field with one's private hobbies just in case one of them may be of benefit! I have no great interest in pure science, but that is a matter of personal taste.

Lozoff and Felt: The chapter also emphasizes that beginning with "real life phenomena" is a worthwhile undertaking. For those of us who have focussed on careful behavioural description and have sometimes been challenged because we did not postulate a mechanism, such comments are encouraging.

Smart: Dobbing makes the interesting statement that "Much shorter periods of growth failure, either within that period or outside it, might be expected to be followed by catch-up on the return of favourable conditions." I accept that a short period of growth failure *after* the brain growth spurt will be followed by catch-up growth, because there is abundant evidence of this. However, I wonder whether catch-up would necessarily follow short-term growth failure either before or during the brain growth spurt. I certainly do not know of published evidence bearing on this point, from properly conducted experiments. The statement that in babies released from gestational restriction " . . . catch-up is possible, being within the vulnerable period . . . " suggests a theoretical framework but it is not clear what it is.

Author's reply: Smart is correct. There is no satisfactory evidence, and that is why I wrote "might be expected". However my "much shorter periods" also imply a much smaller restriction, in the sense that the effects of developmental undernutrition depend greatly on duration and severity, as well as timing. "Much shorter periods" might be recoverable, or apparently so, because of the consequent mildness of the restriction. This being said, it is possible that a very severe restriction for a similarly shorter time might be roughly equivalent to a less severe one for longer. I know I am being much too simplistic, and the experiments would be much more difficult to design than appears at first sight.

It is, however, the case that small-for-dates human babies do engage on a true postnatal catch-up trajectory after liberation from a restrictive intrauterine environment, provided their intrauterine growth retardation is of the restrictive type, and that postnatal conditions are good: and this in spite of having been growth restricted (albeit mildly) during a portion of the brain growth spurt. I must agree that I am only guessing at the general mechanism, and this may be no more responsible than some uses of the expression "may be" discussed in my replies to Yehuda.

Lozoff and Felt: Galler reported that malnourished humans in Barbados ultimately catch up in physical growth [1]. How do these results fit with the animal data in which the animal is permanently stunted after a period of undernutrition during the brain growth spurt?

Reference

1. Galler JR, Ramsey FC, Salt P, Archer E (1987) Long term effects of early kwashiorkor compared with marasmus. I. Physical growth and sexual maturation. J Pediat Gastroenterol Nutr 6:841–846.

Author's reply: I believe that such claims require closer scrutiny before they can be accepted. There is much misunderstanding of the hypothesis that bodily growth restriction during a greater part of the brain growth spurt leads to permanent restriction of body size. Denials that this occurs in humans usually ignore the proper cross-species extrapolation rules enunciated in my Chapter, and often mistake further rapid growth for catch-up. In addition it is not possible in humans, for obvious ethical reasons, to manipulate the scales of severity, timing and duration which have led to the animal findings. Sometimes, for instance, well-fed treated cases of childhood malnutrition have been compared with siblings who remain chronically subnourished, and who quite reasonably are overtaken by their well-nourished, previously malnourished sibs. At the same time there is little doubt about the secular upward trend in height in several groups whose general conditions of life are improving, suggesting that previously height was permanently restricted due to early impoverishment. Mature adults cannot catch up in the way that those children can whose undernutrition was either of relatively short duration or in the period between 2 years and, say, puberty. Even nutritional intrauterine growth restriction results in ultimately smaller humans (Martorell et al, in press).

Galler studied 9–15-year-old children in Barbados who had been malnourished in their first year of life. She found persisting reduced physical growth relative to comparison children of the same sex and age. She also cites studies in Uganda and South Africa showing persisting deficits in height among such previously malnourished children up to 18 years of age. In a later paper [1] Galler et al. report postpubertal follow-up and have detected converging growth trajectories after puberty in index girls compared with comparison girls, possibly predicting ultimate catch-up. The boys had apparently already caught up. It is hard to know whether these results challenge the extrapolation to humans of the finding of permanent stunting in previously underfed rats. The matching of humans with experimental rats in respect of the timing, duration and severity of the undernutrition inevitably depends on knowing these three parameters in a naturally occurring human population, and this is probably impossible. Also to be taken into account is the promptness of satisfactory treatment of malnutrition in some human populations before 2 years of age, before the end of the "vulnerable period", or the persistence of the nutritional adversity into later life in others. I still think it very likely that nutritional *bodily* growth restriction throughout the human equivalent of the rat *brain* growth spurt period (say from 30 weeks human gestation to the second birthday, compared with the rat's first three postnatal weeks) will have lasting effects on ultimate stature; but that anything of a lesser duration or severity, or with later timing, will be less likely to have the same effect, just as is found in the rat.

Reference

1. Galler JR, Ramsey F, Solimano G (1985) A follow-up study of the effects of early malnutrition on subsequent development. I Physical growth and sexual maturation during adolescence. Pediatr Res 9:518–523

Dallman: It seems appropriate to comment on the possible differences between the effects of deficient energy intake (the focus of much of the previous discussion) and the probably more specific effects when a trace nutrient like iron is lacking but caloric intake is adequate (as seems to be the case in the Lozoff and Walter reports). A lack of iron might be expected to have fewer global effects on brain growth and cell number, but to affect more specifically certain processes or functions that are particularly dependent on a continuous supply of iron (similarly to the more specific effects of certain drugs). This issue is central to our subject and deserves more consideration.

Author's reply: I entirely agree that a lack of iron may have few "global" effects on brain growth and development, and may instead more specifically affect certain particularly dependent processes or functions. As I said at the end of my introductory Chapter, the range of *possibilities* is theoretically very wide. However, specific effects are often easier to demonstrate and I am disappointed with the extent to which this has been achieved.

Yehuda: What is the definition of "vulnerable periods"? Is it the same as "critical periods"?

Author's reply: Terms such as "vulnerable periods" and "critical periods" partly depend on the meaning of the words, and partly on usage. It does not much matter if everyone appreciates what an author means by them. I use "critical periods" as meaning the sort of thing which happens in the teratology of embryogenesis, where an insult which is finely, or "nicely" timed in relation to developmental events produces substantial deformity. I have used "vulnerable periods" to mean longer periods of vulnerability, or susceptibility to equally non-specific environmental interference, resulting in effects which outlast the period of the insult, such as is shown when rats are growth-restricted in their first 25 days or so. To say that the brain growth spurt is a vulnerable period for the brain in no way implies that *all* its developmental processes are vulnerable in this sense, nor that a given process is confined to that period, and certainly not that the brain is invulnerable at other ages. It is simply, I suppose, that in a host of ways the vulnerability of the brain to many kinds of insult is much enhanced during that developmental time. A critical period, for me, implies much greater specificity of time and effect: in the sense of the word "critical" = "nice, exact, punctual" – 1716 *(Shorter Oxford English Dictionary)*.

Lozoff and Felt: How does the concept of vulnerable periods in the developing brain relate to the concept of the brain's plasticity in early development?

Author's reply: I do not know if it does. It has often been supposed (I think reasonably) that plasticity in the brain largely ceases when the brain becomes mature, i.e. by the human age of 2 or 3 years, and this is unlike many other tissues. The ability to modify the placing of synaptic connections later than this in response to external stimulus is much talked about, but to my knowledge has never been directly demonstrated outside amphibia, perhaps because of the technical difficulties.

Yehuda: The differences between the effects of undernutrition prenatally and postnatally are not clear. The statement that "general undernutrition is probably only important for the fetal growth in the last one-third of gestation", would not appear to be in accord with cited studies on the effects of undernutrition during the first 3 years of life in humans. More important – the implications of brain development before and after birth may be different. Development before birth has been described. Post-natal development may involve such issues as establishment of active synapses, proper development of neurotransmitters and peptides, and the rate of myelination. Different factors may play roles in these two periods.

Author's reply: I had hoped to make it clear, in my discussion of species differences in maturity at birth, that it was not possible to speak of differences between the effects of prenatal and postnatal undernutrition unless one specifies a species. As far as I know the only general differences between the two phases relate to the relative protection of fetal life, and the (sometimes) different environmental factors and developmental stages: and this is accepted by Yehuda in his last sentence.

My remarks about fetal undernutrition are not in conflict with Yehuda's on that in postnatal life.

Dallman: Could you briefly state what the cell number/cell size hypothesis was?

Author's reply: The cell number/cell size hypothesis was once widely considered for explaining the phenomenon of early nutritional restriction leading to irreversible deficit in tissues or organs. It was particularly, but not at all exclusively, applied to the brain [see my reference 13]. Its basis was the statement that all tissues grew in two overlapping stages: the first being cell multiplication leading early to adult numbers; and the second a period when these cells increased in size. It was suggested that if nutritional growth restriction occurred during phase I there would be a permanent restriction, in spite of a return to adequate diet; but that restriction of organ or tissue size imposed during phase II was potentially recoverable.

The hypothesis tended to dominate thinking about the aetiology of later obesity (fat cell number and fat cell size), and of the observed effects on brain size and bodily size I have outlined. Unfortunately the very basis of the hypothesis was flawed. Tissues do not grow in the two phases claimed [my reference 10], and therefore the hypothesis is nullified: but it was not denied before a number of scientists had spent a decade or more of their lives working on the false assumption. Perhaps this is a classic example of the dangers and waste which can be incurred by insufficiently supported hypotheses.

Smart: Professor Dobbing has been good enough to comment favourably on the artificial rearing method that we have been using recently in our early undernutrition studies. I should like to take this opportunity to promote it further by pointing out its advantages for other types of developmental studies, including those on iron deficiency or excess. The method involves fitting rat pups with gastric cannulae, through which milk can be infused automatically [1]. Both the volume and the composition of the milk can be varied, including the content of minerals such as iron. The technique is also helpful for studies of drugs or toxic agents during the "suckling period". Such substances might have a growth-retarding effect in animals reared by their mothers, through depressing feeding behaviour. In artificially reared rats such a side effect is controlled for, since they are fed automatically.

Reference

1. Hall WG (1975) Weaning and growth of artificially reared rats. Science 190:1313–1315

Lozoff: The Chapter's emphasis on the active promotion of optimal brain growth, rather than merely protecting the brain, is an important one as we think about health policy in many parts of the world.

Author's reply to other general points: Some of the other authors question the relevance of my Chapter to the theme of the book. Its intention as an introductory Chapter, was to set the scene for the remaining, more specifically "iron-based" Chapters: i.e. to discuss some of the nature of the physical development of the brain and, to some small extent, of behaviour, on which iron may have an effect, as well as to highlight the widespread glibness of common assumptions about the relation between brain and higher mental function. I had not expected to find manifestations of what I believe to be this "glibness" in some of the other Chapters and Commentaries!

I think that the specific effects of iron on developing brain should be considered in the context of the general biological, as well of the specific nature of the subject. I will even dare to say that some of the other, more specific Chapters would have been better had they taken this general neurobiology into account.

In this way we might, for example, have avoided widespread misunderstanding of the nature of cross-species extrapolation, a topic of some present importance if we have to use animal experiment to illuminate a human problem; and we might also have avoided unwarranted and extravagant assumptions about the relation of specific effects on the physical brain to behaviour.

The direct findings of what might be called studies in experimental epidemiology (field studies) are not to be disparaged, but they bristle with problems of interpretation. They seem to indicate that iron lack is associated with changes in higher mental function; but those who have most prominently made these studies, the authors of Chapters in the present book, are the first to accept the difficulties of asserting that the one causes the other. Those, on the other hand, who have demonstrated physical changes in the developing brain as a result of iron lack should not interpret their findings functionally in the apparently desired direction without first telling us how they know that the physical feature which has been altered is important to the higher mental function which the field studies have appeared to find. If this is too severe a test, and I think it is if one takes the complexity of the connection between brain and behaviour into account, then let them say so: but they should not tell those of us who are outside the subject that they have solved a problem which still defies solution in the most learned hands. Nor, in my view, should either field workers or basic scientists pretend so publicly that all is well in the matter of relating brain to mind.

We simply do not know the physical basis of higher mental function, as I have said repeatedly in my Chapter. Until we do, we are not entitled to say of any change, whether of an anatomical, histological, biochemical or metabolic nature, that it will change behaviour.

For example, I am constantly told that deficits in myelin are important to behaviour. These deficits are often measured using neurochemical markers and as such are truly quantitative. Sometimes they are "detected" histologically, and one hears of "myelin pallor", which cannot be measured. Now, it is clear that in primary demyelinating disease, such as multiple sclerosis, considerable disruption of function results from small, circumscribed areas of total myelin loss (the "plaques"), through which pass intact axons. It by no means follows, however, that any dysfunction at all would result if the "myelin deficit" represented the lack of a small number of the laminae from a myelin sheath which may have about 200 already! This is presumably what happens in some nutritional deficiencies, since there are no lesions, either of primary or secondary demyelination to be found. Not even the most optimistic electrophysiologist can think of any disadvantage to the known functions of the myelin sheath from having a few laminae too few, yet it is probably this which is detected as a result of poor nutrition by measuring with neurochemical markers. If iron lack is different, then let us be shown the lesions in structures whose higher mental function is known!

Chapter 2

The Epidemiology of Childhood Iron Deficiency: Evidence for Improving Iron Nutrition among US Children

Ray Yip

Introduction

Iron deficiency is well known as the most common cause of childhood anemia. For this reason, the detection of anemia has been widely used as the primary screening for iron deficiency. Even though anemia represents only one of the many adverse consequences of iron deficiency, it is by far the best known, so that anemia, iron deficiency, and iron-deficiency anemia are often used as interchangeable terms. In a strict clinical definition, the only cases of anemia that can be classified as iron-deficiency anemia are those with biochemical iron deficiency. However, for practical purposes, a presumed clinical diagnosis of iron deficiency and treatment with iron can be justified on the presence of anemia alone, since childhood anemia is so often the result of iron deficiency. For the same reason, monitoring the prevalence of anemia can yield helpful epidemiological information on the iron nutrition status of a population.

In recent years, a series of reports from various parts of the United States showed a declining prevalence of anemia among younger children, and indicated that their iron nutrition status was improving. This Chapter is about the issues and significance of declining childhood iron deficiency.

How Iron Nutritional Status is Defined

Defining Iron Deficiency

Iron deficiency is most often identified by one or more biochemical tests: transferrin saturation, serum ferritin, and erythrocyte protoporphyrin. Each of these reflects different aspects of iron metabolism, and a number of conditions other than iron deficiency can alter the test values, producing either false positives or false negatives. Because of their potential limitations, one strategy to improve the accuracy of diagnosing iron deficiency is to employ them all and regard the individual with multiple test results in the abnormal range as having iron deficiency. In this way the prevalence of iron deficiency based on two or more abnormal values for mean corpuscular volume (MCV), transferrin saturation, and erythrocyte protoporphyrin for US children 1 to 5 years of age was 7.1% (The Second National Health and Nutrition Examination Survey, 1976–1980 (NHANES II)) [1,2]. NHANES II is the latest US survey with complete assessment of hematologic as well as iron nutrition status.

Defining Anemia

In general, a case of anemia is defined as having hemoglobin (Hb) or hematocrit (Hct) values below minus two standard deviations on age- and sex-specific references that exclude the unhealthy subsample [3]. This process of defining the central 95% of a Hb distribution from a healthy reference as the "normal range", and the 2.5th percentile Hb value as the cut-off point for anemia, defines a 2.5% baseline prevalence of anemia. Similarly, if the 5th percentile Hb value were chosen as cut-off, the baseline prevalence of anemia would be 5%. This baseline prevalence of anemia can be regarded as "statistical anemia" because those individuals are at the edge of the healthy sample as selected for the purposes of reference: therefore by definition they are "healthy".

For a population, the prevalence of anemia can vary considerably, depending on the Hb cut-off values chosen to define it. Because of the differences in the Hb or Hct cut-off values used in different clinical settings and in different nutrition surveys, it is imperative to interpret the prevalence of anemia in the light of the cut-off values used. Unfortunately, there are no universally recognized Hb or Hct criteria for anemia, and many reported figures do not include the cut-off used. It is therefore often difficult to make proper comparisons of the prevalence of anemia from different studies.

Based on the healthy US reference sample of NHANES II (excluding individuals with a high likelihood of iron deficiency and inflammatory conditions), the 2.5th percentile of Hb for 1- to 2-year-old children is 10.7 g/dl, and the 5th percentile value is 11.0 g/dl. For children 3 to 5 years of age, the respective Hb cut-offs are 10.9 and 11.2 g/dl. The 5th percentile Hb cut-offs based on NHANES II are similar to the 2.5th percentile cut-offs developed by Dallman et al. as recommended by the American Academy of Pediatrics [4]. The estimated prevalence of anemia for US children 1 to 5 years of age, based on NHANES II was 4.2% (anemia definition: age 1–2 years, Hb < 11.0 g/dl; age 3–5 years, Hb < 11.2).

Defining the Spectrum of Iron Nutritional Status

The availability of multiple iron biochemistry tests and hematologic tests provides a framework for characterizing the spectrum of iron nutritional status. This framework is based on characterizing the results of various tests in progressively severe iron deficiency [5]. Table 2.1 summarizes the spectrum of iron nutritional status (excluding iron overload) based on the presence and absence of abnormal laboratory tests.

Table 2.1 Defining the spectrum of iron nutritional status based on multiple laboratory tests (serum ferritin, transferrin saturation, MCV and erythrocyte protoporphyrin)

Iron nutritional status	Test results	Anemia
Depleted iron store	Low serum ferritin only	Absent
Iron deficiency without anemia	More than one test abnormal	Absent
Iron-deficiency anemia	More than one test abnormal[a]	Present

[a] Low ferritin only and anemia can be regarded as iron-deficiency anemia.

It is important to point out that the spectrum of iron nutrition presented in Table 2.1 represents a simplified scheme for the development of iron deficiency. In reality, because of many other factors that can influence the results of each test (false negative and false positive), test results may not agree with one another. Two important points are related to the schematic spectrum of iron nutrition status: the absence of anemia does not exclude the presence of iron deficiency; and the presence of anemia indicates that iron deficiency is relatively severe.

In addition to the use of multiple biochemical tests for defining iron deficiency, Hb response to oral iron treatment is an alternative and important way of diagnosing it. In general, a rise of one gram or more after a period of oral iron therapy is diagnostic of iron deficiency.

The Relationship between Iron Deficiency and Anemia

The comprehensive battery of hematologic and iron biochemistry test results of children in the NHANES II provided a unique opportunity to define the relationship between iron deficiency and anemia. Using age-specific hemoglobin criteria to define anemia, two or more abnormal results for transferrin saturation and erythrocyte protoporphyrin and MCV to define iron deficiency, Table 2.2 demonstrates the relationship between anemia and iron deficiency for children 1 to 5 years of age [1,2].

The sensitivity of 19% means that only 2 out of 20 cases of iron-deficient children also have anemia. In the US setting, if anemia is the screening test for iron deficiency, 8 out of 10 iron-deficient cases will be missed. The positive predictive value of 33% means that among 10 cases of anemia found, only three are iron deficient. The definition of iron deficiency, two or more of tests showing abnormal results, may represent relatively strict criteria for iron deficiency; if less strict criteria were applied, the positive predictive value would be higher. To determine what proportion of childhood anemia in the US can be attributed to iron deficiency, less strict criteria such as abnormal results for one or more tests, were used to define iron deficiency. With the less strict criteria, 50% of the anemia can be attributed to iron deficiency.

Table 2.2   Relationship between anemia and iron deficiency for US
children 1–5 years old of the NHANES II

Anemia	Iron deficiency		
	Yes	No	Total
Yes	17	34	51[a]
	(1.4%)	(2.8%)	(4.2%)
No	71	1115	1186
	(5.7%)	(90.1%)	(95.8%)
Total	88[b]	1149	1237
	(7.1%)	(92.9%)	(100%)

Iron deficiency was based on two or more abnormal tests of MCV,
Sat, and EP. Anemia was based on Hb <11.0 g/dl for children
1–2 years of age, and Hb <11.2 g/dl for those 3–5 years of age.
[a] Prevalence of anemia: 51/1237 = 4.2%
[b] Prevalence of iron deficiency: 88/1237 = 7.1%
Sensitivity of Hb in detecting iron deficiency: 17/88 = 19.3%
Specificity of Hb in detecting iron deficiency: 1115/1149 = 97%
Positive predictive value of Hb for iron deficiency: 17/51 = 33.3%
Iron deficiency to anemia ratio: 88/51 = 1.73

Because a significant proportion of childhood anemia is related to iron
deficiency, prevalence of anemia would be a useful index to estimate and
monitor the change of iron nutritional status on a population basis. Even though
the actual overlap between anemia and iron-deficiency cases, as shown in Table
2.2, is not great, the ratio of iron deficiency to anemia (1.7) can perhaps be used
to estimate the prevalence of iron deficiency in a population when the
prevalence of anemia is the only information obtainable (estimated prevalence
of iron deficiency = measured prevalence of anemia × 1.7). The iron deficiency:
anemia ratio will also vary from population to population, depending on the
prevalence of other factors that cause anemia. Also the iron deficiency : anemia
ratio will vary in age and sex groups in any single population. Therefore, this
ratio needs to be established by special survey for different parts of the world.
   The relationship between iron deficiency and anemia can be further described
by defining iron deficiency by its increasing severity (Table 2.3). The information
in Table 2.3 indicates that even among the most severe cases of iron deficiency
(three abnormal iron test results), only half have anemia. This suggests that
among US children, anemia is not a very sensitive index for detecting iron
deficiency. The low sensitivity of anemia in detecting iron deficiency is disturbing, since some of the adverse effects of iron deficiency, including altered
behavior and development, may occur among children with iron deficiency but
without anemia [6]. If future research evidence can support the need to detect
and treat infants and children with iron deficiency regardless of anemia status,
laboratory screening tests for iron deficiency, in addition to Hb or Hct, may need
to be adopted.

Table 2.3. The relationship of anemia and the severity of iron deficiency

No. of tests abnormal	No. of subjects	Prevalence of anemia
0	1219	6.7%
1	429	10.7%
2	79	16.5%
3	26	50.0%
All	1753	8.6%

The severity of iron deficiency is based on the number of abnormal tests among MCV (<73fl), EP (≤80 μg/dlRBC) and Sat (< 12%) NHANES II data of children 1–5 years of age.

Declining Prevalence of Anemia among US Children: Evidence to Support Improvement of Infant Iron Nutrition

Evidence of Improved Iron Nutritional Status among Low-Income Children

In recent years, several reports have described a declining prevalence of anemia among low-income children and have provided evidence that iron nutrition in infancy and early childhood has improved [7–10].

Vazquez-Seoane et al. compared the Hb results of low-income children seen in 1971 with those seen in 1984, at a New Haven inner-city public health clinic, and found a significant upward shift of Hb distribution between the two time periods [7]. The prevalence of anemia (Hb < 9.8 g/dl) amongst children attending this clinic had decreased from 23% in 1971 to 1% in 1984. The authors attribute this marked improvement to the Special Supplemental Food Program for Women, Infants and Children (WIC), which was instituted between the two study periods.

In agreement with this study, Miller et al. found a significant reduction of iron-deficiency prevalence, based on low serum ferritin (< 10 ng/ml) among children seen in a public health clinic in downtown Minneapolis: 43% in 1973 and 2% in 1977 [8]. However, the prevalence of anemia did not decline significantly during this period. Because the WIC program was started in this clinic in 1975, the observed improvement of iron nutrition status was also attributed to the program. However, this proposed association, not only in this study but in the New Haven one as well, was an ecological one and required further examination.

The hematologic data collected by the CDC (Centers for Disease Control) Pediatric Nutrition Surveillance System were studied to verify the impression of improved iron nutrition status from the two clinics in New Haven and Minneapolis [9]. This surveillance system collects the hematologic and growth data of children attending public health and nutrition programs. In 1988, a total of 42 states participated in this system. Of the approximately 2 million records received, 85% of them came from the WIC program. Between 1975 and 1986, the observed prevalence of anemia based on this surveillance system appeared to be declining, particularly in the late 1970s. However, it was not easy to rule out the possibilities of confounding by a change in composition of the sample, since this has grown from the initial six states in 1975 to 42 states in 1988. To overcome this, six states (Arizona, Kentucky, Louisiana, Montana, Oregon, and Tennessee) that have been consistently participating in the surveillance system were selected to determine the trend in anemia prevalence [9]. From 1976 to 1985, a total of 1.68 million Hb and Hct measurements were collected from nearly half a million children aged 6 months to 5 years. Because of possible reporting bias for anemia cases near the program cut-off point for anemia (e.g. Hct < 34%), strict cut-off points were used to define anemia in this study: Hb < 10.3 g/dl or Hct < 31% for children aged 6 to 23 months, and Hb < 10.6 g/dl or Hct < 32% for those aged 24 to 60 months. The lower cut-off values resulted in a perceived lower prevalence of anemia but provided a better assessment of anemia trend. The prevalence of anemia from the six selected states is shown in Fig. 2.1. Overall, the prevalence of anemia declined by 54%, from 6.8% in the initial year to 3.1% in the last birth cohort. Had the hematologic data been free from reporting problems, and had the prevalence of anemia been based on a common cut-off point such as Hct < 33% for children under 2 years and Hct < 34% for children aged 2 to 5 years, the estimated prevalence of anemia based on Hct distribution would have been about 18%–19% for the initial year and about 8%–9% for the last year.

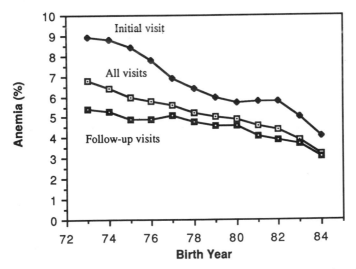

Fig 2.1. Prevalence of anemia in children aged 6–59 months in six selected states; CDC Pediatric Nutrition Surveillance System 1976–1985. The *upper line* represents children seen at the initial visit for enrolment into WIC programs. The *lower line* represents children seen at follow-up visits. (Reproduced with permission from JAMA 258:1619, 1987.)

The CDC Pediatric Nutrition Surveillance System provided an opportunity to look more closely for evidence that the WIC program had contributed to improved iron nutrition status among WIC children. Children were considered "pre-WIC" or "non-WIC" when seen for the initial WIC enrolment or first visit. In contrast, children with at least two visits to the program, or on WIC programs 6 months or longer, were regarded as "WIC" children. Also shown in Fig. 2.1 are the anemia trends for those "non-WIC" children (initial visit) and WIC children (follow-up visit). Although both groups of children showed a decline of anemia prevalence, "WIC" children consistently had a lower prevalence of anemia than "non-WIC" children, a finding compatible with the possibility that the WIC program was indeed beneficial. This difference persisted after adjusting for age and socio-economic variations [9]. Also significant was the decline of prevalence of anemia observed among "non-WIC" children, and therefore factors other than WIC are also playing a role in the improvement. One possibility is that infant iron nutritional status has improved for the nation as a whole and has thereby contributed to the decline of anemia among "non-WIC" children.

Evidence for a Generalized Improvement of Childhood Iron Nutritional Status in the US

If the improvement of iron nutrition in infancy and childhood was not restricted to low-income children, one would expect that middle-class children would show evidence of improvement also. To examine this possibility, a retrospective review of Hct results was conducted for a stable middle-class pediatric practice in Minneapolis [10]. Between 1969 and 1986, a total of 6162 Hct values were collected from the medical records of 2432 children; 91% of these were from well-child visits and 9% were from sick visits. Also collected were 1846 values of erythrocyte protoporphyrin (EP) measured since 1981 by using a portable hematofluorometer. The criteria of anemia for this study were: Hct < 33% for children less than 2 years old; Hct < 34% for children aged 2 to 5 years; and Hct < 35% for children 6 to 7 years. EP values ≥ 35 µg/dl of whole blood were considered elevated and used as evidence of iron deficiency (Fig. 2.2) [10].

In this middle-class clinic population, the prevalence of anemia declined significantly between 1969 and 1986, as it had for the previously mentioned low-income settings. Fig. 2.2 also demonstrates that the decline of anemia occurred for younger as well as older children, suggesting that improvement of the iron nutritional status at a younger age may positively influence their iron nutritional status in later childhood. The observed prevalence of anemia from 1982 to 1986 was very low, less than 3%, which is near the statistical baseline level of 2.5% for a normal population.

The low prevalence of anemia in recent years suggests that this study population has little or no iron deficiency. The few cases of anemia may represent part of the normal Hct distribution or variation related to laboratory errors. The EP data from this study population in the 1980s confirmed the impression that iron deficiency is uncommon: 3% of the children had elevated EP, whereas only 7% of the few anemic children also had elevated EP.

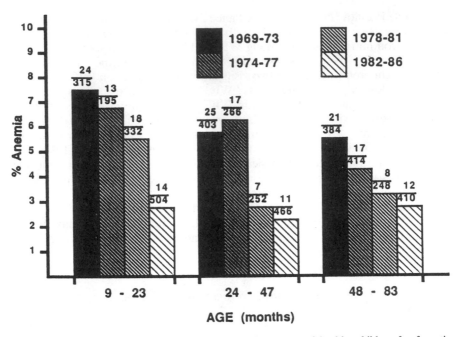

Fig 2.2. Prevalence of anemia for three age-specific groups of healthy children for four time periods. The number on each bar represents the number of subjects with anemia as the numerator and all children who had Hct measurements performed as the denominator. (Reproduced with permisson from *Pediatrics* 80:333, 1987.)

Other evidence indicates that such improvement is not restricted to low-income children. Serum iron (Fe) and total iron-binding capacity (TIBC) were among the biochemistry tests performed consistently between the First National Health and Nutrition Examination Survey (NHANES I, 1970–1975) and NHANES II, 1976–1980. Because both surveys were based on national representative samples, prevalence of iron deficiency in children based on low transferrin saturation were compared for children in both (Table 2.4) [11]. The criteria for defining iron deficiency were transferrin saturation < 8% for children less than 2 years of age, < 9% for children aged 2 to 3 years, and < 10% for those aged 4 to 6.

Table 2.4. Comparison of the prevalence of iron deficiency among US children 1–5 years of age, between NHANES I (1970–1975) and the NHANES II (1976–1980)

Age groups (years)	Prevalence of low Fe/TIBC (%)		
	NHANES I	NHANES II	P value
< 2	14.5	5.3	0.01
2–3	4.8	4.0	0.6
4–6	4.7	4.0	0.5

The findings from these comparisons indicate a significant reduction of iron deficiency in early childhood from the early 1970s to the late 1970s. Since the NHANES samples are nationally representative and not restricted to lower-income families, these findings strengthen the proposition of a generalized improvement of iron nutrition in infancy and childhood.

Evidence for Increased Iron Intake among US Infants and Children

In addition to the evidence for improving iron nutritional status from the studies discussed [7–11], there is also evidence for improved iron intake among infants and children. The National Food Consumption Survey – Continuing Survey of Food Intakes by Individuals (CSFII), a nationwide dietary intake survey based on 24-hour recall conducted by the Department of Agriculture, showed a significant increase of iron intake between the 1977 and the 1985 surveys (Table 2.5) [12]. Iron intake increased for infants and children from all income groups. The WIC program probably contributed to the higher infant iron intake for those low-income infants enrolled; however, this survey information cannot determine the relative contribution of the WIC program to this improvement.

Table 2.5. CSFII mean iron intake per person per day by income level, Spring 1977 and Spring 1985.

Income level	Age (years)	Daily iron intake (mg)	
		1977	1985
<130% poverty	1–3	8.7	10.3
(low-income)	4–5	9.6	11.1
130–300% poverty	1–3	8.2	10.6
(middle-income)	4–5	9.7	10.9
≤300% poverty	1–3	8.8	10.6
(high-income)	4–5	9.8	13.7

The poverty level is a family index based on the number of individuals in a household. For enrolment into public health programs 130% is a level commonly used.

Evidence that the iron intake of WIC infants and children has been beneficial came from the National WIC Evaluation, which was conducted to assess the effects of the WIC program on pregnant women and children [13]. The infant and child portion of the study was cross-sectional in design and included 2619 preschool children whose mothers were also being studied. Approximately one-third of the children were currently enrolled in the WIC program, one-third had been enrolled in the past, and one-third had never been enrolled. The dietary intake revealed significantly higher iron and vitamin C intake among WIC infants than among non-WIC infants (Table 2.6) [13].

The findings indicated that infants and children currently enrolled in the WIC program had greater iron and vitamin C intake than those not enrolled. These findings complement those showing a lower prevalence of anemia among WIC children than non-WIC children based on the CDC Pediatric Nutrition Surveillance System [9].

Table 2.6. Comparison of total mean intake of iron and vitamin C for infants and children from 24-hour dietary recalls, National WIC Evaluation.

Nutrients	Age (months)	Current WIC	Past WIC	Controls
Iron (mg)	0–11	21.4	14.3	13.5
	12–59	11.1	9.8	9.9
Vitamin C (mg)	0–11	113.1	98.5	85.7
	12–59	103.9	88.7	92.1

Evidence of Improved Infant Feeding Patterns in the US

One likely explanation for the improved iron nutritional status and increased intake of iron observed among US children is improved infant feeding practices. Certain infant feeding practices, such as breast-feeding and the use of iron-fortified formula, are known to engender better iron nutritional status; other practices, such as the use of whole milk or non-iron-fortified formula, tend to increase the risk of iron deficiency [14]. Since the 1960s, the Ross Mother's Survey, a nationwide market survey, has been consistently collecting detailed information on infant feeding [15]. This survey has demonstrated a substantial shift in infant feeding practices over the past two decades (Fig. 2.3).

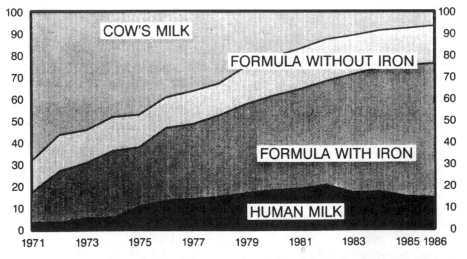

Fig. 2.3. Relative proportion of US infant feeding methods at 5–6 months of age; Ross Mother's Survey, 1971–1986.

Fig. 2.3 shows a marked shift from feeding practices conducive to poor iron nutrution to those conducive to good iron nutrition. This change appears to be a likely explanation for the improved iron nutrition status observed among US children. In addition, the quality as well as the quantity of iron in infant cereal has increased in the past decade, which also contributes to the iron nutrition in infancy and early childhood.

These changing practices can perhaps be attributed to the work of a number of investigators more than two decades ago who demonstrated how the use of whole milk in early infancy can contribute to iron deficiency, whereas breast-feeding and iron-fortified formula can guard against iron deficiency [16,17]. These important findings led to policy recommendations, education, and promotion of better infant feeding practices [14,18,19].

Thus far the evidence points to a significant reduction of childhood anemia among infants and children in the United States. The best explanation of the decline in anemia is the improvement of infant and childhood iron nutrition. The changing pattern of infant feeding (Ross Mother's Survey) and the increased oral intake (CSFII) complements the observations of declined prevalences of anemia or improved iron nutritional status. Low-income children appear to be affected by the trend of generalized improvement of iron nutrition as evidenced by the decline of anemia prevalence among those pre-enrolment to WIC (Fig. 2.1). There is also evidence to suggest that low-income children also benefit from the WIC program (National WIC Evaluation). The potential explanation for the WIC program affecting iron nutrition positively in infancy is the optimal iron nutrition provided in infancy in the form of iron-fortified formula for the eligible infants who were not breast-feeding.

The Public Health Significance of Childhood Iron Deficiency

The NHANES II data indicated that in the late 1970s the prevalence of iron deficiency for US children 1 to 5 years of age, was about 4%–5%. For children under 2 years of age, the estimated prevalence was 9%–10%. Each year approximately 3.5 million children are born in the United States. Using the NHANES II prevalence and taking the declining trend of iron-deficiency anemia into account, potentially 150000 to 300000 children from each birth cohort could be adversely affected by iron deficiency.

The growing awareness of various adverse physiological consequences has highlighted the need to prevent and to treat childhood iron deficiency. Altered behavior and development of younger children are perhaps the best studied and have generated the greatest concern. Two issues are of public health relevance here. One is that although some of the adverse effects of iron deficiency can be reversed with iron treatment, recent studies have indicated the possibility of a non-reversible component of set-back in child development [20]. If this is indeed the case, the best strategy for avoiding any irreversible adverse effect of iron deficiency on behavior is to prevent its occurrence. Such prevention is feasible;

the declining trend of anemia among US children related to improved iron nutrition demonstrates that iron deficiency can be successfully prevented. Primary prevention efforts would rely on adequate iron supplementation in the diet and educational efforts to improve infant feeding practices known to improve better iron nutritional status: breast-feeding, using iron-fortified formula, and avoiding the early use of large quantities of whole milk. Secondary prevention of iron deficiency based on anemia screening with Hb or Hct would result in missing substantial numbers of iron-deficient children without anemia as illustrated in Table 2.1. For this reason, current screening methods for iron deficiency may need to be reassessed, and more sensitive methods may need to be developed.

The other issue of public health significance also indirectly involves behavior and child development: the enhanced heavy metal absorption related to iron deficiency. NHANES II data provided an opportunity to examine the interaction of childhood lead poisoning and iron deficiency. The children with iron deficiency defined as Sat < 10% were three times more likely to be found with increased blood lead (Pb > 30 mg/dl), than were children with Sat $\geq$ 30%. Those children with intermediate Sat (10%–29%) were twice as likely to have elevated blood lead [21].

This epidemiological evidence of association (not necessarily causal) of childhood lead poisoning with iron deficiency agrees with evidence from clinical studies which found a very high prevalence of iron deficiency among lead-poisoned children [22], and from animal and human lead absorption studies which found iron deficiency resulted in increased lead absorption and tissue lead retention [23,24]. Since lead poisoning is a major contributor to neurological damage and developmental delay in many urban areas of the United States, for those children living in an at-risk environment for lead poisoning, iron deficiency may very well be contributing to the adverse effect on brain related to lead. Because of the interaction of iron deficiency and childhood lead poisoning, lead exposure and its adverse effect on the central nervous system can potentially confound the study of the effect of iron deficiency on brain function [25]. For this reason, it may be necessary to control for lead-exposure status in studying the brain function of iron-deficient children, since they are more likely to absorb lead than control (non-iron-deficient) children. Most of the existing neuropsychological studies on iron deficiency have not performed strict control for lead status. Similarly, for the proper study of neuropsychological outcomes of low-level lead exposure in children, controlling for iron nutritional status is also necessary.

From a public health perspective, the improved iron nutritional status of infants and children represents another success in prevention. Improved infant feeding practices have likely resulted in a significant reduction of one of the most common nutrition disorders of US children. In general, prevention is a superior approach to screening and treatment. As with other preventive practices such as childhood immunization, continuing effort is needed to ensure further reduction of childhood iron deficiency.

References

1. Dallman PR, Yip R, Johnson C (1984) Prevalence and causes of anemia in the United States, 1976 to 1980. Am J Clin Nutr 39:437–445
2. Expert Scientific Working Group (1985) Summary of a report on assessment of the iron nutrition status of the United States population. Am J Clin Nutr 42:1318–1330
3. Galen RS, Gambino SR (1975) Beyond normality: the predictive value and efficiency of medical diagnosis. John Wiley and Sons, New York
4. Committee on Nutrition, American Academy of Pediatrics (1985) Nutrition Handbook American Academy of Pediatrics, Elk Grove Village, Illinois
5. Hillman RS, Finch CA (1985) Red cell manual, 5th edn. FA Davis, Philadelphia, pp 56–98
6. Lozoff B, Brittenham GM, Viteri FE, Wolf AW, Urrutia JJ (1982) Developmental deficits in iron deficient infants: effects of age and severity of iron lack. J Pediatr 101:948–952
7. Vazquez-Seoane, P, Windom R, Pearson HA (1985) Disappearance of iron deficiency anemia in a high risk infant population given supplemental iron. N Engl J Med 313:1239–1240
8. Miller V, Swaney S, Deinard AS (1985) Impact of the WIC program on the iron status of infants. Pediatrics 75:100–105
9. Yip R, Binkin NJ, Flashood L, Trowbridge FL (1987) Declining prevalence of anemia among low-income children in the United States. JAMA 258:1619–1623
10. Yip R, Walsh KM, Goldfarb MG, Binkin NJ (1987) Declining prevalence of anemia in childhood in a middle-class setting: a pediatric success story? Pediatrics 80:330–334
11. Yip R, Binkin NJ, Trowbridge FL (1986) Declining childhood anemia prevalence in the US: evidence of improving iron nutrition. Blood 68:51a
12. Human Nutrition Information Service (1985) National food consumption survey: continuing survey of food intakes by individuals: women 19–50 years and their children 1–5 years, 1 day, 1985, US Dept of Agriculture NFCS, CSFII report 85–1
13. Rush D, Leighton JL, Slaon NL, Alvir JM, et al. (1988) The national WIC evaluation, VI. Study of infants and children. Am J Clin Nutr 48:484–511
14. Committee on Nutrition, American Academy of Pediatrics (1976) Iron supplementation for infants. Pediatrics 58:765–768
15. Martinez GA, Nalezienski JP (1979) The recent trend in breast-feeding. Pediatrics 64:686–692
16. MacKay HMM (1931) Anemia in infancy with special reference to iron deficiency. Med Res Counc Spec Rep Series No.157
17. Anyon CP, Clarkson KG (1974) Cow's milk, a cause of iron deficiency anemia in infants. NZ Med J 74:24
18. Committee on Nutrition, American Academy of Pediatrics (1969) Iron balance and requirements in infancy. Pediatrics 43:134
19. Committee on Nutrition, American Academy of Pediatrics (1971) Iron fortified formula. Pediatrics 47:786
20. Lozoff B, Brittenham GM, Wolf AW, et al. (1987) Iron deficiency anemia and iron therapy effects on infant developmental test performance. Pediatrics 79:981–995
21. Centers for Disease Control (1985) Preventing lead poisoning in young children: a statement for Centers for Disease Control, Atlanta, DHSS pub no. 99–2230
22. Yip R, Norris TN, Anderson AS (1985) Iron status of children with elevated blood lead concentrations. J Pediatr 98:922–925
23. Mahaffey-Six KR, Goyer RA (1972) The influence of iron deficiency on tissue iron content and toxicity in ingested lead in the rat. J Lab Clin Med 79:128–136
24. Watson WS, Hume R, Moore MR (1980) Oral absorption of lead and iron. Lancet 2:236–237
25. Rutter M (1980) Raised lead levels and impaired cognitive/behavioral functioning: a review of the evidence. Dev Med Child Neurol 22 (Suppl):1–26

Commentary

Walter: There seems to me to be no really good evidence that iron deficit short of anaemia may produce behavioural consequences. It is a disturbing fact that so many infants, even in the US, are allowed to become anaemic and that many more are at high risk of reaching that stage.

Lozoff and Felt: We are somewhat concerned by the Chapter's comments on brain function. To our knowledge, none of the studies of infants and children can be sure that they study brain function apart from peripheral changes. It therefore may be premature to use the term "brain function" at the present time. Furthermore, comments about the ill effects of iron deficiency in the absence of anemia perhaps need to be stated more tentatively, given that neither Walter nor our group were able to identify such ill effects in two recent, large studies [1,2]. The only explanation we have for the discrepancy between our results in Costa Rica [2] and in Guatemala [3], where ill effects in the absence of anemia were suggested, is that the Guatemalan findings were restricted to older infants (in the 19–24-month age range), who may have had their iron deficiency for an extended period of time, with other associated problems.

References

1. Walter T, DeAndraca I, Chadud P, Perales CG (1989) Iron deficiency anemia: Adverse effects on infant psychomotor development. Pediatrics 84:7–14
2. Lozoff B, Brittenham GM, Wolf AW, et al. (1987) Iron deficiency anemia and iron therapy: Effects on infant developmental test performance. Pediatrics 79:981–995
3. Lozoff B, Brittenham GM, Viteri FE, Wolf AW, Urrutia JJ (1982) Developmental deficits in iron-deficient infants: Effects of age and severity of iron lack. J Pediatr 101:948–952

Finberg: Since iron deficiency (at least iron-deficient anemia) is disappearing, do we have any evidence of improved cognition in United States children? Will SAT scores rise in 10–12 years?

Author's reply: I do not know.

Walter: The statistical acrobatics to prove that iron nutrition in infancy (with or without the WIC) has improved in North American infants could have been avoided by using the simple prospective follow-up of a WIC compared with a non-WIC cohort, with careful surveillance of intervening variables. However, I understand the ethical constraints that may now preclude this study. It should have been performed before WIC began.

Table 2.4 is very convincing. However I wonder if the bioavailability of the iron consumed by the poorest was similar to that in the less poor? If the WIC was the main cause of the increase, the relatively high bioavailability of the iron in WIC (iron-fortified formula) should have induced a more marked change in iron status in this group. However, this change, if it occurred, may also be due to the "ceiling effect", the poor having more room for improvement than the less poor.

Parks: The decline in the prevalence of iron-deficiency anaemia in the USA is very impressive. The overall changes in infant diet makes interpretation of the impact of the WIC program more complicated. Does the author think the WIC program should be available to all low income families now that the prevalence of anaemia is so low?

Author's reply: Yes, it should. Like immunization it needs to continue to keep the prevalence low.

Smart: The inference from the finding that the incidence of anaemia declined between 1969 and 1986 in younger and older children, that improvement of the iron nutritional status at an early age may positively influence iron nutritional status at a later age seems unwarranted. It may be the case, I suppose, but it seems much more likely that the benefits result from improved iron nutrition throughout childhood.

Lozoff and Felt: Regarding Yip's comments that the iron status of the US population improved in general, not only among those infants receiving WIC support, it is important to repeat that during the last couple of decades, infant feeding has changed throughout the country in ways that support improved iron nutrition – increased breast-feeding, iron-fortified formulas and cereals, and delayed introduction of whole cow's milk. Given these dramatic changes in feeding practices, it would surely be difficult to attribute improved iron status solely to WIC. However, the value of the WIC program in making iron-fortified products more readily available to the poor cannot be emphasized enough in view of Yip's data showing that the prevalence of anemia drops even further when such infants go on the WIC program.

Larkin: One interesting aspect of iron deficiency raised by the author is the enhanced heavy metal absorption related to iron deficiency, especially with regard to lead poisoning. This adds yet another confounding note in unravelling the specific effects of iron deficiency from other variables both in the patients and the experimental models.

Finberg: The association of lead poisoning with iron deficiency may have some causal connection but also may have little or none. Both are seen in certain circumstances of poverty and ignorance.

Author's reply: I agree. I wrote that iron deficiency can contribute to lead absorption, not that there was a direct causal relationship.

Smart: The finding of increased heavy metal absorption associated with iron deficiency and the suggestion that the iron deficiency directly enhances absorption of lead is extremely interesting. Is there any possibility that the relationship might be the converse of that suggested, i.e. that increased ingestion of heavy metals causes iron deficiency?

Lozoff and Felt: Another interesting contrast between the US and the Costa Rican data is that the Costa Rican infants with iron deficiency did not seem to be at any increased risk for having an elevated blood lead level. Of the 318 totally healthy children for whom we have venipuncture specimens, only two had blood levels above 25 µg/dl and neither was in the iron-deficient anemic group [1].

Reference

1. Lozoff B, Brittenham GM, Wolf AW, et al. (1987) Iron deficiency anemia and iron therapy: Effects on infant developmental test performance. Pediatrics 79:981–995

Dobbing: Could we avoid the expression "lead poisoning" in this context? For doctors and pathologists (at least in the UK) it has a connotation whole orders different from the small increases in lead being discussed here. Also I strongly disagree that the degree of lead exposure mentioned here "is a major contributor to neurological *damage*" and developmental delay.

Parks: In the anaemic group what was the presumed cause of the anaemia in those who were *not* iron deficient?

Author's reply: "Statistical anemia": 2%–5% is the expected baseline due to laboratory errors, and other causes such as infection and thalassemia traits.

Parks: Even though checking the haemoglobin alone may fail to detect up to 50% of iron-deficient children this still remains the best screening test for "significant" iron deficiency.

Lozoff and Felt: Yip makes a point that cannot be emphasized enough: that the iron deficiency: anemia ratio is likely to vary from population to population. This point is well illustrated by data from the Costa Rican study. In this study we had iron measures for 318 children with completely normal medical histories, normal lead levels (< 25 µg/dl), and AA hemoglobin patterns on electrophoresis. One hundred and thirty-three of these children (42%) had two or more iron measures in the deficient range and 58 (15%) of them were anemic as well, giving an iron deficiency: anemia ratio of 2.3. In addition, 45% of the remaining children had a single iron measure in the abnormal range, and only 12% had normal measures on all three iron parameters. These data contrast not only with the US data in terms of the iron deficiency: anemia ratio but also markedly with respect to the prevalence both of iron deficiency and of anemia. Furthermore, in contrast to the finding in the NHANES II data, in which only one of ten anemic cases was iron deficient, nine of ten anemic children were iron deficient in the Costa Rican sample. This comparison emphasizes the need for caution in making general statements from US data. This caution may also apply to data from any country in which iron-fortified cereals and formulas are widely available and there is a delay in the introduction of solid foods.

Chapter 3

Importance of Fetal and Neonatal Iron: Adequacy for Normal Development of Central Nervous System

Edward C. Larkin and G. Ananda Rao

Iron is an integral component or an essential cofactor of several enzymes such as aconitase, catalase, cytochrome C, cytochrome C reductase, cytochrome C oxidase, formiminotransferase, monoamine oxidase, myeloperoxidase, peroxidase, ribonucleotidyl reductase, succinic dehydrogenase, tyrosine hydroxylase, tryptophan pyrrolase and xanthine oxidase [1]. These enzymes are involved in a number of important pathways such as DNA synthesis, mitochondrial electron transport, catecholamine metabolism, neurotransmitter levels, and detoxification [1]. Iron is also involved in lipid metabolism. The multienzyme complex which catalyses the desaturation of stearoyl-CoA to yield the monounsaturated oleoyl-Coa ($\triangle$ 9-desaturase) contains not only cytochrome b_5 but also a terminal desaturase enzyme which is a non-heme iron protein [2–4]. Thus, each desaturase enzyme complex contains two atoms of iron. Iron is also required for the production of polyunsaturated fatty acids [5]. Carnitine is necessary for the transport of long-chain fatty acids into the mitochondria for beta-oxidation. Its synthesis from trimethyl lysine involves two hydroxylases which require ferrous iron [6,7]. Hepatic levels of carnitine have been reported to be reduced in iron-deficient rat pups compared to iron-supplemented controls [8]. Thus iron has an important role in various metabolic events related to lipids, such as oxidative degradation of fatty acids, synthesis of mono- and polyunsaturated fatty acids, plasmalogens and prostaglandins [9]. Although lipids play a key role in many health-related problems such as obesity, cancer and heart disease, investigations on the effects of iron deficiency on tissue lipid metabolism have been sparse.

Since myelin is composed of 80% lipid, myelination culminates in a rapid increase in brain lipid per gram tissue [10]. The lipid content of rat brain increases about three fold from birth to 4 weeks. Brain has a low lipogenic capacity compared with other organs such as liver, and therefore it depends on an external source of lipids such as those from the diet or hepatic synthesis. The blood–brain barrier is not considered to be a barrier for lipids. Hence, the effect of iron deficiency on lipid metabolism in tissues such as liver or plasma may be reflected in brain, thereby altering the normal function and development of the central nervous system. Increase in DNA, protein and lipid in brain during development [10] suggests that iron may have an important role in this process. However, in this review we restrict our discussion to only those effects which are related to the role of prenatal iron deficiency on the metabolism of lipids. This includes (a) hypertriglyceridemia, (b) fatty liver, (c) changes in tissue fatty acid composition (d) hypomyelination and (e) fatty acid oxidation by the cerebral tissue.

Hypertriglyceridemia

Since the early report by Boggs and Morris [11] that repeated bleeding of rabbits caused lipemic blood, many investigators have reported lipemia when anemia was produced by hemorrhage [12–16]. Association of nutritional iron deficiency and lipemia was later recognized by Amine and Hegsted [17]. When chicks or weanling rats were fed iron-deficient diets for 5 weeks, a significant rise in their plasma triacylglycerol (TG) content was observed compared to controls fed the iron-supplemented diet. The extent of lipemia was found to be a function of the degree of iron-deficiency [17]. In subsequent studies by Lewis and Iammarino, when male rats weaned at 3 weeks of age were fed an iron-deficient diet for 5 weeks, the serum TG content was 135 mg% while it was only 28 mg% in the controls [18]. In numerous investigations, Sherman and colleagues have reported that maternal dietary iron restriction during gestation and lactation caused lipemia in the pups [19–23]. Even though pups developed lipemia, iron-deficient dams did not [19]. Furthermore, in some experiments with iron-deficient female or male adult rats, serum contained a lower level of TG compared to that in the controls [24,25]. Thus, it would appear that hyperlipemia which is associated with iron deficiency is related to the age of the animal and is observed only at a young age. However, this may not be a valid conclusion since in some experiments, the serum TG levels of not only iron-deficient pups but also of dams was found to be markedly greater than the levels in the corresponding controls [26]. Conflicting results have also been obtained on serum lipid levels of anemic human subjects. Many investigations have demonstrated an enchanced serum lipid level during iron deficiency in humans [27–30]. In contrast, other studies have shown either no significant relationship between anemia and serum lipids [31] or a hypolipemia in patients with anemias of different origins [32–35]. These observations show that it is difficult always to equate iron deficiency with occurrence of lipemia. However, one can conclude that maternal iron deficiency during pregnancy and lactation in rats consistently produces hypertriglyceridemia in the offspring.

Several investigations have been carried out to understand the mechanisms responsible for the production of lipemia. The contents of TG and cholesterol in the milk produced by the iron-deficient dams were similar to those of controls and hence were considered to have no role in causing lipemia [21]. Assay of lipoprotein lipase activity suggested that the clearance of lipids from blood in iron-deficient pups was similar to that in controls [21]. Since incorporation in vitro of $[1-^{14}C]$ glucose into TG was found to be significantly greater with liver slices from iron-deficient pups than in controls, it was suggested that lipemia is related to increased endogenous synthesis of TG [21]. This may not be true since the hepatic lipogenic potential is low in iron-deficient pups [36]. The fatty acid synthetase activity in the livers of iron-deficient pups is even lower than that in the iron-supplemented controls (Table 3.1). When the lipogenic capacity of liver is enhanced in rats fasted for 2 days and then maintained on a fat-free, high carbohydrate diet for a week, the hepatic fatty acid synthetase activity is increased several-fold compared to that in the livers of iron-deficient or iron-supplemented pups (61.5 ± 4.9 units/mg cytosolic protein) [36]. The capacity of liver to synthesize TG from [1-^{14}C] palmitate was also found to be not significantly different from that in the iron-supplemented controls [21].

Table 3.1. Body weight, hemoglobin, hematocrit, plasma triacylglycerol (TG), and hepatic fatty acid synthetase levels in iron-deficient or iron-supplemented 17-day-old rat pups

	Iron-deficient	Iron-supplemented
Body weight (g)	24.7 ± 3.1	46.8 ± 2.8
Hemoglobin (g/dl)	5.8 ± 0.6	10.7 ± 0.4
Hematocrit (%)	14.7 ± 1.1	34.6 ± 1.5
Plasma TG (mg/dl)	482 ± 73	41 ± 8
Hepatic fatty acid synthetase (units/mg cytosolic protein)	6.6 ± 0.4	8.2 ± 0.6

Values given are mean ± s.d. with 5 pups in each diet group [36].

Table 3.2. Fatty acid composition of plasma triacylglycerol (TG) from iron-deficient or iron-supplemented 17-day-old rat pups

Fatty acid	Rat milk fat (% total)	Plasma TG	
		Iron-deficient (% total)	Iron-supplemented (% total)
6:0	0.4	24.1 −	24.1 −
8:0	7.6	−	−
10:0	20.3	1.2 ± 0.1	−
12:0	13.0	8.1 ± 0.6	4.1 ± 0.5
14:0	10.2	13.1 ± 2.7	4.8 ± 0.9
16:0	26.3	27.0 ± 5.2	25.0 ± 3.7
16:1 ω9	1.6	4.4 ± 0.8	1.7 ± 0.3
18:0	3.3	2.6 ± 0.5	5.9 ± 0.4
18:1 ω9	12.6	24.1 ± 1.1	25.5 ± 3.2
18:2 ω6	4.8	19.6 ± 2.4	32.8 ± 6.8

Fatty acid composition of plasma TG is given as mean ± s.d. from 4 pups in each diet group [36]. The fatty acid composition of rat milk fat is from Smith and Abraham [37].

The mechanism for the production of lipemia in iron-deficient pups is unknown. Comparison of the fatty acid composition of plasma TG with that of rat milk TG indicate that the fatty acid in plasma may have originated from mother's milk fat [36] (Table 3.2). Capric (10:0), lauric (12:0), myristic (14:0) and linoleic (18:2 ω6) acids in plasma TG comprised about 40% of total fatty acids. These acids are not produced in the liver and must have originated from milk fat where they are present. Most of palmitic (16:0) and oleic (18:1 ω9) acids, the major acids in plasma TG, along with stearic (18:0) acid may not also be produced endogenously due to the low lipogenic capacity of liver.

Presence of a large amount of short- and medium-chain fatty acids in plasma TG in iron-deficient pups compared to controls suggests that their oxidation for the production of energy or utilization for chain elongation may be depressed. Iron-containing proteins involved in oxidation metabolism are known to be decreased during iron deficiency [38]. Morphological changes in the tissues of iron-deficient rat pups have also been observed [38]. Carnitine, required for the transport of long-chain fatty acids into the mitochondria for beta-oxidation is reduced in the liver of iron-deficient pups compared to controls [8]. Due to these changes, it is likely that iron deficiency can cause a profound effect on tissue fatty acid utilization resulting in increased levels of circulating TG.

Plasma lecithin cholesterol acyl transferase (LCAT) has been considered to play a role in altering the lipoprotein composition and a reduction of activity of this enzyme has been suggested to be responsible for the production of lipemia due to iron deficiency [39]. However, in iron-deficient rats, even in the absence of lipemia, the plasma LCAT activity has been found to be reduced [25,40]. The mechanism by which the plasma LCAT activity is affected by iron deficiency is not known. This enzyme is mainly extracellular and is secreted into plasma by liver. The role of iron in the production of LCAT remains to be investigated. Earlier studies on the effect of iron deficiency on LCAT activity were carried out using adult rats. The effect of prenatal iron deficiency on the plasma LCAT levels of the offspring and during development has not been examined.

Fatty Liver

Eighteen-day-old rat pups from iron-deficient dams show not only lipemia but also centrilobular liver lesions with the hepatocytes in these areas showing deposition of enlarged fat globules [23]. Liver lipid analysis revealed an accumulation of TG (132.3 ± 16.8 mg/g) compared to the controls (18.2 ± 1.8 mg/g) [26] which was appreciably greater than that observed in rats with alcoholic fatty liver [41] or due to choline deficiency [42]. However, it was not known whether the hepatic fat accumulation occurred prenatally or subsequent to the birth of pups. Recent studies to examine this question showed a progressive development of fatty liver and changes in hepatocyte ultrastructure in the iron-deficient neonatal rat [43]. Livers of one-day-old iron-deficient and control pups did not exhibit a difference between one another. An increase in lipid vacuoles per hepatocyte was observed in the iron-deficient neonates with age. Five-day-old iron-deficient pups showed a 340% increase in lipid content, 11-day-old 925% and 18-day-old 1397% compared to the iron-supplemented corresponding controls [43]. The progressive fat accumulation observed by morphometric measurements was further confirmed by an analysis of lipid content of neonatal rat livers [44]. The hepatic TG content of one-day-old rat pups born to female rats which were fed an iron-deficient diet during pregnancy and lactation was similar to that in the one-day-old pups born to the controls. However, as the iron-deficient pups grew, their liver TG content increased. At weaning, the hepatic TG level in iron-deficient pups was about nine-fold greater than that in the corresponding controls [44] (Table 3.3). These observations clearly demonstrate that fatty liver does not occur at birth but rather develops due to iron deficiency during postnatal growth.

Table 3.3. Liver lipid content of rat pups at various ages.

Age of pups	TG		PL		Cholesterol		Cholesterol ester	
(days)	Fe$^+$	Fe$^-$	Fe$^+$	Fe$^-$	Fe +	Fe$^-$	Fe$^+$	Fe −
1	17.4	16.8	22.8	24.7	2.1	3.8	1.9	3.6
5	12.6	29.7	25.1	23.5	1.8	4.2	2.0	4.5
12	10.8	56.9	22.5	24.6	1.9	3.7	2.2	4.4
21	12.7	115.3	25.7	26.5	2.4	4.6	2.5	4.7

Values given are mg/g liver and are mean values from separate analyses of liver lipids from 4 pups at each age [44].

Enhanced accumulation of TG in the liver may not be due to increased lipogenesis. This conclusion is supported by the fact that the liver fatty acid synthetase activity in iron-deficient pups is even less than that in the controls (Table 3.1) and meager compared to the conditions under which lipogenesis is stimulated [36]. Increased levels of TG in both plasma and liver compared to those in the controls indicate that the utilization of lipids for storage or energy production may be hampered due to iron deficiency.

Fatty Acid Composition of Liver Lipids

Since iron is required for the fatty acid desaturase activity, the ratio of monoenoic to saturated acids (16:1/16:0 and 18:1/18:0) in tissue lipids is reduced by iron deficiency [45]. Iron deprivation has also been shown to diminish the hepatic microsomal $\triangle$9-desaturase activity [46]. These studies of the role of dietary iron in influencing the tissue fatty acid composition and acyl-desaturase activity were conducted with adult rats. Such effects of iron deprivation can also occur in pups. In liver, 16:1ω9 is generated by the desaturation of 16:0 and 20:4ω6 is produced by the desaturation and elongation of 18:2ω6. Levels of both 16:1ω9 and 20:4ω6 were reduced in liver phospholipids from iron-deficient pups compared to the controls [44] (Table 3.4). Analysis of the content and fatty acid composition of liver lipids shows that many changes in lipid metabolism occur in the liver during the initial growth period of pups due to iron deficiency [44]. These will reflect in the lipids in circulation and so may influence the lipid composition and development of the brain.

Table 3.4. Fatty acid composition of liver phospholipids of rat pups at various ages

Age of pups (days)		14:0	16:0	16:1	18:0	18:1ω9	18:2ω6	20:4 ω6
1	Fe$^+$	T	24.8	1.2	10.6	18.7	22.6	21.7
	Fe$^-$	3.2	22.5	T	12.1	20.6	30.4	10.5
5	Fe$^+$	0.8	26.2	1.8	11.3	20.2	24.5	15.2
	Fe$^-$	2.6	24.8	T	10.6	22.8	28.4	10.5
12	Fe$^+$	T	25.0	2.6	10.8	21.6	23.6	16.3
	Fe$^-$	1.8	24.2	1.2	11.7	22.8	29.7	8.6
21	Fe$^+$	1.2	22.5	1.7	12.4	22.1	24.6	15.5
	Fe$^-$	2.8	23.2	T	12.6	24.8	28.6	7.4

Values given are as per cent of total fatty acids. Values less than 0.5% are given as T [44].

Hypomyelination

Myelin from adult brain contains cholesterol, phospholipids and galactolipids (cerebrosides + sulphatides) in a molar ratio of approximately 2:2:1 and this composition is similar in all vertebrate species [47]. However, this ratio is approximately 2:3.5:0.2 in myelin from brains of 12-day-old rats [48]. The high proportion of phospholipid and the low proportion of cerebroside are characteristic of the outer membrane of many animal cells and may reflect the lower surface to volume ratio of cells in the growing brain. Myelin accounts for a higher proportion of lipid than any other brain subcellular structure and its lipid content is greater than that of other types of biological membrane. At least 44% of the total brain cholesterol and 68% of the cerebroside is present in the myelin [49]. About 25%–30% of the dry weight of myelin consists of protein.

Myelination has been regarded as a "once and for all process" since the mature central nervous system has no capacity to remyelinate following demyelination [50]. In adult brain, lipid biosynthesis occurs at a slow rate while in the developing brain many brain lipids are actively synthesized during the myelination period. This period has been considered as a vulnerable period for the myelinating brain. Inhibition of lipid and protein biosynthesis as a result of nutritional restriction or disease in the developing animals may lead to incomplete or faulty myelination [50]. On the contrary, it can be anticipated that deprivation of the mature nervous system would have little effect on the metabolically stable myelin [51]. Thus, although conditions unfavorable for the formation of myelin may not reduce the amount of myelin in adult animals, if they occur during active myelination, they can cause a permanent and irreversible deficiency of myelin in the brain. There are several factors such as malnutrition [52,53], and specific deficiencies of either thyroid hormone [54], vitamin B$_6$ [55] or copper [56] which are known to reduce myelination. Recent studies from our laboratory show that dietary deprivation of iron during the fetal and neonatal period can also reduce or retard myelination [57].

Brains of young rats have a greater capacity than any other tissue for synthesizing cholesterol from acetate in vitro but adult brain cannot synthesize cholesterol in vitro [58]. Although it is likely that most of the cholesterol in the brain is made in situ, some of it must be also deprived from plasma since ^{14}C-cholesterol in vitro [58]. Although it is likely that most of the cholesterol in the brain is made in situ, some of it must be also derived from plasma since ^{14}C-acid synthesis based on maximum enzyme capacity is sufficient to account for the accumulation of saturated fatty acids in the cerebral lipids [60]. However, fatty acids originating from dietary fat such as $18:2\omega6$ needed for the synthesis of $20:4\omega6$ or $18:3\omega3$ for the synthesis of $22:6\omega3$ have to be obtained from circulation. Other unsaturated fatty acids such as $18:1\omega9$ or $20:4\omega6$ can be produced in the brain and/or derived from plasma lipoproteins. Iron appears to influence myelination by its effect on lipid metabolism not only in liver thereby causing changes in the fatty acid composition and contents of lipids in circulation but also in the brain itself.

The production of monoenoic fatty acids by $\triangle9$ – desaturase is most active in fetal rat brain and declines throughout the neonatal period while the enzyme activity increases in the liver [61,62]. The $\triangle9$-desaturase only occurs in the fetal and neonatal brain up to 20 days of age [63,64]. Arachidonic acid ($20:4\omega6$) is a major fatty acid of fetal brain phospholipids. Late in gestation, the fetal brain can synthesize $20:4\omega6$ from $18:2\omega6$ indicating that the $\triangle5$-desaturase and elongation systems are functional [65]. Thus, it would appear that at the time of most active differentiation, nervous tissue has the necessary enzyme machinery to adapt fatty acids synthesized within the brain or, as in the case of the $\omega3$ and $\omega6$ fatty acids, taken up from circulation to meet the changing requirements of the specialized membrane formation. However, the capacity for fatty acid desaturation in nervous tissue is low compared to fatty acid biosynthesis and a greater proportion of unsaturated fatty acids compared to saturated acids must be taken up from circulation by the developing brain [60].

Several studies have shown that hepatic fatty acid synthetase and desaturase activities are influenced by the nutritional status of the animal such as fasting, or ingestion of diets with a high level of fat or a high level of carbohydrate. However, these nutritional changes have no effect on the fatty acid synthetase and desaturase activities in the brain [60]. On the other hand, due to the essential requirement of iron for the desaturase, as in the case of liver [46], iron deprivation can be expected to depress the enzyme activity in the fetal and neonatal brain. An assay of desaturase in the developing brain during iron deficiency has not been carried out. Analysis of the fatty acid composition of brain lipids suggests that iron deprivation when young may be able to reduce the desaturase activity in the brain unlike in the case of adult rats. In the total lipids of rat brain, the levels of nervonic acid ($24:1\omega9$) and lignoceric acid ($24:0$) are relatively small when compared to other fatty acids such as $16:0$, $18:0$ and $18:1\omega9$ [66,67]. The $24:1\omega9$ and $24:0$ are present mostly in sphingolipids. Brain cerebrosides and sulfatides contain only a small level of $16:0$ or $18:0$ and are mainly esters of $24:1\omega9$ and $24:0$ [66]. When weaned iron-deficient rat pups were fed for 2 weeks an iron-deficient diet, the ratio of $24:1\omega9$ to $24:0$ in their brain total lipids decreased by about four-fold when compared to the iron-supplemented controls [67]. When the brain sphingolipids were analyzed for their fatty acid composition, those from iron-deficient pups but not adults exhibited a reduced ratio for $24:1\omega9$ to $24:0$ and $18:1\omega9$ to $18:0$ [67] (Table 3.5). When the iron-deficient pups were fed for 5 days an iron-supplemented diet, $18:1\omega9/18:0$ ratio increased to the control values. The relative level of $24:1\omega9$ to $24:0$ also increased markedly but did not achieve the normal value found in the iron-supplemented control pups [67]. Whether iron supplementation for a longer period would have further increased the relative level of $24:1\omega9$ to $24:0$ was not investigated. These observations demonstrate that iron deficiency in young rats can cause dramatic changes in the fatty acid composition of myelin-specific lipids such as cerebrosides.

Table 3.5. Fatty acid composition of brain sphingolipids from iron-deficient and iron-supplemented rats

	Pups (% total)			Adults (% total)	
Fatty acid	Iron-supplemented	Iron-deficient	Iron-repleted	Iron-supplemented	Iron-deficient
16:0	6.5	7.4	9.8	10.4	11.6
16:1 ω9	T	T	T	T	T
17:0	2.6	2.6	2.6	1.7	1.6
18:0	31.6	33.4	32.8	23.1	22.7
18:1ω9	5.8	2.3	6.2	13.2	14.4
19:0	2.6	3.1	2.1	2.2	1.8
20:0	T	T	T	1.9	2.2
22:0	4.8	6.1	3.7	3.1	2.8
22:1 ω9	6.2	4.0	7.3	7.6	8.5
24:0	10.3	15.2	11.7	6.7	6.0
24:1 ω9	15.7	13.5	12.3	15.2	12.0
22:5 ω6	1.9	4.4	6.9	2.6	2.6
22:6 ω3	11.3	8.0	4.6	11.3	13.4
$\dfrac{18:1}{18:0}$	0.18	0.07	0.19	0.57	0.63
$\dfrac{24:1}{24:0}$	1.52	0.89	1.05	2.27	2.00

Values given are mean from separate analyses with 5 rats in each group [67]. Values less than 0.5% are given as T.

In total fatty acids of brain sphingolipids, $24:1\omega9$ is a major component [66]. Myelin-deficient mutant mice such as Quaking and Jimpy are deficient in $24:1$ [68–70], indicating that this monounsaturated acid may have a role in myelinogenesis. Our results on the changes in the relative levels of $24:1\omega9$ in brain sphingolipids suggested that iron deficiency may also reduce myelinogenesis. In order to ascertain this, a histopathological examination of the brain from iron-deficient or iron-supplemented rat pups was carried out [57]. Pups were obtained from female rats which were fed an iron-deficient diet or iron-supplemented diet during both pregnancy and lactation. Immediately after anesthesia and the collection of blood, pups were fixed by intracardiac infusion of 2% gluteralde-hyde. Brain and cervical cord were fixed, embedded in paraffin wax and cut at 6µ thickness. Myelin was identified using Luxol fast blue stain. As compared with controls, 11-day-old iron-deficient pups showed reduced myelination in spinal cord. Although myelination increased somewhat in the iron-deficient 17-day-old pups, the amount of myelin in the spinal cord and white matter of cerebellar folds was reduced compared with that of the corresponding controls [57]. These studies have demonstrated the importance of prenatal iron adequacy in myelinogenesis.

Table 3.6. Effect of iron deficiency on brain lipids of rat pups

	Iron-supplemented	Iron-deficient
Body weight of pups (g)		
10 day	24.8 ± 3.2	16.4 ± 1.8
17 day	41.7 ± 4.6	25.2 ± 3.7
Brain weight (g)		
10 day	1.26 ± 0.23	1.02 ± 0.11
17 day	1.49 ± 0.35	1.20 ± 0.26
Hematocrit (%)		
10 day	35.5 ± 3.1	15.6 ± 2.4
17 day	42.6 ± 2.9	16.1 ± 1.7
Lipid content (µmol/g brain)		
Cerebroside		
10 day	4.82 ± 0.28	2.75 ± 0.35
17 day	7.82 ± 0.46	4.06 ± 0.27
Cholesterol		
10 day	13.8 ± 1.1	6.2 ± 0.7
17 day	18.4 ± 1.3	9.5 ± 0.6
Phospholipid		
10 day	30.1 ± 4.6	26.4 ± 6.2
17 day	27.2 ± 2.4	27.7 ± 4.8

Values given are mean ± s.d. from 5 pups in each group. Total lipid of brain was extracted [71]. Cerebroside was analysed by estimating the content of hexose [72], cholesterol, by using phthalaldehyde [73] and phospholipids by measuring the content of total phosphorus [72].

Additional support for the role of iron in myelinogenesis was obtained from an analysis of some myelin-specific lipids and myelin protein from the brain. In the iron-deficient pups, the level of cerebrosides and cholesterol, which are mostly present in the myelin fraction of brain, was less at 10 days of age compared to 17 days (Table 3.6). This may be related to the fact that in rats, myelination begins about 10 days after birth and thereafter continued growth of brain with deposition of myelin occurs [50]. At either age, the levels of these lipids in the brain of the control pups were greater compared to those in the iron-deficient pups indicating a reduced myelination due to iron deficiency. This is further supported by the fact that the amount of myelin protein (3.04 mg/g brain) from the brain of 17-day-old iron-deficient rat pups was markedly less than that from the brain of 17-day-old controls (4.83 mg/g brain). However, the relative content of protein, cholesterol, cerebroside and phospholipid was similar in the myelin fraction from the brain of iron-deficient and iron-supplemented pups (Table 3.7). These results further show that in the brain of 17-day-old iron-deficient pups, myelin content is reduced compared to that in the corresponding iron-supplemented controls. Due to the important role of iron in the production of unsaturated fatty acids, it is likely that the fatty acid composition of myelin lipids in the iron-deficient rat pups is different from that in the controls. If this is so, not only the content of myelin is reduced but also an altered myelin is produced due to iron deficiency. Further studies are needed to investigate these aspects of qualitative changes in myelination.

Table 3.7. Content of protein and lipids in the myelin fraction of brain from iron-deficient or iron-supplemented 17-day-old rat pups.

	Iron-deficient (%)	Iron-supplemented (%)
Protein	31.9	33.6
Cerebroside	13.6	16.8
Cholesterol	19.3	18.2
Phospholipid	35.2	31.4

Myelin was isolated as described by Norton and Poduslo [74]. Protein content was measured as described by Lowry et al. [75]. Myelin fractions from four brains were pooled to analyze the content of cerebroside [72], cholesterol [73] and phospholipid [72].

Fatty Acid Oxidation by Cerebral Tissue

Fatty acid oxidation does not occur in the cerebral tissue of the adult but has been shown to occur in the brain of fetal and neonatal rat [76], the human fetus [77] and the neonatal dog [78]. The peak activity for the carnitine translocation system involving mitochondrial fatty acyl-CoA:carnitine acyl transferase is reached in the neonatal brain at 10 days of age [79]. This activity is low before birth. The induction of fatty acid oxidation around birth may be hormonal or due to elevated levels of non-esterified fatty acids in circulation and their increased uptake [60]. The fatty acyl-CoA synthetase of cerebral mitochondria required for fatty acid activation has maximal activity prior to birth [80]. However, the carnitine acyl transferase and the fatty acyl-CoA synthetase activities of mitochondria begin to decline in the mid suckling period in the rat (81). The activation system for short-chain fatty acids is also known to increase in rat brain postnatally [82].

The inability of fatty acids to be utilized as a source of energy in the adult brain has been considered to be due to the absence of the mitochondrial translocation system and the low levels of carnitine [79]. While the potential for fatty acid oxidation in neonatal brain is evident from the activities of various enzymes involved, the quantitative importance of this process for the overall energy supply in the brain is unknown. In the neonatal dog, fatty acid oxidation has been suggested to contribute 25% of the oxidizable metabolites entering the TCA cycle [78]. Iron has a role in the fatty acid oxidation not only because it is a component of cytochromes, but also because it is involved in the production of carnitine [6,7]. Although iron deficiency has been shown to result in reduced levels of carnitine in the liver of pups [8] it remains to be determined whether the brain levels of this metabolite are also decreased under these conditions. Due to a reduced production of carnitine in the liver, the amount of this metabolite transported to brain will also be depressed by iron deficiency. To our knowledge, the effect of iron deficiency on fatty acid oxidation in neonatal brain has not been studied.

Conclusions

Earlier investigations on the effects of prenatal iron inadequacy were carried out by feeding rats iron-depleted diets containing only 5–10 mg/kg diet. Clinical iron deficiency in humans is usually not as severe as that achieved in laboratory animals. It is likely that some of the effects of iron deficiency discussed above may also be observed to some extent even if the animals are iron depleted with little or no anemia. This is supported by the results of recent studies in which rats were fed a diet containing 27 mg iron/kg [83]. An analysis of fatty acid composition of tissues revealed a mild impairment in essential fatty acid metabolism in moderately iron-deficient rats. A significant alteration in the total lipid content of plasma and erythrocytes also occurred as compared to the iron-supplemented controls (83). Effects of moderate iron deficiency on myelination and brain lipid metabolism remain to be investigated.

Some of the effects of iron deficiency during pregnancy and lactation are reversible by iron supplementation. Hypertriglyceridemia present in the iron-deficient weaned rats disappears when fed a control diet for nine days [22]. Iron supplementation also causes an increase in the hematocrit to control values [22]. However, to what extent the effects of iron deficiency during the neonatal period on the brain lipid changes and myelination can be corrected by iron supplementation will be ascertained only by further studies. When iron-deficient pups were fostered by normal control dams during the neonatal period, the degree of myelination was improved but was not comparable to that observed in the controls [57]. Many rehabilitation studies have been carried out in developing rats and pigs after subjection to various periods of undernutrition [84,85]. Evidence has been presented that effects of the lipid composition of the brain may be produced by nutritional restriction only during the vulnerable period of development and that this may be permanent [86]. It may be that most of the effects of iron deprivation on brain are irreversible and can occur only during the fetal and neonatal period.

Evidence from malnourished rats and pups suggests that poor mental performance may be related to restrictions imposed during the vulnerable period of brain development [53,84,87]. Iron deficiency during the vulnerable period can also have a similar effect. Many studies have shown that iron deficiency has adverse effects on attention, intelligence test performance and school achievement in children [88,89]. It has been demonstrated that iron supplementation among iron-deficient anemic children benefits the learning process as measured by the school achievement test scores [90]. Hence an adequacy of iron during the fetal and neonatal period may play an important role in the normal development of brain and intellectual performance of the animal.

Acknowledgements. Studies from our laboratory which were referred to in this review were supported by the Veterans Administration. We thank Mr Donald H. Cook for assistance in the preparation of this script.

References

1. Vyas D, Chandra RK (1984) Functional implications of iron deficiency. In Stekel A (ed): Iron nutrition in infancy and childhood. Raven Press, New York, pp 45–59
2. Shimakata T, Mihara K, Sato R (1972) Reconstitution of hepatic microsomal stearoyl coenzyme. A desaturase system from solubilized components. J Biochem (Tokyo) 72:1163–1174
3. Holloway PW, Katz JT (1972) A requirement for cytochrome b_5 in microsomal stearyl coenzyme A desaturation. Biochemistry 11:3689–3696
4. Strittmatter P, Spatz L, Corcoran D, Rogers MJ, Setlow B, Redline R (1974) Purification and properties of rat liver microsomal stearyl coenzyme desaturase. Proc Natl Acad Sci USA 71:4565–4569
5. Okayasu T, Nagao M, Ishibashi T, Imai Y (1981) Purification and partial characterization of linoleoyl-CoA desaturase from rat liver microsomes. Arch Biochem Biophys 206:21–28
6. Lindstedt G (1967) Hydroxylation of γ-butyrobetaine to carnitine in rat liver. Biochemistry 5:1271–1281
7. Hulse JD, Ellis SE, Henderson LM (1978) Carnitine biosynthesis. ß-Hydroxylation of trimethyl lysine by an α-ketoglutarate-dependent mitochondrial dioxygenase. J Biol Chem 253:1654–1659
8. Bartholmey SJ, Sherman AR (1985) Carnitine levels in iron-deficient pups. J Nutr 115:138–145
9. Rao GA, Larkin EC (1984) Role of dietary iron in lipid metabolism. Nutr Res 4:145–151
10. Dhopeshwarker GA (1983) Growth characteristics of the brain. Nutrition and brain development. Plenum Press, New York, pp 13–22
11. Boggs TR, Morris RS (1909) Experimental lipemia in rabbits. J Exp Med 11:553–560
12. Horiuchi Y (1920) Studies on blood fat. II Lipemia in acute anemia. J Biol Chem 44:363–379
13. Bloor WR (1921) Lipemia. J Biol Chem 49:201–227
14. Fishberg EH, Fishberg AM (1928) The mechanism of the lipemia of bleeding. Proc Soc Exp Biol Med 25:296–299
15. Johansen AH (1930) Lipemia in hemorrhagic anemia in rabbits. J Biol Chem 88:669–673
16. Spitzer JJ, Spitzer JA (1955) Hemorrhagic lipemia: a derangement of fat metabolism. J Lab Clin Med 46:461–470
17. Amine EK, Hegsted DM (1971) Iron deficiency lipemia in the rat and chick. J Nutr 101:1575–1582
18. Lewis M, Iammarino M (1971) Lipemia in rodent iron-deficiency anemia. J Lab Clin Med 78:546–554
19. Guthrie HA, Froozani HA, Wolinsky I (1974) Hyperlipidemia in offspring of iron deficient rats. J Nutr 104:1273–1278

20. Sherman AR, Guthrie HA, Wolinsky I (1977) Interrelationships between dietary iron and tissue zinc and copper levels and serum lipids in rats. Proc Soc Exp Biol Med 156:396–401
21. Sherman AR, Guthrie HA, Wolinsky I, Zulak IM (1978) Iron deficiency hyperlipidemia in 18-day-old rat pups: effects of milk lipids, lipoprotein lipase and triglyceride synthesis. J Nutr 108:152–162
22. Sherman AR (1979) Serum lipids in suckling and post-weanling iron-deficient rats. Lipids 14:888–892
23. Rothenbacher H, Sherman AR (1980) Target organ pathology in iron deficient suckling rats. J Nutr 110:1648–1654
24. Sherman AR (1978) Lipogenesis in iron deficient adult rats. Lipids 13:473–478
25. Rao GA, Crane RT, Larkin EC (1983) Reduced plasma lecithin cholesterol acyl transferase activity in rats fed iron deficient diets. Lipids 18:673–676
26. Sherman AR, Bartholmey SJ, Perkins EG (1982) Fatty acid patterns in iron deficient maternal and neonatal rats. Lipids 17:639–643
27. Bloor WR, MacPherson DJ (1917) Blood lipids in anemia. J Biol Chem 31:79–95
28. Erickson BN, Williams HH, Hummel FC, Lee P, Macy IG (1937) The lipids and mineral distribution of the serum and erythrocytes in the hemolytic and hypochromic anemias of childhood. J Biol Chem 18:569–597
29. Skrede S, Seip M (1979) Seum lipoproteins in children with anemia. Scand J Haematol 23:232–238
30. Ohira Y, Edgerton R, Gardner CW, Senewiratne B (1980) Serum lipid levels in iron deficiency anemia and effects of various treatments. J Nutr Sci Vitaminol 26:375–379
31. Fujii T, Shimizu H (1973) Investigations on serum lipid components and serum vitamin E in iron deficiency anemia. J Nutr Sci Vitaminol 19:23–28
32. Rifkind BM, Gale M (1967) Hypolipidemia in anemia. Lancet ii:640–642
33. Rifkind BM, Gale M (1968) Hypolipidemia in anemia. Am Heart J 76:849
34. Hashmi JA, Afroz N (1969) Hypolipidemia in anemia. Am Heart J 78:840
35. Bottiger LE, Carlson LA (1972) Relation between serum cholesterol and triglyceride concentration and haemoglobin values in non-anemic healthy persons. Brit Med J 3:731–733
36. Rao GA, Larkin EC (1988) Hypertriglyceridemia in iron-deficient neonatal rats: possible origin of fatty acids from milk fat. Biochem Arch 4:125–130
37. Smith S, Abraham S (1975) The composition and biosynthesis of milk fat. Adv Lipid Res 13:195–239
38. Dallman PR, Goodman JR (1971) The effects of iron deficiency on the hepatocyte: a biochemical and ultrastructural study. J Cell Biol. 48:79–90
39. Jain SK, Yip R, Pramanik AK, Dallman PR, Shohet SB (1982) Reduced plasma lecithin cholesterol acyl transferase activity in iron deficient rats: its possible role in the lipemia of iron deficiency. J Nutr 112:1230–1232
40. Rao GA, Jarratt BA, Larkin EC (1985) Decreased lecithin cholesterol acyl transferase activity in the plasma of rats due to iron deficiency. Biochem Arch 1:191–197
41. Rao GA, Larkin EC (1984) Alcoholic fatty liver : a nutritional problem of carbohydrate deprivation and concomitant ethanol ingestion. Nutr Res 4:903–912
42. Takada A, Porta EA, Hartroft WS (1967) Regression of dietary cirrhosis in rats fed alcohol and a "super diet". Am J Clin Nutr 20:213–225
43. Yu GSM, Larkin EC, Rao GA (1989) Progressive development of fatty liver and changes in hepatocyte ultrastructure in iron-deficient neonatal rats. Biochem Arch 5:91–99
44. Rao GA, Larkin EC (1989) Changes in liver lipids of iron-deficient rat pups during suckling period. Biochem Arch 5:125–132
45. Rao GA, Manix M, Larkin EC (1980) Reduction of essential fatty acid deficiency in rats fed a low iron fat free diet. Lipids 15:55–60
46. Rao GA, Crane RT, Larkin EC (1983) Reduction of hepatic stearoyl-CoA desaturase activity in rats fed iron-deficient diets. Lipids 18:573–575
47. Cuzner ML, Davison AN, Gregson NA (1966) Turnover of brain mitochondrial membrane lipids. Biochem J 101:618
48. Cuzner ML, Davison AN (1968) The lipid composition of rat brain myelin and subcellular fractions during development. Biochem J 106:29–34
49. Davison AN (1969) The biochemistry of myelinogenesis. Neuropat Pol 3:251–254
50. Davison AN (1969) Biochemistry of the myelin sheath. Ann Rev Sci Basis Med 220–235

51. Davison AN, Dobbing J (1966) Myelination as a vulnerable period in brain development. Br Med Bull 22:40–44
52. Dobbing J (1964) The influence of early nutrition on the development and myelination of the brain. Proc R Soc Lond (Biol) 159:503–509
53. Dobbing J (1968) Vulnerable periods in developing brain. In: Davison AN, Dobbing J. (eds) Applied neurochemistry. Blackwell, Oxford, pp 287–316
54. Dalal KB, Valcana T, Timiras S, Einstein ER (1971) Regulatory role of thyroxine on myelinogenesis in the developing rat. Neurobiol 1:211–224
55. Kurtz DJ, Kanfer JN (1973) Composition of myelin lipids and synthesis of 3-ketodihydrosphingosine in the vitamin B_6-deficient developing rat. J Neurochem 20:963–968
56. Zimmerman AW, Matthieu JM, Quarles RH, Brady RO, Hsu JM (1976) Hypomyelination in copper-deficient rats. Arch Neurol 33:111–119
57. Yu GSM, Steinkirchner TM, Rao GA, Larkin EC (1986) Effect of prenatal iron deficiency on myelination in rat pups. Am J Pathol 125:620–624
58. Srere PA, Chaikoff IL, Treitman SS, Burstein LS (1950) The extrahepatic synthesis of cholesterol. J Biol Chem 182:629–634
59. Davison AN, Dobbing J, Morgan RS, Payling Wright G (1959) Metabolism of myelin : the persistence of [4-^{14}C] cholesterol in the mammalian central nervous system. Lancet i:658–660
60. Carey EM (1982) The biochemistry of fetal brain development and myelination. In : Jones CT (ed) The biochemical development of the fetus and neonate. Elsevier, Amsterdam, pp 287–336
61. Cook HW, Spence MW (1973) Formation of monoenoic fatty acids by desaturation in rat brain homogenate. Some properties of the enzyme system of 10-day old brain. J Biol Chem 248:1786–1793
62. Cook HW, Spence MW (1973) Formation of monoenoic fatty acids by desaturation in rat brain homogenate. Effects of age, fasting and refeeding and comparison with the liver enzyme. J Biol Chem 248:1793–1796
63. Cook HW (1979) Differential alteration of $\triangle$9- and $\triangle$6-desaturation of fatty acids in brain preparations in vitro. Lipids 16:763–767
64. Cook HW, Spence MW (1974) Biosynthesis of fatty acids in vitro by homogenate of developing rat brain: desaturation and chain-elongation. Biochim Biophys Acta 369:129–141
65. Sanders TAB, Naismith DJ (1979) Synthesis of arachidonic acid by fetal rat brain. Proc Nutr Soc 38:94A
66. Pullarkat RK, Maddow J, Reha H (1976) Effect of early postnatal dietary sterculate on the fatty acid composition of rat liver and brain lipids. Lipids 11:802–807
67. Larkin EC, Jarratt BA, Rao GA (1986) Reduction of relative levels of nervonic to lignoceric acid in the brain of rat pups due to iron deficiency. Nutr Res 6:309–317
68. Baumann NA, Jacque CM, Pollet SA, Harpin ML (1968) Fatty acid and lipid composition of the brain of a myelin deficient mutant, the "quaking" mouse. Europ J Biochem 4:340–344
69. Nussbaum JL, Neskovic N, Mandel P (1971) Fatty acid composition of phospholipids and glycolipids in jimpy mouse brain. J Neurochem 18:1529–1543
70. Joseph KC, Druse MJ, Newell LR, Hogan EL (1972) Fatty acid composition of cerebrosides, sulphatides and ceramides in murine leucodystrophy : quaking mutant. J Neurochem 19:307–312
71. Folch J, Lees M, Sloane-Stanley GS (1957) A simple method for the isolation and purification of total lipids from animal tissues. J Biol Chem 226:497–509
72. Dittmer JC, Wells MA (1969) Quantitative and qualitative analysis of lipids and lipid components. Methods Enzymol 14:482–530
73. Rudel LL, Morris MD (1973) Determination of cholesterol using O-phthalaldehyde. J Lipid Res 14:364–366
74. Norton WT, Poduslo SE (1973) Myelination in rat brain: method of myelin isolation. J Neurochem 21:749–757
75. Lowry OH, Rosebrough NJ, Farr AL, Randall RJ (1951). Protein measurement with folin phenol reagent. J Biol Chem 193:265–275
76. Ramsay RB, Nicholas HJ (1972) Brain lipids. Adv Lipid Res 10:143–232
77. Yoshioka T, Roux JF (1972) In vitro metabolism of palmitic acid in human fetal tissue. Pediatr Res 6:675–681
78. Spitzer JJ (1975) Application of tracers in studying free fatty acid metabolism of various organs in vivo. Fed Proc 36:2242–2245

79. Warshaw JB, Terry ML (1976) Cellular energy metabolism during fetal development. VI, Fatty acid oxidation by developing brain. Dev Biol 52:161–166
80. Cantrill RC, Carey EM (1975) Changes in the activities of de novo fatty acid synthesis and palmitoyl-CoA synthetase in relation to myelination in rabbit brain. Biochim Biophys Acta 380:165–175
81. Gross I, Warshaw JB (1974) Fatty acid synthesis in developing brain. Biol Neonate 25:365–375
82. Reijnierse GLA, Veldstra H, Vandenberg CJ (1975) Short-chain fatty acid synthesis in brain. Subcellular localization and changes during development. Biochem J 152:477–484
83. Cunnane SC, MacAdoo KR (1987) Iron intake influences essential fatty acid and lipid composition of rat plasma and erythrocytes. J Nutr 117:1514–1519
84. Dobbing J (1987) Early nutrition and later achievement. Academic Press, London.
85. Dobbing J, Widdowson EM (1965) The effect of undernutrition and subsequent rehabilitation on myelination of rat brain as measured by its composition. Brain 88:357–366
86. Dobbing J (1966) Effect of undernutrition on myelination in central nervous system. Biol Neonat 9:132–147
87. Davison AN (1968) The influence of nutritional disorder in the lipid composition of the central nervous system. Proc Nutr Soc 27:83–85
88. Pollitt E, Leibel RL (1976) Iron deficiency and behavior. J Pediatr 88:372–381
89. Pollitt E, Saco-Pollitt C, Leibel RL, Viteri FE (1986) Iron deficiency and behavioral development in infants and preschool children. Am J Clin Nutr 43:555–565
90. Soemantri AG, Pollitt E, Kim I (1985) Iron deficiency anemia and educational achievement. Am J Clin Nutr 42:1221–1228

Commentary

Walter: I am surprised by the research that shows lipaemia in iron-deficiency anaemia. Commonly in clinical practice, one of the characteristics is precisely how pale and transparent is the serum when seen, for example, in the spun hematocrit tube.

Pearson: The authors relate lipidemia to iron deficiency. In the "old days" when patients with thalassemia major were permitted to drop their hemoglobin levels to 5 or 6 g/dl before transfusions, it was common to note grossly lipidemic sera that rapidly cleared with transfusion. Such patients had iron overload and hemosiderosis. Also, the usual finding in children with iron-deficiency anemia is pale, clear serum.

Finberg: Moving from the biochemical to the cognitive and behavioral consequences is a great and largely unsupported leap.

Walter: That DNA, lipid and iron accumulate during brain development cannot be adduced as implying that iron, lipid or DNA may be important to each other. This and other statements in the introductory paragraph need clarification. I do not see how plasma, liver, and dietary lipids may influence brain lipids with the possible exception of essential omega 3 and 6 series.

Assay of lipoprotein lipase (LPL) and ^{14}C-glucose incorporation in liver slices may give insufficient data to explain lipid clearance (transport). Levels of serum lipoproteins transporting fatty acids synthesized in the liver to LPL in the periphery are not accounted for. Moreover, the results of this study cannot be interpreted adequately if Table 3.1 is examined. The body weight of the iron-deficient pups is about half of that of the iron-supplemented animals. The enormous influence that undernutrition has at all levels of lipid metabolism should have been controlled for with pair-fed animals. Here it may be important to remember that, for example, the fatty liver of kwashiorkor is not a derangement of lipid metabolism, but rather a lack of protein-carrier molecules (lipoproteins). This may account for the findings described.

Omega-9-desaturase is influenced by insulin, temperature, protein, zinc and other factors. Is the effect of iron possibly mediated by any of these in experiments without optimal controls?

Yehuda: I am not an expert on brain lipid metabolism. My knowledge in this field is limited and mainly based on Dhopenshwarkar's book [1]. Reading this paper, I am impressed by the great advances in research and understanding since the publication of the book. Therefore I will limit my comments to general ones.

I am very much interested in a field in which lipids may play a major role. We are examining the role of the neuronal plasma membrane in mediating cognition and behaviour. Changes in the composition of the neuronal membrane may be expressed as changes in the "membrane fluidity index". There is no need here to describe the importance of the neuronal membrane in conducting neuronal potentials. The assumption is that changes in the composition of the neuronal membrane will be reflected in its functional level [2]. Many studies have indicated that the neuronal membrane should be at an optimal state: not too hard and not too soft. Changes in the functional level are expected to modify the conduction of neuronal impulses and the "behaviour" of neurotransmitter receptors [2]. Therefore, any major effect on the level of lipids or fatty acids in the brain is of great interest.

It is interesting to note that iron-deficient rats are very poor learners [3]. In our preliminary study we found that by using the gas chromatographic method, we can demonstrate a *significant increase* in the amount of cholesterol in the plasma membranes of the hippocampus, striatum and cortex of iron-deficient rats, but not in the brain stem or the cerebellum. An increase in cholesterol levels leads to decreases in the membrane fluidity index, i.e., a hardening of the membrane.

While these two phenomena (learning and cholesterol level in the plasma membrane) might not be related to one another, they justify a closer look at the influence of iron in brain lipids and fatty acids on behaviour.

References

1. Dhopeshwarkar GA (1983) Nutrition and brain development. Plenum Press, New York, pp 59–69
2. Yehuda S (1987) Nutrients, brain biochemistry and behavior: a possible role for the nuronal membrane. Int J Neurosci 35: 21–36
3. Yehuda S, Youdim MBH, Mostofsky DI (1986) Brain iron deficiency causes reduced learning capacity in rats. Pharmacol Biochem Behav 25:141–144

Author's reply: As noted in Table 3.5, the fatty acid 22:6ω3 is present in significant amounts in brain sphingolipids. This acid is derived from linolenic acid by the action of desaturases in the brain. The absence from brain of linolenic acid, an essential fatty acid, has been shown to result in defects in ethanolamines in rat brain, especially in the cerebellum. This absence of linolenic acid, and thereby loss of 22:6ω3 in brain sphingolipids, is associated with abnormal animal behavior.

Reference

Laatsch RH (1962) J Neurochem 9:487–492

Smart: Larkin and Rao describe a most interesting histophathological study from their laboratory of myelination in the offspring of iron-deficient female rats. They found reduced myelination of the spinal cord and cerebellar folds in 17-day old experimental pups as compared to "corresponding controls". I was prompted to comment that, presumably, these were controls of the same age and not controls of the same body weight, knowing that the iron deficiency was likely to have caused a general growth retardation and thinking that the effect on myelination might be a reflection of that rather than a specific effect of iron deficiency. In fact, Table 3.6 from a further experiment fortuitously affords the comparison I was looking for. It so happens that the 10-day old iron-supplemented rats are the same body weight as 17-day-old iron-deficient rats and are, therefore, effectively "weight controls" for them. Following this comparison down the table, brain weight is similar in these two groups, but brain cholesterol concentration is markedly low, and perhaps also cerebroside concentration, in the deficient group. Hence there would appear to be some specific effects of neonatal iron deficiency, over and above those of general growth restriction.

Larkin and Rao seem to be determined to sign off with a flourish in the last two pages of their review, throwing prudence to the winds and, I think, uncharacteristically indulging in some over-statement and over-simplification. I hope that they can be persuaded to take a dose of caution – perhaps from Lozoff's plentiful supply – and to consider revising this section.

Dobbing: Almost all its cholesterol, the most abundant substance in the brain, is synthesized in situ [1], as is acknowledged later. I know of no evidence that other lipids are transferred from blood to brain as the preformed molecule. If this is correct there need be no automatic effect of disturbances of liver or plasma lipids on the development of the central nervous system. Also a direct effect on behavioural or other function cannot be automatically assumed from a change in composition [2].

In any case it is not clear to me how hyperlipidaemia, which appears to be one result of iron deficiency, can lead to anything but an excessive supply to the developing brain, with which its relative metabolic autonomy might be expected to cope.

Although it may be "likely" that iron deficiency "can cause a profound effect on tissue fatty acid utilization", the same cannot be assumed for the brain as for other tissues. We have been taught that developing brain has considerable metabolic autonomy compared with other tissues, especially liver, and especially with respect to lipids. The relatively minor effects of severe undernutrition on the brain compared with those on other tissues are a good example.

Thus it cannot be *assumed* that changes in circulating lipid composition "can influence the lipid composition and development of the brain". Nor is it necessarily true that, "as in the case of liver, iron deprivation can be expected to depress the enzyme activity in the fetal and neonatal brain", especially when this activity has not been directly measured in developing brain during iron deficiency.

So many of the direct examinations of brain lipids in this context seem to have been carried out after weaning in the rat, i.e. at an equivalent age of more than 2 human years, and therefore later than the period at which lasting effects on brain structure or composition might be expected.

I do not know how much the views on the metabolic stability of the myelin sheath we expressed in the late 1960s (references 47–53 and 59) are still current, however archival they seemed at the time. Is it not the case that some constituents of myelin are apparently metabolically stable (reference 59), while others are very labile? I would have expected much of the 25-year-old literature to have been superseded by now.

The statement that "Iron can influence myelination . . . etc " appears to be unsupported, except by theory.

I am not clear whether the work described in reference 57 and Table 3.6 distinguished between delayed myelination on the one hand and persistently deficient myelination on the other. "Reduced" myelination, whether detected histochemically or biochemically, may signify nothing more than a potentially recoverable delay, part of a general growth retardation coinciding with a period of fast myelination. In this case there need be no specific role for iron deficiency in myelinogenesis.

I have never been able to attribute malfunction in the nervous system to moderately or slightly reduced myelination. Clearly, where small areas of myelin are completely destroyed, as in primary demyelination in the plaques of multiple sclerosis, there will be a loss of function. Equally where axons or whole tracts are subject to secondary demyelination following injury, there will also be loss of function. But nothing approaching these examples occurs in malnutrition, or, as far as is known, in iron deficiency. It may be that only a few laminae are lost in a myelin sheath in malnutrition, or do not appear, and I know of no neurophysiological reason why this should affect nerve impulse conduction. Is there any proposed model for the "reduced" myelination of iron deficiency producing functional impairment?

As a spectator of neurochemistry of long standing, my feeling of frustration is not specifically with this Chapter, but non-specifically with the biochemical *genre* of which it is an example [2]. Mechanisms are postulated for phenomena with little or no evidence that the phenomena themselves exist: indeed it seems to be suggested that the very possibility of a mechanism is itself evidence for the phenomena, and I think this is a hazardous line of reasoning. If no one has investigated directly whether lack of iron actually does cause changes in lipid composition, is it merely because this would be difficult to show? If not, then perhaps this should be the starting point? There seems to me little to be said for postulating a mechanism for something we do not know happens.

References

1. Dobbing J (1963) The entry of cholesterol into rat brain during development. J Neurochem 10:739–742
2. Dobbing J (1990) Vulnerable periods in developing brain. Chapter 1, this volume

Lozoff and Felt: Reports of reduced myelination of the spinal cord in iron-deficient animals may be particularly relevant to human studies. Although Dobbing is unaware of any functional effects of altered myelination in the CNS, could reduced myelination in the spinal cord affect motor function? Balancing and coordination were clearly altered in iron-deficient anemic infants in both the recent Chilean and Costa Rican studies [1,2]. Could reduced myelination of the spinal cord affect such functions? [See Dobbing's comments on Chapter 6.] In any case, it seems useful not to restrict ourselves too rapidly to hypotheses that behavioral alterations in iron deficiency are due to altered higher brain function when there may be other significant changes, for example: in the peripheral nervous system or in muscle.

References

1. Walter T, DeAndraca I, Chadud P, Perales CG (1989) Iron deficiency anemia: Adverse effects on infant psychomotor development. Pediatrics 84:7–17
2. Lozoff B, Brittenham GM, Wolf AW, et al. (1987) Iron deficiency anemia and iron therapy: effects on infant developmental test performance. Pediatrics 79:981–995

Dallman: This article is very interesting and useful in that it reviews for the first time the effects of iron deficiency on fat metabolism. I have only a few suggestions.

It seems that the concepts could be clarified if vulnerability of pups compared to adults and hepatic versus brain fatty acid synthesis in situ could be discussed in one section of the Chapter. At present, the emphasis on hepatic sources of fatty acids for brain lipids seems at odds with the later focus on brain synthetic processes. Similarly, the recovery of normal 18:1 to 18:0 fatty acid ratios after iron treatment seems at odds with the concept of a "once and for all process" for myelinization mentioned. Just a bit of reorganization and clarification would help to make the findings much more coherent.

There is a tendency to predict, by implication, the results of experiments that remain to be done, as though such experiments would be merely demonstrations, since the results are virtually a foregone conclusion. Extrapolations to man should recognize that the human fetus is much more protected from iron deficiency than the rat and that human iron deficiency is almost always much milder. Similarly, it seems worth indicating that you recognize that iron deficiency can affect the brain in many other ways than by altered fat metabolism, and that establishing specific relationships with infant behavior will be difficult.

In relation to the "Conclusions" it is difficult to consider the group of rats fed a 27 mg iron/kg diet as representing mild iron deficiency since their hemoglobin concentration did not differ significantly from an iron supplemented group (reference 83). It might be safer to attribute the differences in lipid metabolism in the supplemented group to a greater than physiological intake of iron. These findings are interesting and may deserve a little more discussion.

The space devoted to lipemia seems excessive and the distinction between a non-specific lipemia with anemia and that associated with iron-deficiency anemia should be clarified.

Chapter 4

Neurochemical Basis of Behavioural Effects of Brain Iron Deficiency in Animals

Shlomo Yehuda

Iron deficiency and anaemia are the most common nutritional disorders in both Third World and industrialized countries today. The numerous behavioural manifestations of iron deficiency in adults include lethargy, irritability, apathy, listlessness, fatigue, lack of concentration, pagophagia (pathological craving for ice) and pica (perverted craving for substances unfit for food), inattention, hypoactivity and, sometimes, a decreased performance on the IQ test. In children, iron deficiency may also lead to hyperactivity.

Despite the widespread nature of iron deficiency, until recently the only evidence connecting it to these symptoms was of an indirect nature, namely, that the symptoms could, in some cases, be reversed by iron therapy. Today, however, a number of studies have succeeded in showing a direct connection between these behavioural symptoms and low iron levels.

One of the key ingredients in this success was the development of an animal model for nutritionally induced iron deficiency, which was necessitated by the obvious restrictions imposed by the use of human subjects in behavioural studies. Weinberg et al.'s [2,3] animal model used rats to examine the role played by environmental and nutritional variables, during the rats' early development, on their behaviour as adults. Using this model the authors found that adult rats fed an iron-deficient diet when young, exhibited a significant decrease in various aspects of learning capacity, such as responsiveness to environmental stimuli, passive and active avoidance tasks, taste-aversion and open-field tasks, and tasks involving transfer of learning [1].

Animal Models

Animal models possess certain limitations which must be recognized if their use is to benefit research in iron deficiency in humans. Lozoff and Brittenham [1], in their review of studies of the behavioural aspects of iron deficiency, point out that the use of the rat model may cause scientists to underestimate its effects due to the fact that the behavioural repertoire of humans is more complex than that of rats, whose relatively simple behaviours are less vulnerable to insult. On the other hand, the use of the rat model may also lead to an overestimation of the effects of iron deficiency on behaviour because "rats place a larger burden on their dams both pre- and postnatally than humans, are less mature at birth, and their rate of growth and development is more rapid over weeks rather than years". Furthermore, rats and humans differ in their rates of neuronal and biochemical development. Lastly, these researchers point out that, to date, all studies in the field have suffered from a lack of sufficient control. Specifically, they have failed to control for the "timing, duration and severity of the deficiency" as well as to differentiate between decreased energy intake, iron deficiency and iron-deficiency-induced anaemia. Lozoff and Brittenham suggest employing exchange transfusion studies to investigate further the effects of iron deficiency on behaviour.

These cautionary points aside, two basic types of animal models have been used with success in medical and biological research. In the first, an attempt is made to mimic a given disorder (e.g., can a given virus induce fever in a rat, and if so, does a substance reducing virus-induced fever in the rat act on humans in a similar manner?). In the second, the focus is the mode of action of a given disorder. For instance, the action of anti-psychotic medication in rats can be predicted by means of the rotational model, which is able to mimic the mode of action of schizophrenia. This, despite the fact that rotational behaviour is not found among schizophrenic patients, while rats do not appear to hallucinate.

In this paper a series of studies using animal models will be presented which are concerned either with manifestations of iron deficiency (learning capacity) or with the neurochemical basis of brain iron deficiency (dopamine-mediated behaviours; effects on the blood–brain barrier). All of the studies were carried out on post-weanling rats, and most included time-course investigations of the effects of different feeding periods. In our studies the age of the rats was varied. The youngest rats were 6 weeks old at the beginning of the iron-deficiency treatment. Other groups were 6, 9 and 18 months old. The data presented in this chapter are on 6-week-old rats. This is approximately comparable to puberty in human children. In all of them, the effects on brain iron were differentiated from general anaemia. In addition, the developmental aspects of iron deficiency will be discussed, as will its effects on the immune system.

Learning Capacity

The decrease in learning capacity (IQ level) in children deprived of iron has been extensively documented [1]. While the effects of iron deficiency on learning capacity of rats have been studied, using both active and passive avoidance designs [2,3], the experimental animals employed were either the offspring of iron-deficient mothers, or rats in whom iron deficiency was induced at a very early age.

Interested as we were in the manipulation of iron deficiency in post-weanling rats, we developed an experimental model of nutritionally induced iron deficiency involving exposing the rats to an iron-free diet for a period of 4 weeks.

Biochemical studies showed brain iron levels to be significantly reduced after such a period of time. The ability of our experimental model to reproduce the effects of iron deficiency on cognitive functions such as learning was a crucial issue, which was investigated using 5 to 6-week-old rats in a maze-learning task. In order to avoid the confounding use of water and food as positive reinforcers in a nutritional study, a water maze was employed [4]. The other requirements for testing rats in the learning paradigm were: (a) that electric shock should not be used as reinforcement, because the pain threshold of iron-deficient rats is significantly increased; and (b) that the learning of the new task should be fast, in order to avoid longer feed periods.

Our study showed that the learning capacity of iron-deficient rats was significantly inferior to that of controls, and that this learning deficit became greater, the longer the rats were kept on an iron-deficient diet (see Table 4.1). Furthermore, the deficit was evident even before the rats' haemoglobin level had decreased to a significant degree.

Table 4.1. Effects of diet on water maze learning

	Learning	
Days on diet	Control rats	Iron-deficient rats
0	11.5+0.4	12.1+0.3
7	11.5+0.4	15.1+0.3*
14	12.3+0.7	18.1+0.3*
21	12.5+0.8	19.9+0.4*
28	11.8+0.8	20.1+0.4*

Data are expressed as mean + s.d. of number of trials to reach learning criterion; 6–7 animals per group.
*Statistically significant difference ($P < 0.01$) from day 0.

Recently (Yehuda and Youdim, unpublished results), a similar deficit in learning and memory was found in iron-deficient rats trained in a Morris Water Tank. The task of the rats in this apparatus was to locate a submerged platform (7.5 cm in diameter) in a large water tank (1.0 m in diameter). The tank was filled with water (22 ± 2 °C) which had been made opaque. The animals were unable to see the platform, and thus had to rely on environmental cues in order to reach it. While control rats (n = 18) needed 19.6 ± 3.3 trials to reach the learning criterion, iron-deficient rats (n = 19) needed 26.4 ± 1.1 trials to reach the same level of performance (all results ± s.e. (mean), $P < 0.001$). The temperature of the water did not affect the results.

At the end of both of these experiments, the rats were fed an iron-supplemented diet, and were re-tested either in the same water maze, or in the Morris Water Tank 2, 4, 6 and 8 weeks later. No restoration of learning and/or memory was found. This latter was particularly interesting in the light of the fact that the effects of iron deficiency on other behaviours such as motor activity, thermoregulation, stereotyped behaviour and pain threshold, are reversible by such treatment. The learning deficits, in contrast, persisted for at least 2 months after treatment for iron deficiency. While the level of haemoglobin in the blood was restored after such a period, the level of brain iron remained low for a very long time after treatment [5]. This may explain the long-term nature of iron deficiency on cognitive functions.

Dopamine-Mediated Behaviours

It was hypothesized that the effects of iron deficiency on behaviour are mediated by a decrease in the functional activity of DA-Dd2 (dopamine Dd2) receptors. This hypothesis was based on two sets of findings, namely, that in many respects iron-deficient rats resemble neuroleptic-treated rats (see below), and the fact that many DA-mediated behaviours have been found to be modified in iron-deficient rats. Indeed, one of the major effects of iron deficiency was found to be the reversal of the circadian cycles of pain threshold, stereotypy, motor activity and thermoregulation. These phenomena will be presented below. Beaton [6] has presented data indicating clear circadian cycles in the levels of haemoglobin, haematocrit, serum iron and transferrin saturation in adult male and female rats. The levels of these blood indices are also age-dependent. In normal populations the levels are higher at ages 0–13 years than at ages 14–20 years, and they increase again later in life.

Pain Threshold

We were able to show that pain threshold, as indicated by response time to a hot plate at 58 °C, is circadian cycle-dependent [7]. The level of activity of the dopaminergic system seems to be inversely related to the level of opiate (beta-endorphin and enkephalines) activity. It was hypothesized that iron-deficient rats would exhibit higher pain thresholds. Pain threshold level was assessed in nutritionally induced iron-deficient rats during the feeding periods. It was found that: (a) pain threshold levels are circadian cycle-dependent, such that the pain threshold was higher during the light period in control rats. No change in pain threshold was found over 4 weeks (a new group was tested every week). (b) The pain threshold of iron-deficient rats during the light period was identical to that of controls during the light period, while an increase in pain threshold was observed in iron-deficient rats during the dark period. After 2 weeks on the diet the pain threshold was identical during the light and the dark periods, while after 4 weeks, the pain threshold became significantly elevated during the dark period ($P < 0.001$). (See Fig. 4.1.)

The involvement of the dopaminergic system in mediating pain threshold responses was indicated by the fact that some neuroleptics had effects on pain threshold which were very similar to that of iron-deficiency treatment [7].

Peripheral administration of opiates (beta-endorphin and enkephalines) did not change the pain threshold of control rats. However, when iron-deficient rats were treated with peripheral doses of beta-endorphin or enkaphalines, a significant non-linear increase in pain threshold was found (Fig. 4.2). This unexpected result can be explained by assuming either that in iron-deficient rats

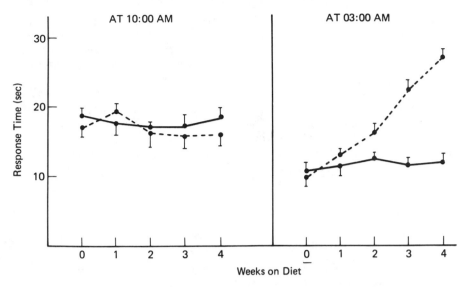

Fig 4.1.   Effects of iron deficiency treatment on pain threshold (latency time in seconds) during light and dark periods. *Continuous lines* (_____) represent control rats and *broken lines* (– – –) represent iron-deficient rats. Each dot represents data from an independent group ($m \pm$ s.d.).

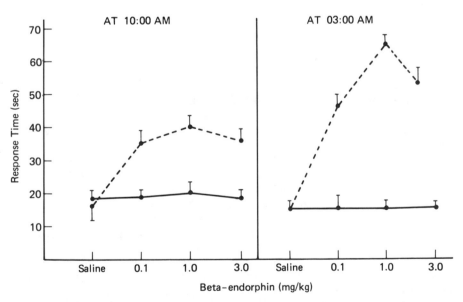

Fig. 4.2.   Effects of various doses of beta-endorphin (i.p.) on the pain threshold of control *(continuous line)* and iron-deficient *(broken line)* rats during light and dark periods. Each dot represents data from an independent group ($m \pm$ s.d.).

the enzymes which degrade the beta-endorphin and enkaphalines are iron-dependent and their activity was diminished, or that the iron-deficient state modified the blood–brain barrier activity, and thus more beta-endorphin was able to penetrate into the brain. An indirect study showed that the pattern of penetration of several compounds into the brains of iron-deficient rats is different from that in controls. It is interesting to note that the iron-deficient state does not damage the blood-brain barrier, but rather induces specific changes in penetration rate, e.g. a significant increase in glucose and insulin penetration rates [8]. The changes in pain threshold during the dark period and the effects of beta-endorphin in iron-deficient rats are naloxone sensitive [7].

An iron-supplemented diet restores the reversed circadian cycle of the pain threshold.

Stereotypy

Activation of the dopamine system clearly mediated stereotyped behaviour, as represented by head movement, circling activity and biting. Drug-induced stereotypy was also found to be circadian cycle-dependent. The same dose of a dopaminergic agonist induced a significantly higher degree of stereotypy during the dark period in control rats. However, apomorphine (2.5 mg/kg, i.p.) induced a higher degree of stereotypy during the light period among iron-deficient rats. The circadian cycle of stereotypy in iron-deficient rats is also reversed. Placing the iron-deficient rats on an iron-enriched diet restored the circadian cycle to its usual phases [9].

Motor activity

We recently replicated Glover and Jacobs' 1972 study [10] showing that iron-deficient rats had lower motor activity levels that did controls. These results had been confirmed by Youdim and Green [9] who reported that the levels of NE (norepinephrine), 5-HT (serotonin) and DA (dopamine) were unchanged in iron-deficient rats.

In our study the rats were kept under light regime of 12:12 L:D periods. Level of motor activity was measured by means of an LKB Animex activity meter at day 28 on the diet. While in a number of studies carried out over a period of a few years, it had been found that control rats are very active during the dark period, with the highest peak at about 03:00 am and a smaller peak around midnight, and with the lowest activity levels occurring between 10:00 am and mid-day, our results showed iron-deficient rats to be very active during the light period, with peak activity between 10:00 am and mid-day, and to be very inactive during the dark period. The changes in the circadian cycle of motor activity were positively correlated with the length of time on the iron-deficient diet. Furthermore, the general level of motor activity during the 24-hour period was lower among iron-deficient rats [11]. Thus, the iron-deficient state induced a reversal of the circadian cycle of motor activity level (Fig. 4.3).

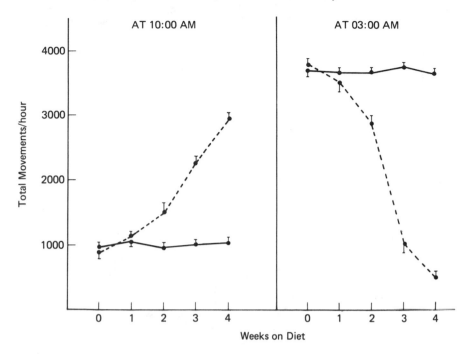

Fig. 4.3. Effects of iron deficiency on motor activity level during light (10:00 am) and dark (03:00 am) periods as a function of the length of feeding period. Each dot represents data from an independent group of rats ($m \pm$ s.d.). *Continuous line,* control rats; *broken line,* iron-deficient rats.

A significantly higher level of motor activity was found in both control and iron-deficient rats following treatment with d-amphetamine, which, however, did not restore the reversed circadian cycle [11]. The motor activity cycle returned to normal after treatment with ferrous sulphate, or after administration of TRH (thyrotrophin releasing hormone), which caused an increase in motor activity level while reversing the reversed iron-deficient cycle [12]. These differential effects of TRH and d-amphetamine may be explained by the different modes of action of the two drugs. While TRH has greater affinity to the noradrenergic system, d-amphetamine has greater affinity to the dopaminergic system.

Thermoregulation

Previous findings have shown that d-amphetamine induces significant hypothermia among rats kept in an environmental chamber at 4 °C [13], and pharmacological and anatomical studies have proved that the hypothermic effects of d-amphetamine are mediated by the release of dopamine in the nucleus accumbens [14]. The hypothermic effect of d-amphetamine is circadian cycle-dependent [15].

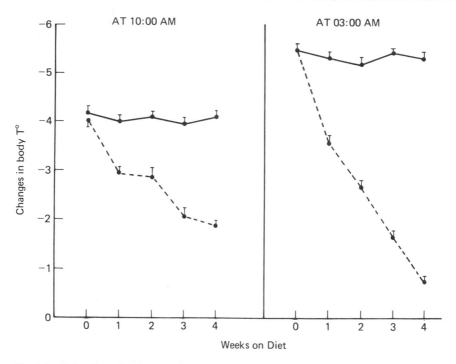

Fig 4.4. *d*-Amphetamine-induced hypothermia in control *(continuous line)* and iron-deficient *(broken line)* rats during light and dark periods. Colonic temperatures were measured 30 minutes after *d*-amphetamine injection and placement in a room at 4 °C. Each dot represents data from an independent group (*m* ± s.d.).

The effects of drugs which act on the dopaminergic system seem to be attenuated in iron-deficient rats. When *d*-amphetamine (15 mg/kg, i.p.) was given to iron-deficient rats on the 28th day of feeding treatment, the magnitude of the hypothermic effect was much reduced ($P < 0.01$) compared to the effect of the drug in control rats [11]. Moreover, in this respect the effect of iron deficiency was similar to the action of neuroleptics, e.g. pimozide and haloperidol [13]. The magnitude of the decrease in the hypothermic effect of *d*-amphetamine is positively correlated with the length of the feeding period (Fig. 4.4). The effects of iron deficiency were greater during the dark period. The rate of decrease in the hypothermic effect of the drug is correlated with the length of the feeding period and with the rate of decrease in the blood Hb.

After the animals were fed on an iron-rich diet or treated with ferrous sulphate, the cycle was reversed. Similarly, treatment with TRH temporarily reversed the cycle [12].

Specific Brain Lesions

Yehuda and Youdim [16] examined the effects of specific brain lesions in the pineal, hypophysis and area postrema regions, on the reversed thermoregulatory and motor activity cycles of iron-deficient rats. The pineal area was selected in order to evaluate the effects of melatonin on the circadian cycles, and the hypophysis in order to evaluate the possible role of the endocrine system. Previous studies [15] had shown that area-postrema-lesioned rats showed a marked decrease in body temperature with no circadian cycle.

Sham-operated and lesioned rats were fed either an iron-free or a control diet for 3 weeks after surgery. Their colonic temperatures were measured with a Yellow Spring telethermometer. Their motor activity was measured by means of an LKB Animex motor activity meter over a 24-hour (12:12, L:D) period. The results showed that the sham-operated rats showed the same reversed thermal and motor activity cycles as non-lesioned, intact iron-deficient rats.

Among the pinealectomized rats, the peak of the thermoregulatory cycle was delayed by 3 hours. However, pinealectomized iron-deficient rats had the same reversed cycle as the control iron-deficient rats. The motor activity cycle of the pinealectomized rats was not effected by either the lesion or by the treatment for iron deficiency.

Hypophysectomized rats, however, kept their thermal circadian cycle and were insensitive to either the lesion or to the iron-deficiency treatment, while their motor activity cycle was affected by the treatment but not by the lesion. The thermoregulatory cycle of the area-postrema-lesioned rats (both control and iron deficient) was abolished. The motor activity cycle of control area postrema rats was a phase-shifted cycle. These rats were sensitive to the iron-deficiency treatment, exhibiting another phase-shifted reversal cycle.

While it is difficult to explain these results, it may be important to note that the pineal and area postrema areas are among those in which the level of iron is highest, while the iron level in the hypothalamus is very low [17]. Both pinealectomized and area-postrema-lesioned rats exhibited phase-shifted thermoregulatory circadian cycles. As stated above, dopamine plays a major role in the thermoregulatory cycle, while norepinephrine mediates the motor activity cycle. The combination of lesions and iron deficiency have different effects on this latter cycle than on the thermoregulatory cycle.

Iron Deficiency and Neuroleptic Drugs

As mentioned above, the hypothesis that iron-deficiency effects are mediated by the dopaminergic system fits Youdhim's suggestion that, in many respects, iron-deficient rats resemble neuroleptic-treated (e.g., with haloperidol) rats. In both cases, (a) the behavioural response to presynaptic (amphetamine) and postsynaptic- (apomorphine) acting drugs is significantly diminished; (b) the amphetamine-induced hypothermia is blocked; (c) neuroleptic drugs mimic iron-deficiency effects on pain threshold; (d) sleeping time following administration of phenobarbitone is significantly increased; (e) plasma prolactin is elevated; and (f) the prolactin receptor binding sites ($beta_{max}$) in the liver increase in number. However, unlike the neuroleptic-treated animals, iron-deficient rats do not exhibit catatonia [5].

Iron in the brain

The use of Fe^{2+} or Fe^{3+} salt injection into the cortex or amygdala-hippocampus complex for the induction of epileptogenic discharges is well known [18]. The effects include lipid peroxidation and persistent behavioural and electrical abnormalities, which can be blocked by anti-oxidants. The occurrence of epileptic (convulsive) discharges as a result of bleeding after head injury is thought to be due to neuronal damage caused by the increase in iron released from red blood cells. Czernansky et al. [18], while studying epileptic foci (seizures) of rats injected with $FeCl_3$ into the amygdala–hippocampus complex according to the procedure originated by Willmore et al. [19], noted extensive

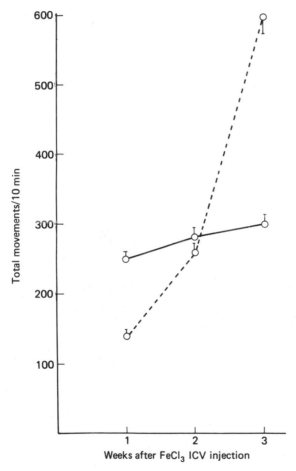

Fig. 4.5. Motor activity induced by apomorphine (0.5 mg/kg i.p.) in control (*continuous line*) and intraventricular FeC₃ (*broken line*) rats, as function of weeks after $FeCl_3$ treatment. Each dot represents data from an independent group ($m \pm$ s.d.).

facial twitching in these animals. They also reported a time-dependent (3-week) period and highly significant dopamine D_2 receptor supersensitivity, as indicated by increased caudate nucleus binding of ^{3}H-spiperone- and apomorphine-induced circling and hyperactivity. We have confirmed the latter data with respect to dopamine D_2 receptor supersensitivity in rats injected intraventricularly with $FeCl_3$ [16]. These rats manifested a motor activity supersensitivity to apomorphine (Fig. 4.5), and excessive gnawing on low doses of morphine (0.1–0.2 mg/kg) which are not normally observed in control animals [8].

Development and Iron Deficiency

Very few systematic studies have been done on the effects of iron deficiency on developmental processes. Recently, Youdim (personal communication) was able to show that the earlier in life the nutritionally-induced iron deficiency occurs, the more severe the consequences. Several key developmental issues have yet to be satisfactorily understood. Among these issues are:

(a) Experience. Iron-deficiency-induced hypomotility and lack of responsiveness to environmental stimuli. One of the most important developmental principles is the relationship between the organism and the environment, namely, the fact that early experience is necessary for the proper development of the biological system. Without the necessary sensory feedback from the environment, the biological system will not develop properly and will not prepare the organism for the next developmental state. Thus, damage to the sensory system during development is not limited in its effect to the sensory system alone, but also interferes with the important feedback loop to the brain, thus amplifying the damage.

(b) Potential. While it is true that the magnitude of the effects of iron deficiency in children, for example, is at times not considerable, and that the performance on IQ tests of such children can be brought up to normal by iron therapy, the main issue is whether or not the individual is now able, with or without treatment, in the "best" possible environment, to fulfil his biological and cognitive potential. This point is illustrated by the following episode. A group of adopted 7-year-old Korean children [20] were tested in the USA. The children, who had suffered from severe early childhood malnutrition, received IQ scores in the normal range. On the basis of this finding, it might be concluded that no cognitive damage occurred due to severe malnutrition. However, a comparable group of adopted Korean children, who had lived in the US for the same amount of time and who had never suffered from malnutrition, exhibited significantly higher IQ scores. One of the conclusions which can be drawn from these findings is that the first group of children did not realize their cognitive potential, and can, in fact, be regarded as "underachievers".

(c) Brain Plasticity. The important role of the plasticity of the brain has been expressed several times in this paper. Although many studies [e.g. 21–23] have

shown that the organism may overcome prenatal and/or postnatal damage or injury, either by means of alternative neuronal routes or by synaptogenesis, there are many other studies which indicate that the organism is often unable to overcome such insults. For example, administration of the neurotoxin 6-hydroxy-dopamine to a specific brain area in young kittens results in a permanently non-functioning visual system; specific prenatal stress [24] will permanently impair the cognitive development of the offspring; sleep deprivation in young rats will cause a decrease in the number of dendrites and retarded cognitive development. More importantly, we do not yet know when and why the effects of brain plasticity appear; at this stage, all of our knowledge is *post factum* information. Until such time as all the variables involved in the plasticity of brain mechanisms are known to us, we should be careful in our use of this principle to evelute and predict the extent of brain damage.

(d) Developmental "Index". At this stage, we lack sufficient knowledge regarding the effects of iron deficiency on several developmental "indices" such as the rate of synaptogenesis and that of myelination.

Iron Deficiency and the Immune System

It is not surprising that nutritionally-induced iron deficiency results in changes in other body systems in addition to brain biochemistry. Modifications in the endocrinological system [e.g. 25–27] have been reported. Special attention should be directed to the possible damaging effects of iron deficiency on the immune system [27,28]. Several aspects of the relationship between iron deficiency and cell-mediated immunity have been described [30]. Only recently, the role of iron deficiency in the regulation of the lymphokine system has been investigated. Interleukin–1 causes a decrease in serum iron [31]. Preliminary studies (Yehuda and Sredny, unpublished) showed that many of the lymphokine components respond to iron-deficiency treatment, and that these changes are circadian cycle dependent. In general, there is a tendency towards an increase in interleukin–1 and a decrease in interleukin–2 levels. Because of the recent findings [32] regarding the possible involvement of iron in learning processes, these effects of iron deficiency on the immune system should be investigated further.

Conclusion

The use of animal models in iron-deficiency research has enabled us to document the important role played by it in a wide range of behavioural changes, the majority of which are dopamine-mediated. These changes include the reversal of the circadian cycles of pain threshold, stereotypy, motor activity and thermoregulation, and a lowered sensitivity to drug treatment and to environmental stimuli. Rats made nutritionally iron deficient, compared to controls, demonstrated inferior ability to learn the Morris Water Tank task, which requires attending to environmental cues.

These findings testify to the valuable nature of animal models of iron deficiency (particularly those which are designed to avoid the possible shortcomings outlined by Lozoff and Brittenham [1]. They mimic both the cognitive deficits demonstrated in learning and memory tasks in humans, as well as the apparent mode of action of iron deficiency, which is believed to be caused by a decrease in the functional activity of the D_2 dopaminergic system. Animal models constitute a powerful tool with which to study and verify various approaches to the neurobiochemical basis of iron deficiency and anaemia.

References

1. Lozoff B, Brittenham GM (1986) Behavioural aspects of iron deficiency. Prog Hematol xiv:23–53
2. Weinberg J, Dallman PR, Levine S (1980) Iron deficiency during development in the rat: behavioural and physiological consequences. Pharmacol Biochem Behav 12:493–502
3. Weinberg J, Bert LP, Levine S, Dallman P (1981) Long term effects of early iron deficiency on consummatory behavior in the rat. Pharmacol Biochem Behav 14:447–453
4. Yehuda S, Youdim MBH, Mostofsky DI (1986) Brain iron deficiency causes reduced learning capacity in rats. Pharmacol Biochem Behav 25:141–144
5. Youdim MBH, Ben-Shachar D (1987) Minimal brain damage induced by early iron deficiency: modified dopaminergic neurotransmission. Isr J Med Sci 23:19–25
6. Beaton GH, Corey P, Steele C (1989) Conceptual and methodological issues regarding the epidemiology of iron deficiency and their implications for the functional consequences of iron deficiency. Am J Clin Nutr 50:[Suppl] 575–588
7. Yehuda S, Youdim MBH (1984) The increased opiate action of beta-endorphin in iron-deficient rats: the possible involvement of dopamine. Eur J Pharmacol 104:245–251
8. Ben-Shachar D, Yehuda S, Finberg JPM, Spanier I, Youdim MBH (1988) Selective alteration in blood brain barrier and insulin transport in iron deficient rats. J Neurochem 43:139–143
9. Youdim MBH, Green AR (1977) Biogenic monoamine metabolism and functional activity in iron-deficient rats: behavioral correlates. In: Porter RR, Knight J (eds) Iron metabolism. CIBA Foundation Symposium 51 (New Series) Elsevier, Amsterdam, 51:pp. 201–223
10. Glover J, Jacobs A (1972) Activity pattern of iron-deficient rats. Br Med J ii:627–628
11. Youdim MBH, Yehuda S, Ben Uriah Y (1981) Iron deficiency induced circadian rhythm reversal of dopaminergic mediated behaviors and thermoregulation in rats. Eur J Pharmacol 74:295–301
12. Youdim MBH, Yehuda S (1972) Iron deficiency-induced reversed circadian cycles: differential effects of d-amphetamine. Nature 240:477–478
13. Yehuda S, Wurtman RJ (1972) Release of brain dopamine as a probable mechanism for the hypothermic effects of d-amphetamine. Nature 240:477–478
14. Yehuda S, Wurtman RJ (1975) Dopaminergic neurons in the nigrostriatal and mesolimbic pathways: mediation of specific effects of d-amphetamine. Eur J Pharmacol 30:154–158
15. Yehuda S, Mostofsky DI (1984) Modification of the hypothermic circadian cycle induced by DSIP and melatonin in pinealectomized and hypophysectomized rats. Peptides 5:495–497
16. Yehuda S, Youdim MBH (1987) Effects of ID and brain lesions on the motor activity and body temperature circadian cycles in rats. Soc Neurosci 27:6010
17. Hill JM (1988) The distribution of iron in the brain. In: Youdim MBH (ed) Brain iron: neurochemical and behavioral aspects. Taylor and Francis, London pp 1–24

18. Csernansky JG, Holman CA, Bonnett KA, Grabowsky K, King R, Mollister L (1983) Dopaminergic supersensitivity at distant sites following induced epileptic foci. Life Sci 32:385–390
19. Willmore LJ, Sypert GW, Manson JV, Hurd RW (1978) Chronic focal epileptiform discharges induced by injection of iron into rat and cat cortex. Science 200:1501–1503
20. Hamilton EM, Whitney EN, Siser FS (1985) Nutrition: Concepts and controversies, 3rd edn. West Publishing Co, St. Paul
21. Cottman CW (1985) Synaptic plasticity. The Guildford Press, New York
22. Morris RGM, Halliwell RF, Bowery N (1989) Synaptic plasticity and learning. II. Do different kinds of plasticity underlie different kinds of learning? Neuropsychologia 27:41–59
23. Murnmoto K, Kobayashi K, Nakanishi S, Matsuda Y, Kuroda Y (1988) Functional synaptic formation between cultured neurons of rat cerebral cortex. Proc Jpn Acad 64B:319–322
24. Weller A, Glaubman H, Yehuda S, Caspy T, Ben-Uriah Y (1988) Acute and repeated gestational stress affect offspring learning and activity in rats. Physiol Behav 43:139–143
25. Beard J, Finch CA, Green WL (1982) Interactions of iron deficiency, anemia and thyroid hormone levels in the response of rats to cold exposure. Life Sci 30:691–697
26. Chen SCH, Shirati MRS, Orr RA (1983) Triiodothyroxine (T_3) and thyroxine (T_4) levels in iron deficient, hypertriglyceridemic rats. Nutr Res 3:91–106
27. Farrell PA, Beard SL, Bruckenmiller M (1989) Increased insulin sensitivity in iron deficient rats. J Nutr 118:1104–1109
28. Bhaskaram P (1988) Immunology of iron deficient subjects. Nutr Immunol 1:149–168
29. Weinberg ED (1978) Iron and infection. Microbiol Rev 42:45–66
30. Chandra RK (1977) In: Iron metabolism. CIBA Foundation Symposium 51, Elsevier, Amsterdam
31. Kuribidila S (1987) Iron deficiency, cell-mediated immunity and resistance against infections: present knowledge and controversies. Nutr Res 7:989–1103
32. Goldblum SE, Cohen DA, Jay M, McClain LJ (1987) Interleukin-1 induced depression of iron and zinc. Am J Physiol 252:E27–E32

Commentary

Smart: I am prompted to comment again on the question of severity of iron deficiency in animal experiments (see my Commentary on Youdim). It would appear that Yehuda's and Youdim's usual regime is to give their rats an *iron-free* diet for 28 days. Given that a day in the life of a rat is said to be equivalent to something like a month of human existence, this regime is comparable to feeding a human being an iron-free diet for a period of about 2.5 years, severe deprivation indeed. I feel, now that Yehuda and Youdim have demonstrated a battery of fascinating effects of this severe regime, that it would be most helpful if the experiments were repeated using levels of iron deprivation that are more akin to those found in human populations.

Next I should like to comment on the tests of learning in iron-deficient rats reported by Yehuda. First, a general comment stemming from the very basic physiological differences he describes in iron-deficient rats. The reversed circadian rhythm of activity and altered thermoregulation are changes which might well predispose to different performance in a test of learning, though whether in the direction of improving or impairing performance is difficult to say. Altered thermoregulation in particular might be important in the water maze test in which rats were placed in water at 18 °C. [Yehuda's reference 4)], which is quite cold for a test of this type. The statement with respect to the

Morris water tank test that "The temperature of the water did not affect the results", indicates that Yehuda has taken account of this factor in his most recent study. I am reassured and look forward to seeing the results in detail in due course.

The result of the study of position learning in a Y water maze [Yehuda's reference 4] are undoubtedly impressive, even though I might query a few aspects: that the water temperature was low, that the criterion of learning was lax, and, indeed, that the task is a very simple one. Notwithstanding all of this, the findings are impressive and if one reads the original paper they appear even more so than in the review. For instance, it is clear from the original that different groups of rats were tested at each stage up to 28 days, which is good methodologically. Perhaps the most remarkable finding was that, when re-tested after 3 weeks of feeding on the control diet, the former iron-deficient rats took 27 trials to reach criterion compared to 7 trials by re-tested controls. The magnitude of the difference is staggering, and my only comment is to wonder whether the concept of "state-dependent" learning might be applicable to these results. Learning is said to be state-dependent when optimum task performance depends on the animal being in the same physiological state under which the original learning took place [1]. The state of the iron-deficient rats changed from being iron deficient at the time of original testing to being iron replete at retesting, and their performance may have been especially poor then as a result.

What I should like to see are comparisons of performance by control rats and rats recovered from iron deficiency on new tests of learning (in situations they had not encountered before). This would address the question whether there are lasting effects of a period of iron deficiency on ability to learn.

The results of the Morris water tank test are not yet published and the review format does not allow scope for a detailed description. Therefore I cannot comment in an informed manner. I must confess to being slightly puzzled, however, as to why this particular test was chosen, since it is usually used as a test of hippocampal function [2]. I had not supposed that hippocampal function was thought to be impared in iron-deficient animals.

It is interesting to note that Youdim talks about *damage* to the blood–brain barrier, but Yehuda comments that ". . . the iron-deficient state *does not damage* the blood–brain barrier . . .". I prefer Yehuda's rather more cautious and interpretive statement.

References

1. Overton DA (1974) Experimental methods for the study of state-dependent learning. Fed Proc 33:1800–1813
2. Morris RGM, Garrud P, Rawlins JN, O'Keefe J (1982) Place navigation is impaired in rats with hippocampal lesions. Nature 297:681–683

Felt and Lozoff: In this chapter Yehuda describes the large body of research that he, Youdim and others have performed assessing the role of the dopaminergic system in centrally mediated behaviors in the currently iron-deficient or previously iron-deficient rat model. This concentrated effort has generated a number of intriguing hypotheses. Interpretation of the work is greatly facilitated by the fact that several study design parameters have been conserved across studies. These parameters include developmental stage or age (primarily the post-weanling 6-week-old animal), time of institution of low iron diet, duration of diet and thus, presumably the severity of anemia, time and duration of dietary rehabilitation, and analyses to dissociate iron deficiency from frank anemia. That the majority of the work, however, uses the post-weanling model limits the studies' ability to observe the effects of iron deficiency on the developing brain.

This issue is important in assessing two early statements in Yehuda's paper. First, the potential hazards of attempting direct comparisons between animal and human studies notwithstanding, one must at a minimum carefully attend to the stage of brain development in each system. While Yehuda's work on "learning capacity" using the Y-maze and Morris Water Tank tasks in the post-weanling rat [1,2] may in some way be compared with studies of the effects of iron deficiency in older children (both after the brain growth spurt), Weinberg's work [3,4] should not be. Weinberg's studies used a rat model of iron deficiency *during* the brain growth spurt. Secondly, Yehuda, here as in previous writings, attributes the persistence of a deficit in "learning capacity" to a persistence of lower brain iron despite prolonged iron treatment. From the work of this group and others, we know that iron deficiency during the brain growth spurt (specifically from 10 days of age in the reference cited by Yehuda) causes an irreversible deficit of brain iron. However their own work shows that later iron deficiency results in a brain iron deficit that can be remediated [5]. Thus, since the animals in the Y-maze and Morris Water Tank studies were post-weanling, to postulate that a lasting deficit in brain iron explains the altered "learning capacity" does not seem to take into account these developmental considerations.

Along this same line, it is not obvious that Weinberg's findings, on responsiveness to environmental stimuli and passive and active avoidance tasks, are evidence for decreased learning capacity. Rather, Weinberg and associates, studying 28-day-old anemic rats and adult rats rehabilitated by dietary iron after a period of iron deficiency during the brain growth spurt, hypothesized an altered threshold of arousal that seemed to persist despite iron treatment. In fact, improved performance on passive avoidance testing was noted in the previously iron-deficient animals of both sexes [3,4]. Similarly, Findlay et al. [6], in a study of 100-day-old rats who had been iron-deprived during gestation and lactation, showed no deficit on number of trials to extinction in a passive avoidance shuttlebox task and showed shorter escape latencies and fewer false entries. Thus, Yehuda's summary of these findings as a "decrease in various aspects of learning capacity" does not seem entirely accurate. Finally, the issue of "transfer of learning" comes from the work of Massaro and Widmayer [7] in a post-weanling rat model and thus may not be directly comparable to the work of Weinberg and Findlay.

The description of the Y–maze and Morris Water Tank findings as evidence for persistent, diminished "learning capacity" raises several questions that, if addressed by Yehuda, may help clarify what we may conclude from these data. First, this group's prior work has demonstrated circadian cycle reversal for several parameters including motor activity in the iron-deficient rat, with lower motor activity for these animals overall. Given that Y–maze testing occurred from 10:00am–2:00pm (the Morris Tank testing times are not similarly described here), can we infer that the deficits observed for the anemic rats may actually have been minimized due to their relatively greater activity during this time period? Would it make more sense to compare each group's performance during their most active period? Alternatively, might the anemic group's poorer performance be attributed to some other factor, such as lower "motivation" or even "altered threshold or arousal", given the "lower motor activity" for iron-deficient animals overall? Similarly, might the persistence of poor performance after iron rehabilitation be due to some other factor such as a different "learning state" [8]? That is, these previously iron-deficient animals are now asked to demonstrate conservation of memory for a task learned in a reversed circadian cycle and perhaps at an altered threshold of arousal. Or, might persistence of that altered threshold of arousal be a factor that interferes with improved performance later? Although Brittenham and Lozoff have stated that rats have "relatively simple behaviors" [9], we must take care to avoid relatively simple and potentially hazardously incorrect conclusions regarding those behaviors.

The summary of this group's work, using various approaches to describe central dopaminergic processes is important and intriguing. But is the focus on the dopamine system an oversimplification, given the complex interrelatedness of numerous neurotransmitter systems involved in brain development, function and potentially behavior? Although the work by others investigating the serotonin and GABA systems, for instance, is far less extensive, it may be premature to limit our scope to dopaminergic mechanisms only. In truth, the prospect of defining simple central neurotransmitter mechanisms for the behavior alterations observed in iron-deficiency anemia seems remote.

Two final comments concern the developmental issues raised near the end of this paper: first, the importance of the age or developmental stage at which iron deficiency occurs is raised with attention to a potential for loss of sensory input and experience due to the animals' hypomotility and decreased responsiveness. We would also stress the importance of developmental stage consideration for potentially critical windows in brain development at the subcellular, cellular, and regional levels. In other words, the timing of an iron-deficiency insult may be important on many, likely interrelated, levels. Second, given our current limited knowledge of the possible effects of iron deficiency on the brain, it seems premature to use the label "damage". "Altered function" is perhaps a more suitable general description for what we think we know at this point.

References

1. Yehuda S, Youdim MBH, Mostofsky DI (1986) Brain iron deficiency causes reduced learning capacity in rats. Pharmacol Biochem Behav 25:141–144
2. Yehuda S (1989) Unpublished results presented in paper
3. Weinberg J, Levine S, Dallman PR (1979) Long-term consequences of early iron deficiency in the rat. Pharmacol Biochem Behav 11:631–638
4. Weinberg J, Dallman PR, Levine S (1980) Iron deficiency during early development in the rat: behavioral and psychological consequences. Pharmacol Biochem Behav 12:493–502
5. Youdim MBH, Ben-Shachar D (1987) Minimal brain damage induced by early iron deficiency: modified dopaminergic neurotransmission. Isr J Med Sci 23:19–25

6. Findlay E, Ng KT, Reid RL, Armstrong SM (1981) The effect of iron deficiency during development on passive avoidance learning in the adult rat. Physiol Behav 27:1089–1096
7. Massaro TF, Widmayer P (1981) The effect of iron deficiency on cognitive performance in the rat. Am J Clin Nutr 34:864–870
8. Levitsky D (1989) Review of Yehuda, S. Brain iron: a lesson from animal models. Am J Clin Nutr (in press)
9. Lozoff B, Brittenham GM (1986) Behavioral aspects of iron deficiency. Prog Hematol XIV:23–53

Dallman: The results of the water maze studies were particularly interesting in terms of the rapidity of onset of the abnormalities and the persistence of the learning deficits despite iron treatment. In addition to learning ability, there are a few characteristics that might conceivably affect the performance of the iron-deficient rats.

1. Their body temperature might fall more than that of controls since the temperature of the water bath is considerably below thermoneutral and iron deficiency impairs thermogenesis.
2. They might become more fatigued since iron deficiency decreases work capacity.
3. Their elevated blood norepinephrine levels might be associated with changes in behavior.

How would these considerations influence your interpretation? Also, how do you deal with testing the animals at the same time of the day when their circadian pattern of activity is reversed? Have you tested the iron-deficient rats at a comparable part of their circadian activity pattern (with a reversed light cycle)?

Yip: Concerning the use of the water maze and the Morris water tank for studying the learning capacity of rats, does the performance of a rat in a water maze require significant energy expenditure or muscle work such as swimming? If it does, the effect of iron deficiency on reduced muscle function, especially endurance, may adversely affect the performance. Reduced performance of learning or memory of muscle-dependent activities may represent a combined effect of iron deficiency on brain as well as muscle.

Author's replies: Regarding the possible effect of iron deficiency on muscle, causing rats to become fatigued more quickly and thus possibly explaining the fact that iron deficiency treatment appeared to interfere with the learning mechanism: (a) the duration of exposure of each rat in the water tank was very short: no more than 120 seconds on each run. The animal was put back into the tank only after a resting period; (b) rehabilitated iron-deficient rats, when tested for memory, had a restored Hb level and normal circadian cycle, and performed very poorly, despite the fact that they were now "normal" rats; (c) iron-deficient rats made many more mistakes in the Y water maze, and covered a much longer distance than the controls; and (d) the very long period required for habituating iron-deficient rats cannot be explained by fatigue.

I believe that the term "state-dependent learning" does not explain the poor memory displayed by the iron-deficient rats. The group of iron-deficient rats during the learning period was divided later into two groups: one fed the control diet, the other the iron-deficient diet. Both groups showed a significantly lower level of performance in the Morris water tank, not only compared with the control rats, but even compared with the level of performance they had shown originally.

Regarding the time we tested the animals during the daytime (the light period), while they were in a reversed circadian cycle: in a large scale, hitherto unpublished study we examined the performance of the different groups (control and iron-deficient) in the Morris water tank, tested at different times during the 24 hours. The rats were tested every 3 hours. No statistical differences were found among the various groups. The best learning curve for control and iron-deficient rats was found in the morning. We therefore tested our rats at that time. The results of performance in the Morris water tank are independent of the circadian cycle. This was never published because the results were negative. However, we will include these results in a future paper on the effects of iron deficiency on performance in the Morris water tank.

Finberg: The anecdote about Korean children cannot be interpreted at all. Many variables are at play in severe malnutrition, including some not involving the diet.

Dobbing: Do we know what the blood–brain barrier to iron actually is, and whether it is an "active" mechanism as implied? Or are you merely meaning the blood–brain relationships for the substances? I think that one should not speak of the blood–brain barrier as if it is a structure with similar permeability properties for all substances [1], without mentioning the substance being referred to. The same remark applies to "damage" to the blood–brain barrier, as is presumably illustrated by the word "selective" in the title of Yehuda's reference 8.

Reference

Dobbing J (1961) The blood–brain barrier. Physiol 41:130–188

Larkin and Rao: Animal models: the author points up problems which are of great importance in iron deficiency studies. Studies which are not fully controlled for anemia, the degree of iron deficiency, and the duration of iron deficiency could yield very disparate results.

Developmental "index": the author is quite correct that the effects of iron deficiency on "indices" such as the rate of synaptogenesis and that of myelination are not sufficient. However, we do know that iron deficiency does profoundly affect myelination. The author discusses the use of animal models for iron deficiency research and the role played by iron deficiency in a wide range of behavioral changes. A close association of the discussion with respect to the developing brain is rather tenuous. The discussion appears to address general effects of iron deficiency regardless of age. Are there any special effects pertaining to the neonatal or infant brain?

Chapter 5

Neuropharmacological and Neurobiochemical Aspects of Iron Deficiency

Moussa B.H. Youdim

Introduction

It is well known that iron deficiency represents the most prevalent nutritional disorder in the world, affecting some 50 million subjects. This topic would not have received our attention were it not for the original reports by Oski and colleagues [1, see 2 for review] of the impairment of cognitive and learning processes in iron-deficient children. However, in spite of the well-documented evidence supporting the deleterious effects of undernutrition on brain growth and development during the pre-weaning period [3], such fundamental approaches were not considered or applied to the study of nutritional iron deficiency in man and animals until relatively recently. It is more than possible that the reports of cognitive and learning abnormalities in iron-deficient children were treated with scepticism. This may have had at its root the lack of knowledge and understanding of the function of iron in the central nervous system. The absence of in-depth studies of iron metabolism in the brain and its influence on brain development, biochemistry and function must have been a contributory factor. It is rather curious to be confronted by well-known neuroscientists and neurologists saying, "We have always known of the presence of well-defined and large deposits of iron in specific neurotransmitter-rich brain regions, but, because of its high concentration, no importance was attached to it". It was precisely this phenomenon which prompted us to investigate closely the role of iron in the brain and the long-term consequences of early iron deficiency at different ages on brain biochemistry and function [4].

The first indication that brain may be adversely affected by iron deficiency can be found in the studies of Dallman and coworkers [5,6]. They showed a significantly decreased brain iron in nutritionally iron-deficient rats. The restoration of tissue iron and turnover of brain iron were significantly slower than those in livers from the same animals (Fig. 5.1). Our own studies [4,7–9] demonstrated not only an age-dependent abnormality of brain iron metabolism in iron-deficient rats, but also alterations in behavioural responses to psychotropic drugs known to act pre- and post-synaptically with monoamine neurotransmitter neurons (dopamine, noradrenaline and serotonin) in the brain. Thus a reduction in availability of brain iron could profoundly affect biochemical events in the metabolically active and vulnerable neurons of the brain. The behavioural and cognitive abnormalities reported in children with nutritional iron deficiency may therefore stem from defects within these neurons [1]. The possible peripheral biochemical changes, which are known to occur in iron deficiency, may themselves in turn affect brain function by negative feedback and exacerbate the already altered brain physiology. Therefore, if the biochemical basis of the behavioural effects of iron deficiency was to be understood and dealt with, it was necessary to establish an animal model which closely resembled the human condition. The involvement of iron with DNA and protein synthesis, as a cofactor of enzymes and its association with myelin, ferritin and membrane structural proteins [5,6,10–13] could not be ignored in iron deficiency [9–11]. An earlier study by Glover and Jacobs [14] had shown that iron-deficient rats displayed a significant reduction in 24-hour motility, a finding confirmed by others [4,5,16] but previously attributed to the effect of iron deficiency on myoglobin and muscle-working performance [17,18]. However, the reversal of the 24-hour pattern of motor activity of the iron-deficient rat [4,12,13], such that the animals were more active in the light period than in the dark period, was difficult to explain and implicated central nervous system changes associated with a possible reduction in brain iron. The concentrations in brain of the neurotransmitters dopamine, noradrenaline and serotonin exhibit circadian rhythm, the highest levels being observed in the dark period. A possible consequence of iron deficiency might be alterations in metabolism of these neurotransmitter substances, due to the diminished activities of their iron-dependent synthetic enzymes, tyrosine hydroxylase and tryptophan hydroxylase [4,19,20]. The emphasis placed on monamine neurotransmitters in our studies stems from the fact that these neurotransmitters have been implicated in neuropsychiatric disorders such as depressive illness, schizophrenia, Parkinson's disease and Alzheimer's disease, as well as having major roles in cognitive and learning processes [20].

The major developmental period of rat brain takes place after birth and continues until the animal is 25 days old [21,22]. This contrasts with the human brain which has a very rapid growth rate prior to birth, reaching its peak at the time of birth (see Chapter 1). Thereafter in human and rat brain there is a fall in growth rate. Brain growth is associated with a parallel increase in DNA and protein during its initial phase of development [22]. However, there are significant differences in the rate of DNA synthesis and brain growth in the various regions during the postnatal development [3,23]. Once again the major surge in DNA synthesis occurs during the first part of the brain growth spurt in both species: i.e. from mid-gestation until about 2–3 years in the human, and in the first 10 postnatal days in the rat. The picture is not very different for the appearance of iron in the brain [24,25].

Iron deposition in rat brain takes place up to 5 weeks after birth and thereafter remains constant until ageing commences, when brain iron decreases [24]. In the human brain iron increases during the first decade of life and remains relatively stable throughout life [25,26]. However, when different brain regions are examined, it is found that the iron content of the globus pallidus and substantia nigra can increase well beyond the age of 30, and iron may continue to be deposited until 70–80 years of age [25]. In some instances excessive iron deposition can become pathological as in Parkinson's disease [27] and Haller

Vorden Spatz disease [28] where the substantial increase of iron in the substantia nigra and globus pallidus is thought to contribute to the neurodegenerative processes [27]. Nevertheless the initial association between human and rat brain growth and iron deposition appears to be valid and it has been suggested that one day in rat life is equivalent to 1.36 months in human [21,22]. It is during the first decade of human life, when the brain is rapidly developing, that a major portion of nutritional iron deficiency, with its manifestations of behavioural abnormalities is observed. Thus if an insight into the role of iron metabolism in brain development and function is to be considered, particular attention needs to be paid to this initial period.

In contrast to other transition metals, iron in human and rat brain has a unique uneven distribution [4,25-30]. The extrapyramidal regions (globus pallidus, substantia nigra, red nucleus, putamen, thalamus and caudate nucleus) contain the highest concentrations of iron. Other regions which are rich in iron are the dentate gyrus, interpeduncular nuclei, olfactory tract and cerebellar nuclei. These regions also contain the highest contents of neurotransmitters and neurohormones and neuropeptides, such as dopamine, serotonin, GABA, enkephalins, endorphins and somatostatin. In these regions iron content is surprisingly greater than that in the liver and blood, suggesting either a relatively slow turnover or increased uptake. By contrast other regions of the brain have relatively low iron levels [25-30]. Histochemical examination of iron in human and rat brain has confirmed the more direct biochemical iron determination [29,30]. The most notable and striking feature of iron distribution in the brain is its sharply localized deposition within the globus pallidus, substantia nigra and dente gyrus. These are the brain areas prone to neurodegeneration in Haller Vorden Spatz disease, Parkinson's disease, tardive dyskinesia and Alzheimer's disease. In iron-rich regions the metal appears in nerve bundles or clusters and may be visible in all parts of the neurons or be present in the myelin sheath of neurons [29,30]. It is not known whether iron can be accumulated within the neurons by a specific uptake process.

Subcellular distribution of iron in human and animal brains indicate that the major portion (70%) of iron is present in the myelin fraction. The rest is found in the mitochondrial (15%), microsomal (5%) and soluble (5%-10%) fractions. The presence of iron in the myelin fraction may explain why, during postnatal development, brain iron increases since the development of dentritic trees and their differentiation may be closely associated with myelination. Whether iron participates in this process cannot be answered but needs to be investigated, especially in relation to iron deficiency.

The transport of iron into and out of the central nervous system has received least attention. Limited studies indicate a significantly slower turnover of iron (uptake and metabolism) in the brain [9,11,12,31], as compared with the liver. While liver iron stores can be increased by 20-30 fold in rats placed on iron-rich diet, little change in brain iron can be established [9,11,12] (Fig 5.1). Even so, iron must be transported across the capillary blood-brain barrier by some as yet unknown mechanism. The slow turnover of brain iron is not necessarily due to the absence of a transport system or transferrin [31,34], since iron can be transported in and out of brain, albeit at a very slow rate. Furthermore transferrin receptors have clearly been identified in capillary endothelial cell membrane [31].

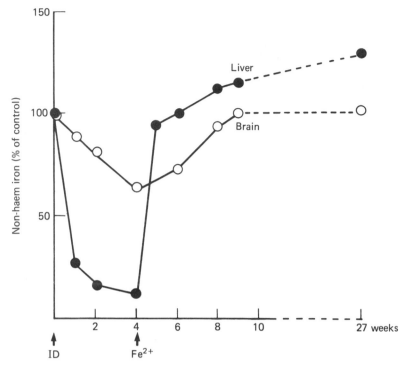

Fig. 5.1. Comparison of the effects of iron deficiency (ID) and iron rehabilitation (FE^{2+}) on liver and brain non-haem iron in 3-week-old rats [9].

Neurochemical and Neuropharmacological Aspects

Most published studies on behavioural aspects of iron deficiency have dealt with measuring the activity of iron-deficient rats in a tread mill. These indicate that iron-deficient rats are less responsive to movements than control rats. Whether this behaviour is centrally mediated has been a matter of considerable debate. The studies of Edgerton and coworkers [17,18] clearly demonstrated that what was being measured was the reduction of the working performance of iron-deficient rats, as indicated by diminished myoglobin [35]. It became necessary to establish some centrally mediated behavioural alteration in an animal model that could explain the deficit of cognition in human iron deficiency.

The inherent problems of animal models for the human condition are well known to most behavioural and neuro-scientists. In the case of iron deficiency, the problems may be simpler since undernutrition of a specific nutrient is being examined and not general undernutrition. In this case the experimenter has control over the constituents of both the control and the experimental diet. At least for the animal model of iron deficiency, the results so far have been as expected. The biochemical and haematological alterations in rat correlate reasonably well with those of the human condition [see 4]. In collaboration with Professor S. Yehuda, who discusses the behavioural aspects (Chapter 4), we have made a three-pronged approach to the study of the central nervous system mediated behavioural effects of iron deficiency. These concern (a) the neurochemistry and neuropharmacology of the brain; (b) specific behaviours mediated by certain neurotransmitters and (c) learning processes.

The initial evidence that iron deficiency may adversely affect centrally mediated behaviours came from studies of the 24-hour motor activity of the iron-deficient rats and the behavioural response of these animals to drugs which are known to act pre- and post-synaptically in dopaminergic and serotonergic neurons [4,15]. Iron-deficient rats showed a reduction and reversal of their 24-hour activity, confirming an earlier study [14]. Furthermore, the behavioural responses to serotonin (5-methoxy-*N, N*-dimethyltryptamine and chloroamphetamine) and dopamine (apomorphine, amphetamine and bromocriptine) agonists were significantly diminished. Stimulation of the post-synaptic receptor by increasing the synthesis of serotonin or dopamine by treating iron-deficient rats with tryptophan or L-dopa (L-dihydroxyphenylalanine), previously given a monoamine oxidase inhibitor, also resulted in similarly diminished behavioural responses [4]. These results were interpreted as indicating either a reduction in neurotransmitter synthesis and release or alterations in pre– and post-synaptic neurotransmitter receptor responsiveness, namely reduced sensitivity of serotonin ($5-HT_2$) and dopamine D_2 receptors.

Indeed determination of the activities of iron-dependent enzymes in the brains of iron-deficient rats, including cytochrome C oxidase, succinic dehydrogenase, monoamine oxidase, aldehyde dehydrogenase, tyrosine hydroxylase, tryptophan hydroxylase, γ-aminobutyric acid transaminase and glutamate decarboxylase have revealed a resistance to change in the activities of these enzymes, even though brain iron concentration was decreased between 40% and 60%. By contrast the activities of the same enzymes in the systemic organs of heart, liver and adrenals were reduced, with the enzymes in the heart showing the largest deficits [4,36–38].

The most surprising aspect of iron deficiency is the unaltered activities of iron-dependent tyrosine and tryptophan hydroxylases, the rate-limiting enzymes of monoamine neurotransmitters. These enzymes are dependent on iron and oxygen for their activity [19]. It might have been expected that they would have shown some deficit due to low oxygen tension in iron deficiency. It is possible that the deficiency of iron stores in the brain may not have been sufficient to induce a decrease in the activities of these enzymes. In any case, these data are matched by unaltered levels in vivo of dopamine, noradrenaline and serotonin and their oxidatively deaminated metabolites in caudate nucleus (striatum) hypothalamus, raphe nucleus and spinal cord [4,38,40]. We cannot explain the discrepancy between our results and those reported for altered catecholamine and serotonin metabolism by Finch and coworkers [36,39]. Indeed even under conditions of unphysiological iron deficiency (i.e. Hb < 4.0 g/dl) no apparent effect on these brain enzymes can be observed [4].

The logical consequence for the reduction in animal behavioural responses to pre- or post-synaptic acting drugs, in the absence of unaltered monoaminergic

neurotransmitter metabolism, is adaptive alterations in receptors mediating the
short- and long-term action of dopamine, noradrenaline and serotonin. The
notion that dietary deficiency of a specific nutrient, namely iron, could alter
receptors was considered novel enough to examine the biochemical nature of
these receptors in iron deficiency. Scatchard analyses of receptor densities for
dopamine D_1 and D_2, serotonin, benzodiazepine, γ-aminobutyric acid,
muscarinic–cholinergic and α- and ß-adrenoreceptors in different brain regions
have revealed diminution only in dopamine D_2 receptor B_{max} [9,41–43] (Fig.
5.2). The time course of the dopamine D_2 receptor decrease (dopamine receptor
subsensitivity) parallels the reduction in serum and brain non-haem iron and the
behavioural response to the putative dopamine agonist, apomorphine. These
results can be interpreted as indicating the importance of serum iron for
maintaining brain iron and dopamine D_2 receptor number and, in addition, iron
supplementation of iron deficient animals can reverse all these effects (Fig. 5.2).
Furthermore phenylhydrazine-induced haemolytic anaemia in rats, which has no
effect on serum iron does not alter brain non-haem iron, dopamine D_2 receptor
number nor the behavioural response to apomorphine [41,43]. The possible
direct involvement of iron in the dopamine D_2 receptor synthesis or regulation
has been discussed on several occasions [4,43]. This suggestion is supported by
observations that dopamine D_2 receptor subsensitivity in iron-deficient rats, like
the neuroleptic-induced (haloperidol and chlorpromazine) dopamine D_2 receptor blockade, modifies other dopamine-dependent physiological responses.
These include increases of serum prolactin and prolactin receptors in the liver

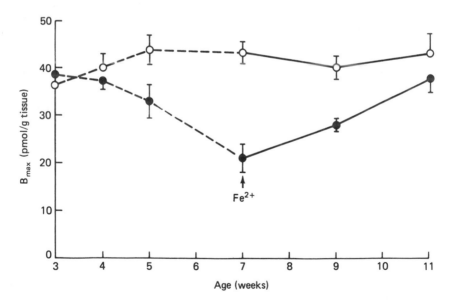

Fig. 5.2. Dopamine D_2 receptor B_{max} as measured by the binding of [³H]spiperone to rat caudate
nucleus in control (○) and iron deficient (●) rats, followed by iron rehabilitation of iron deficiency
[9].

Table 5.1. The induction of iron deficiency and its rehabilitation by iron supplementation in rats of different ages and their effects on dopamine D_2 receptor as measured by the radioligand spiperone (^{3}H–SPIP) in the candate nucleus [9]

Animal	Age at start of iron-deficient diet	Duration of diet	Diet (n)	SP. ^{3}H-SPIP binding (pmol/g) at end of diet	Duration of recovery	SP. ^{3}H-SPIP binding (pmol/g) after recovery
New born	10 days	2 weeks	12 Control Iron-deficient	15.58 ± 0.47^a 12.09 ± 0.68	6 weeks	20.38 ± 0.91^a 15.3 ± 0.54
Young	3 weeks	4 weeks	10 Control Iron-deficient	25.1 ± 4.0^a 12.7 ± 1.6	3 weeks	20.9 ± 3.8 18.0 ± 3.3
Adult	7 weeks	7 weeks	18 Control Iron-deficient	19.5 ± 1.2^a 10.6 ± 1.3	1 week	20.45 ± 2.28 19.97 ± 2.85

$^a P < 0.01$

and prostate, inhibition of amphetamine-induced hypothermia, increase of phenobarbitone sleep time and increased opiate-dependent antinociception [13].

The reversibility of iron deficiency-induced reductions in brain non-haem iron, dopamine D_2 receptor and apomorphine-induced stereotypy are age dependent: immature (10-day-old) animals are more susceptible to the induction of iron deficiency than adult rats (48-days old). However, the reverse is true for the recovery from iron deficiency with iron replacement therapy [9]. Although adult animals can recover from the effects of iron deficiency relatively rapidly after 7–14 days iron supplementation, the immature (10-day-old) animals show only a partial recovery of brain iron, even after 6 months of iron treatment. This is not enough to normalize dopamine D_2 receptor and dopamine-dependent neuro-transmission [9] (Table 5.1). Considering what Dobbing [21] and Bedi [3] have shown regarding the deleterious effects of undernutrition on brain development at an early age, the results of our studies are not totally unexpected. The long-term consequences of early iron deficiency on brain biochemical and functional processes are therefore obvious, but they do require careful assessment in the light of new clinical data showing the continued deficit in mental and motor function of iron-deficient infants reassessed 5 years after their iron deficiency was discovered (see Lozoff in this volume). It is possible that iron deficiency or some other unidentified factor, related to its consequences, produces a long lasting developmental disturbance. Similar to our animal studies with adult iron-deficient rats, the picture appears to be different for children who become iron-deficient at an older age, showing higher achievement test scores with iron supplementation. These results point to improvement with iron therapy in older children in contrast to those in infants. Whether iron deficiency can produce chronic impairment of brain in adolescents but not adults is a matter for speculation but preliminary animal studies have indicated certain defects [9].

Biochemical Basis of Learning Deficit in Iron Deficiency

The cognitive and learning processes reported to be defective in iron-deficient children have not escaped examination in animal models of iron deficiency. If their biochemical basis is to be identified and understood, animal models are crucial even though they can be criticized for their limitations. Because of the limitations and drawbacks of human studies Weinberg et al. [44,45] developed an animal model in which environmental and nutritional reinforcing variables could be carefully monitored and examined during the early development of iron deficiency in rats and after iron rehabilitation. A significant decrease in learning capacity of 10-day-old rats which were exposed to iron deficiency was noted. This age was chosen because of the rapid development of brain at this period. The examination of several other types of learning tests demonstrated that the iron-deficient offspring animals were less responsive to environmental stimuli and slower in learning tasks employing passive and active avoidance, taste aversion, transfer of learning and open field tests [44,45]. The main brain biochemical features of the 10-day-old rats made iron deficient are the fall in both brain iron [9,11,12] and dopamine D_2 receptor which could not be reversed, even after 6 months of iron rehabilitation, even though these animals demonstrated normal haemotology [9]. In these animals reduced dopamine receptor sensitivity was matched by the behavioural deficit in response to the dopamine agonist, apomorphine [9] (Table 5.1). Thus the possible link between reductions of learning ability, brain iron and dopaminergic neurotransmission cannot be ignored even though it is not well understood. The crucial aspects of the latter findings for the present discussion is the long-term irreversible consequences of early iron deficiency on the development and function of the brain dopamine neurons [9]. The effects of previous iron deficiency on learning capacity examined in older (5–6 week old) rats, have given similar results [46,47]. Since water and food could not be used as reinforcements in a nutritional study, the ability of iron-deficient rats to learn a water maze was examined. The iron-deficient groups of rats displayed a significantly inferior learning capacity when compared to matched controls. Furthermore, the longer the animals were kept on the iron-deficient diet, the greater the deficit in learning. One striking feature of these studies was that the deficit in learning was evident even when the level of haemoglobin did not change but when serum iron had fallen [46,47]. A similar deficit in learning and memory can be found in iron-deficient rats trained in a Morris Water Tank [47]. In this system the rats are trained to locate a submerged platform in a large water tank (1.5 m in diameter) filled with water. The water is made opaque by spraying milk powder over it, so that the animals cannot see the platform. Therefore the animals need to rely on environmental cues in order to navigate themselves onto the platform. Once again in this system as in the Y water maze the iron-deficient animals needed a significantly higher number of trials to reach the same level of performance as the control group. In accordance with the results of Weinberg et al. [44,45], the iron-deficient rats rehabilitated with iron supplementation for up to 8 weeks showed no restoration of learning or memory [47], even though levels of Hb and serum iron became normal. The "permanent" deficit in learning capacity contrasts with the ability of iron supplementation to restore the changes in serum prolactin, Hb, and serum iron.

The roles of serotonin and dopamine in learning and cognition are well documented. For the present discussion, where reduced biochemical and behavioural sensitivity of dopamine neurotransmission in iron deficiency has been noted, attention must be turned to this neurotransmitter in the absence of any other brain biochemical abnormality. The inability to restore brain iron, dopamine D_2 receptor density as measured in the caudate nucleus and apomorphine-induced stereotypy may explain the long-term effects of early iron deficiency on cognitive function [47].

The chemical lesion of dopaminergic A–10 neurons using 6–hydroxydopamine induces deficits in retention of an alteration task [48]. This is in accord with the hypothesis that catecholamines in general, and dopamine in particular, may have an important role in mediating learning and memory processes [49,50]. Supportive evidence has come from studies in which the level of delayed alternating learning correlated with the dopamine level in the cortex, but not other amines or metabolites [51]. However, the nature or extent of the dopaminergic system's involvement is not known. What can be inferred at present is the possible down regulation (reduced sensitivity) of cortical dopamine D_2 receptors leading to diminished dopaminergic neurotransmission in the iron-deficient animals. By analogy iron deficiency also induces reduced sensitivity of enriched dopamine neurons in the caudate nucleus, nucleus accumbens and pituitary gland. Thus it may have an adverse dampening effect on the brain dopamine neuronal system as a whole, and if induced early enough may cause irreversible damage to these neurons. Whether damaged dopaminergic neurotransmission is solely responsible for the deficit in learning capacity remains to be established.

The requirement for iron for DNA and protein synthesis must be considered, since these are synthesized at their maximum rate in the first 2 weeks of rat brain postnatal development [3,21–23]. Accordingly, a decreased iron level in the brain might interfere with DNA and protein synthesis [5,52] and with the molecular mechanism of learning. Indeed, we have examined the effect of iron status on protein synthesis and distribution within the caudate nucleus and nucleus accumbens in adult rats [52]. In caudate nucleus, iron deficiency was associated with a significant reduction of glial fibrillary acid protein (GFAP) and increase of albumin. In the nucleus accumbens both albumin and enolase were increased. The iron deficiency induced an increase in albumin in both regions and is thought to result from increased local blood flow in response to reduced oxygen carrying capacity. By a similar line of reasoning the increase in enolase may reflect a need for increased anaerobic metabolism under conditions of reduced oxygen tension.

If iron deficiency does indeed interfere with cognition and learning, as indicated by the animal and human studies, its deleterious effects on brain function may be a result of multifactorial events involving their interaction with dopaminergic inputs. The globus pallidus, substantia nigra, caudate nucleus and putamen not only contain the highest concentration of iron and dopamine in the brain, but these regions also have the highest densities of opiate-peptides

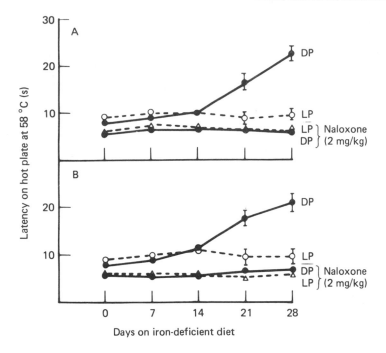

Fig. 5.3. Antinociception responses during light and dark periods in rats made iron deficient and their response to naloxone. LP, light period 10.00 am; DP, dark period 03.00 am. The results are given as latency (seconds) on a hot plate at 58 °C [56].

(enkephalins and endorphins) [55,56]. Opiate peptides, if injected centrally but not peripherally, cause amnesia, forgetfulness and antinociception. Therefore they have been implicated in memory and learning. Consistent with these findings is the ability of centrally active opiate antagonists (e.g. naloxone) to improve memory in human and animals [53,54]. Rats made iron deficient show increased antinociceptive response on a hot plate with increasing severity of the deficiency. Naloxane treatment can prevent this effect (Fig. 5.3). These findings and the highly significant increase of antinociception in the peripheral response to administered opiate peptides (met- and leu-enkaphelins and α-endorphin) in iron-deficient rats, a phenomemon absent in control rats [55,56], has been attributed to the increased uptake of opiates as a result of alteration of the blood–brain barrier [57] and reduced opiate metabolism in the brain (Fig 5.4). The net effect and response could be elevated concentrations of opiates in peptidergic neurons of the globus pallidus, substantia nigra, caudate nucleus and putamen. The peptidases responsible for metabolism of opiates are metallo-enzymes, since iron chelators can inhibit their activities [58]. Therefore the possible alteration in the activities of these enzymes in iron deficiency needs consideration. Indeed, substantiation of this hypothesis has come from experiments in which iron-deficient rats show significant increase of antinociceptive response (Figs. 5.3 and 5.4) and highly significant elevation of met- and leu-enkephalins and dynorphin B in the globus pallidus, substantia nigra, caudate

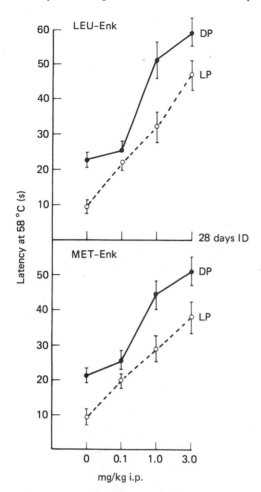

Fig. 5.4. Antinociception responses of 28-day iron-deficient (ID) rats given intraperitoneal injections of leu-enkephalin (LEU-Enk) and met-enkephalin (MET-Enk). LP, light period 10.00 am; DP, dark period 03.00 am. The results are given as latency (seconds) on hot plate at 58 °C [56].

nucleus and putamen [55,56]. Whether naloxane administration to these rats would reverse the deficit in learning has not been examined and such studies are now in progress. However naloxane does inhibit the opiate peptide-induced antinociception in the iron-deficient rats (Figs. 5.5 and 5.6). The increased brain levels of opiate peptides and antinociception in iron-deficient rats may be linked to decreased dopaminergic neurotransmission. Dopamine antagonists (dopamine D_2 receptor blockers), such as haloperidol and chlorpromazine, not only initiate increases in brain enkephalins in rats [59], but also produce highly significant antinociceptive responses in these animals [55,60] which can be blocked by naloxane (Fig. 5.6). The ability of dopamine antagonists to increase brain levels of opiate peptides has been attributed to the inhibitory action of

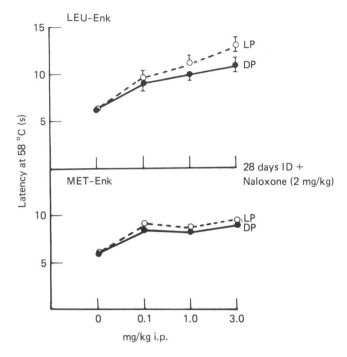

Fig. 5.5. Antinociception responses of naloxone-treated 28-day iron-deficient (ID) rats given intraperitoneal doses of leu- and met-enkephalins. For details see Fig. 5.4 [56].

dopamine in the synthesis of these peptides. Dopamine D_2 receptor antagonists haloperidol and chlorpromazine increase the brain mRNA for opiate peptides [59]. We have noted the elevation of at least four unidentified proteins separated by two dimensional SDS-gel electrophoresis, in the caudate nucleus and nucleus accumbens of iron-deficient animals. It remains to be established whether any of these represent long-chain precursor peptides which give rise to the smaller opiate peptides [52].

Blood–Brain Barrier and Iron Deficiency

The decline in GFAP noted in both the caudate nucleus and nucleus accumbens of iron-deficient rats [52] may be indicative of a lowered content of glia, and other supportive structures as well as changes in the blood–brain barrier [61]. It is now apparent that iron deficiency in rats has a profound effect on the blood–brain barrier as demonstrated by the altered transport of insulin, glucose, valine and endorphin enkephalins and iron into the brain [61,62]. In normal circumstances insulin and glucose and endorphin do not pass the blood–brain barrier. The uptake of these substances is greatly increased in iron deficiency and this

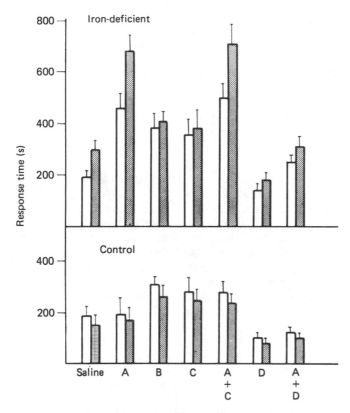

Fig 5.6. Antinociception responses of 30-day iron-deficient and control rats in light and dark periods given intraperitoneal injections of various psychotropic drugs. A, *p*-endorphin 1 mg/kg; B, morphine 10 mg/kg; C, haloperidol 2 mg/kg; D, naloxone 1 mg/kg. The data are obtained in the light period *(open bars)* and dark period *(hatched bars)*. Note the significant difference between iron-deficient and control animals [55].

may be in response to local changes at the level of capillary endothelial cells which constitute the blood–brain barrier. Therefore, the opening of the blood–brain barrier cannot be ignored, and could be of great contributory significance to the pathophysiology of the iron-deficient brain. The change in the blood–brain barrier, as a result of iron deficiency, may allow peripheral "toxic metabolites" to penetrate into the brain. The alterations in the blood–brain barrier in iron deficiency were established in relatively older (7–8-week-old) rats [61] and all indications are that rehabilitation with iron restores the barrier in these animals [9]. Because of their greater susceptibility to iron deficiency, immature (10-day-old) rats might exhibit greater changes in the blood–brain barrier. Phenylketonuria, a deficiency of phenylalanine hydroxylase activity, is known to be associated with brain damage. Interestingly, iron deficiency in rats significantly reduces liver phenylalanine hydroxylase activity resulting in elevated levels of phenylalanine in the serum [63]. Accordingly, decreased iron availability might also result in increased levels of porphyrins [64], leading to a state of toxicity in the brain [64]. Abnormal porphyrin metabolism has been reported to be involved with some psychological disorders [65]. In the final analysis the experiments on brain protein synthesis and the blood–brain barrier must be assessed in immature (10-day-old) animals which, on the face of it, appear to be more susceptible to the nutritional deficiency of iron.

Conclusion and Future Perspectives

There have been few detailed systematic animal behavioural and brain biochemical studies of iron deficiency in immature, young and adult animals. Those that have been performed indicate certain biochemical and behavioural deficits. Although their precise nature is not known, these are expressed as reduced sensitivity of dopaminergic receptor-dependent neurotransmission at behavioural and biochemical levels. Some of these can be prominent, depending on the age at which iron deficiency was induced and iron rehabilitation commenced. This is clearly demonstrated both in immature and adult rats made iron deficient, where rehabilitation of behavioural and biochemical deficits can be achieved in the adult rats but not immature animals. The present data provide evidence that recovery of deficits does not occur with continued iron deficiency. Rehabilitation, if it occurs, is dependent on iron supplementation and iron uptake into the brain. Such a phenomenon appears to support data on human behavioural studies, where long-term treatment with iron does not in all cases correct the cognitive deficit. This provides an area ripe for much future research and a closer examination of the brain.

There is no information whether iron deficiency will alter brain weight as much as it does body weight. An investigation in brain regional weight, growth differences and the capillary blood–brain barrier would be worthwhile. Special attention should be given to the study of regions known to contain relatively high contents of iron and neurotransmitters. Alterations in brain regional weight and proteins might indicate phases of neuronal cell production and proliferation. Quantitative and qualitative neurohistological studies on animal brains with iron deficiency are badly needed, since undernutrition causes alterations in neuron to glial cell ratio [3].

Whether these can be permanent as a result of early iron deficiency is a matter of conjecture. However attention should be given to the considerable body of evidence showing that nutritional deficiency in early life can cause a permanent (irreversible) substantial reduction in the granule to Purkinje cell ratio [3]. The relationship of iron deficiency to these findings requires an in-depth investigation. Undernutrition during early life can cause reversible deficits in some cases and is associated with changes in dendritic spines, dendritic network size, branching patterns, numerical densities of synapses and in the synapse to neuron ratios [3]. The most important question is whether iron deficiency produces similar selective defects within the dopaminergic neuronal systems. The irreversible reduction in dopamine D_2 receptor number and brain iron content observed in immature (10 days old), as compared to adult iron-deficient rats, rehabilitated with iron supplementation, clearly demonstrates susceptibility to a permanent defect in immature animal brain.

In any study of animal models of nutritional iron deficiency it has to be emphasized that great care should be exercised in extrapolating the effects of the deficiency found in animal studies at a given period to the human situation. However, results of animal studies have so far provided enough information to implicate an important role for iron in brain development and function. The most prominent feature of these studies has been the parallelism seen in learning process deficits of iron-deficient animals and those observed in children. Such findings, even though limited, cannot be ignored and must be the basis for future extensive studies.

References

1. Webb TG, Oski FA (1973) Iron deficiency anemia and scholastic achievements: behavioural stability and perceptual sensitivity of adolescents. J Pediatr 82:827–830
2. Lozoff B, Brittenham GM (1986) Behavioral aspects of iron deficiency. Prog Hematol XIV:23–53
3. Bedi KS (1987) Lasting neurochemical changes following undernutrition during early life. In: Dobbing J (ed) Early nutrition and later achievement. Academic Press, London, pp 1–50
4. Youdim MBH, Green AR (1977) Biogenic monoamine metabolism and functional activity in iron-deficient rats: behavioural correlates. In: Porter RR, Knight J (eds) Iron metabolism. Ciba Foundation Symposium 51 (New Series). Elsevier, Amsterdam, pp 201–227
5. Dallman P (1974) Tissue effects of iron deficiency. In: Jacob A, Worwood M (eds) Iron in biochemistry and medicine. Academic Press, London, pp 437–477
6. Bothwell TH, Chorton RW (1981) Iron deficiency in women: International Nutritional Anemia Consultative Group (INACG). The Nutrition Foundation, New York, Washington, pp 1–68
7. Woods HF, Youdim MBH, Boulin D, Callender S (1977) Monoamine metabolism and platelet function in iron deficiency In: Porter RR, Knight J (eds) Iron metabolism, Ciba Foundation Symposium 51 (New Series). Elsevier, Amsterdam, pp 227–249
8. Youdim MBH, Ben-Shachar D, Yehuda S (1989) The putative biological mechanisms of the effects of iron deficiency on brain biochemistry and behaviour. Nutr Rev (in press)
9. Ben-Shachar D, Ashkenazi R, Youdim MBH (1986) Long term consequences of early iron-deficiency on dopaminergic neurotransmission. Int J Devel Neurosci 4:81–88
10. Wriggleworth J, Baum H (1988) Iron-dependent enzymes in brain In: Youdim MBH (ed) Brain iron: neurochemical and behavioural aspects. Taylor and Francis, London, pp 25–66
11. Dallman PR, Siimes MN, Manies EC (1975) Brain iron: persistent deficiency following short term iron deprivation in the young rat. Br J Haematol 31:209–215
12. Dallman PR, Spirito RA (1977) Brain iron in the rat: extremely slow turnover in normal rat may explain the long-lasting effects of early iron-deficiency. J Nutr 107:1075–1081.
13. Youdim MBH, Ben-Shachar D (1987) Minimal brain damage induced by early iron deficiency: modified dopaminergic neurotransmission. Isr J Med Sci 23:19–25
14. Glover J, Jacobs A (1972) Activity pattern of iron-deficient rats. Br Med J ii:627–629
15. Youdim MBH, Yehuda Y, Ben Uria Y (1981) Iron-deficiency induced circadian rhythm reversal of dopaminergic mediated behaviours and thermoregulation in rats. Eur J Pharmacol 74:295–301
16. Williamson AM, Ng KT (1980) Behavioral effects of iron deficiency in the adult rat. Physiol Behav 24:561–567
17. Edgerton VR, Bryant SL, Gillespie CA (1972) Iron deficiency and physical performance and activity of rats. J Nutr 102:381–395
18. Edgerton, VR, Ohira Y, Gardner, GW, Senewirante B (1982) In: Pollitt E, Leibel RL (eds) Iron-deficiency: brain biochemistry and behaviour. Raven Press, New York, pp 141–160

19. Youdim MBH, (ed) (1979) L. aromatic amino acid hydroxylases and mental disease. Wiley, Chichester
20. Usdin E, Hamburg D, Barchas J (eds) (1977) Neuroregulators and psychiatric disorders. Oxford University Press, New York
21. Dobbing J (1976) Vulnerable periods of brain growth and somatic growth. In: Roberts DF, Thomas PM (eds) The biology of human fetal growth. Taylor and Francis, London, pp 137–147
22. Dobbing J, Sands J (1970) Timing of neuroblast multiplication in developing human brain. Nature 226:639–640
23. Essman WB (1987) Perspectives for nutrients and brain function In: Essman WB (ed) Nutrients and brain function. Karger, Basel, pp 1–11
24. Youdim MBH, Ben-Shachar D (1984) Early nutritional iron deficiency causes an irreversible diminution of dopamine D_2 receptor. Fed Proc 43:1095
25. Hallgren B, Sourander P (1988) The effect of age on the non-haem iron in the human brain. J Neurochem 3:41–51
26. Hallgren B, Sourander P (1960) The non-haem iron in the cerebral cortex in Alzheimer's disease. J Neurochem 5:307–310
27. Riederer P, Sofic E, Rausch WD et al. (1989) Transition metals, ferritin, glutathione and ascorbic acid in Parkinsonian brains. J Neurochem 52:515–520
28. Youdim MBH (1985) Brain iron metabolism: biochemical and behavioural aspects in relation to dopaminergic neurotransmission In: Lajtha A (ed) Handbook of neurochemistry, vol 10. Plenum Press, New York, pp 731–757
29. Hill JM, Switzer RC (1984) The regional distribution and cellular localization of iron in the rat brain. Neuroscience 11:595–603
30. Hill JM (1988) The distribution of iron in the brain In: Youdim MBH (ed) Brain iron: neurochemical and behavioural aspects. Taylor and Francis, London, pp 1–25
31. Banks WA, Kastin AJ, Fasold MB, Barrera CM, Augereau G (1988) Studies of the slow bidirectional transport of iron and transferrin across the blood–brain barrier. Brain Res Bull 21:881–885
32. Hill JM, Ruff MR, Weber RJ, Pert CB (1985) Transferrin receptors in rat brain: neuropeptide-like pattern and relationship to iron distribution. Proc Natl Acad Sci USA 82:4553–4557
33. Jeffries WA, Brandon MR, Hunt SV, Williams AF, Gatter KC, Mason DY (1984) Transferrin receptor on endothelium of brain capillaries. Nature 312:162–163
34. Dwork AJ, Schon EA, Herbert J (1988) Non-identical distribution of transferrin and ferric iron in human brain. Neuroscience 27:333–345
35. Finch CA, Miller LR, Indamar AR, Person R, Seiler K, Mackler B (1976) Iron deficiency in the rat: physiological and biochemical studies of muscle dysfunction. J Clin Invest 58:447–554
36. Mackler B, Person R, Miller LR, Indamar AP, Finch CA (1978) Iron deficiency in the rat: biochemical studies of brain metabolism. Pediat Res 12:217–229
37. Taneg V, Mishra K, Agarval KM (1986) Alteration in brain GABA metabolism and enzymes in iron-deficient rats. J Neurochem 46:1670–1675
38. Youdim MBH, Green AR, Bloomfield D, Mitchell B, Heal DJ, Grahame-Smith D (1980) The effects of iron deficiency on brain biogenic amine biochemistry and function in rats. Neuropharmacology 19:259–267
39. Dillman E, Johnson DG, Martin J, Mackler B, Finch C (1979) Catecholamine elevation in iron deficiency. Am J Physiol 237:297–304
40. Tovi A, Ben-Shachar D, Wolfe W, Kuhn D, Youdim MBH (1990) Dopamine and serotonin metabolism is unaltered in brains of iron-deficient rats. J Neurochem (submitted)
41. Ashkenazi R, Ben-Shachar D, Youdim MBH (1982) Nutritional iron deficiency and dopamine binding sites in the rat brain. Pharmacol Biochem Behav 17:43–47
42. Youdim MBH, Ben-Shachar D, Ashkenazi R, Yehuda S (1983) Brain iron and dopamine receptor function In: Mandel P, de Feudis FV (eds) OMS receptors from molecular pharmacology to behaviour. Raven Press, New York, pp 309–322
43. Ben-Shachar D, Finberg JPM, Youdim MBH (1985) The effect of iron chelators on dopamine D_2 receptors J Neurochem 45:999–1005
44. Weinberg J, Levin S, Dallman PR (1979) Long term consequences of early iron deficiency in the rat. Pharmacol Biochem Behav 11:631–638
45. Weinberg J (1982) Behavioral and physiological effects of early iron deficiency in the rat. In: Pollitt E, Leibel RL, (eds) Iron-deficiency: brain biochemistry and behavior. Raven Press, New York, pp 93–123

46. Yehuda S, Youdim MBH, Mostofsky DI (1986) Brain iron deficiency causes reduced learning capacity in rats. Pharmacol Biochem Behav 25:141–144
47. Yehuda S, Youdim MBH (1989) Brain: a lesson from animal models. Am J Clin Nutr (in press)
48. Simon HB, Scartton B, LeMoal M (1980) Dopaminergic A10 neurons are involved in cognitive functions. Nature 286:150–152
49. Iversen SD (1977) Brain dopamine and behaviour. In: Iversen LL, Iversen S, Snyder SH (eds) Handbook of psychopharmacology, vol. 8. Raven Press, New York, pp 333–384
50. Tucker DM, Sandstead HH, Penland JG, Dawson SL, Milne DB (1985) Iron status and brain function: serum ferritin levels associated with asymmetrics of cortical electrophysiology and cognitive performance. Am J Clin Nutr 39:105–113
51. Sahakian B, Sarna GS, Kantamanei BD, Jackson A, Huston PH, Curzon G (1985) Association between learning and cortical catecholamines in non-drug treated rats. Psychopharmacology 56:381–388
52. Youdim MBH, Sills MA, Heydron WE, Creed GJ, Jacobowitz DM (1986) Iron deficiency alters discrete proteins in rat caudate nucleus and nucleus accumbens. J Neurochem 47:794–799
53. Pablo Huidobro-Toro J, Leong-Way E (1983) Opiates. In: Grahame-Smith, DG, Cowen PH (eds) Psychopharmacology I. Part I: Preclinical. Excerpta Medica, Amsterdam, pp 300–343
54. Pablo Huidobro-Toro J, Leong-Way E (1985) Opiates. In: Grahame-Smith, DG, Cowen PJ (eds) Psychopharmacology II. Part I: Preclinical. Elsevier, Amsterdam, pp 283–343
55. Yehuda S, Youdim MBH (1984) Increased opiate action of ß–endorphin in iron-deficient rats: the possible involvement of dopamine. Eur J Pharmacol 104:245–251
56. Yehuda S, Youdim MBH, Zamir N (1986) Iron-deficiency induces increased brain met-enkephalin and dynorphin B and pain threshold in response to opiate peptides. Br J Pharmacol 87:44
57. Ben-Shachar D, Yehuda S, Finberg JPM, Youdim MBH (1988) Selective alteration in blood brain barrier and insulin transport in iron-deficient rats. J Neurochem 50:1434–1437
58. Youdim MBH (ed) (1988) Brain iron: neurochemical and behavioural aspects. Topics in neurochemistry and neuropharmacology, vol. 2. Taylor and Francis, London
59. Tang F, Costa E, Schwartz JP (1983) Increase of proenkephalin mRNA and enkephalin content of rat striatum after daily injection of haloperidol for 2 to 3 weeks. Proc Natl Acad Sci USA 80:3841–3846
60. Lin MT, Wu JJ, Chandara A, Tsay BL (1981) Activation of striatal dopamine receptors inducing pain inhibition in rats. J Neural Transm 51:213–219
61. Ben-Shachar D, Yehuda S, Finberg JPM, Spanier I, Youdim MBH (1988) Selective alteration in blood–brain barrier and insulin transport in iron-deficient rats. J Neurochem 50:1434–1437
62. Ben-Shachar D, Youdim MBH (1989) Unpublished data
63. Lehmann WD, Heinrich HC (1988) Impaired phenylalanine–tyrosine conversion in patients with iron-deficiency anemia studied by a L-(^{3}H)-phenylalanine-loading test. Am J Clin Nutr 44, 468–474
64. Leibel L, Greenfield D, Pollitt E (1979) Biochemical and behavioural aspects of sideropenia. Br J Haematol 41:145–150
65. Bruinvels J, Pepplinkhuizen L, Van Tuiji HR, Moleman P, Blom W (1980) Role of serine, glycine and the tetrahydrofolic acid cycle in schizoaffective psychosis: a hypothesis relating porphyrin biosynthesis and transmethylation. In: Usdin E, Sourkes TL, Youdim MBH (eds) Enzymes and neurotransmitters in mental disease. Wiley, Chichester, pp 11–138

Commentary

Parks: Could the meanings of "subsensitivity" and "down regulation" be more clearly explained?

Author's reply: Subsensitivity or down regulation of a receptor is a pharmacological expression denoting not only the decrease in the function of the receptor in question, but also decreases either in the receptor affinity (K_D) or maximum number of binding sites (B_{max}). In the case of iron deficiency we have noted a reduction in the dopamine D_2 receptor number (B_{max}) as measured in the rat brain caudate nucleus, using the radioligand ^{3}H-spiperone.

Dobbing: Have changes in the blood–brain barrier been demonstrated morphologically (the word "damage" is used)? Or are these merely changes in the blood–tissue relationships of the CNS with regard to these substances? Is it not dangerous to infer penetration of substances from changes in others?

Author's reply: The alteration in the blood–brain barrier noted in the iron-deficient rats is selective. However our recent (unpublished) studies do clearly show that during iron deficiency there is a highly significant increase of ^{59}Fe uptake. Histochemical analysis and radioautographs indicate accumulation of iron in the iron-rich brain regions of globus pallida and substantia nigra.

Smart: One of the behavioural changes in iron-deficient rats, which most impressed me on reading Youdim's paper, was the reversal of the normal diurnal rhythm of activity. Assuming that this is a reliable phenomenon (and presumably it is, being supported by three references), I would have expected it to be the launching pad for a great deal of research. But this does not seem to have been the case. At least, I did not come across any explanation of the reversal, or findings from investigations of other bodily rhythms in iron-deficient animals in Youdim's paper. The question whether there are changes in the rhythms of hormones and neurotransmitters would appear to be a fruitful area of research.

The finding of altered activity rhythms in rats prompts two further comments. (a) The reversed rhythm poses difficult problems with respect to any other behavioural testing of iron-deficient animals. When should one test them? If iron-deficient and control rats are tested at the same time of day, this will be at a time when one of the groups is usually active and the other is usually inactive (even asleep?). The problems for the interpretation of the findings are obvious. The best solution would appear to be to compare the performance of animals at different times of day (minimally two groups of controls, one tested during the light and the other during the dark phase, and two groups of experimentals treated likewise).

(b) I do not remember ever hearing any suggestion of an altered circadian rhythm in iron-deficient children. Is there any change in their sleep-wakefulness cycle, for instance? If there is no evidence of such a change, why the apparent species difference? Could this be due to the much greater severity of iron deficiency in experimental animal studies than in the human situation (cf. Larkin and Rao, Chapter 3). If so, extrapolation from rat to man should be made with caution until further animal studies are conducted, utilizing more realistic levels of iron deficiency.

The crucially important topic of the reversibility or otherwise of the effects of iron deficiency is considered in several places. Youdim and Yehuda are amongst the very few who have investigated this subject and are earnestly to be encouraged to continue to do so. I am a little confused regarding one of the findings, which Youdim quotes twice, that brain iron content is irreversibly reduced by early iron deficiency. This seems to be completely at variance with Fig. 5.1 which shows that non-haem iron levels return to normal by 9 weeks of age in rats which had been iron deficient for the first 4 weeks postnatally. Evidence of a "permanent" deficit in dopamine dependent neurotransmission is given in Table 5.1. I accept that at this one time point, after 6 weeks of recovery, there is a significant and substantial deficit (25%). To be entirely convinced of the irreversibility of this deficit, I should like to see some additional, later time points, say after 3 and 6 months of recovery.

Dallman: Youdim's paper provides an excellent review of recent progress in the neurobiochemical and pharmacological aspects of iron deficiency in the rat. Much of this work comes from his group. The results are stimulating and open up many new areas of investigation and speculation. However, in places the paper seems to have an evangelical tone that may arouse skepticism in the reader. There is an understandable tendency to consider one's favorite nutrient to be of unique importance. However all *essential* nutrients, by definition, play critical roles in normal development. It is true that iron deficiency is very common in man but it is almost invariably quite mild in comparison with the very stringent conditions used in the much more rapidly growing rat.

Table C.1. Circadian activity patterns in male rats with iron-deficiency anemia: varying results from different groups of investigators. A dash signifies that the information was not provided.

	Age (weeks)	Hemoglobin Deficient	g/dl Control	Temp	Light/dark cycle (h)	Measure of activity
A. Normal circadian pattern (active in the dark)						
Edgerton et al. (1972)	5–10	6–8	⁻14	24–25	–	Voluntary exercise wheel for 5 weeks
Dallman et al. (1984)[a]	4–6	5.7 8.5	12.4 12.4	20–22	12/12	Food and water consumption
B. Reversed circadian pattern (active in the light)						
Glover and Jacobs (1972)	⁻8	5.0 12.0	14.6 14.6	–	–	Activity meter
Youdim et al (1981)[b]	⁻8	6.9	14.8	22	12/12	Activity meter

[a]ACTH and corticosterone also maintained normal circadian pattern.
[b]Circadian patterns of body temperature and motor activity in response to *d*-amphetamine and apomorphine were also reversed.

There are two exmples of questionable attribution of unique importance to iron. It seems to be suggested that the mere presence of iron in the brain makes behavioral deficits a virtual certainty in iron deficiency. There are very good reasons why early reports of deficits in cognition and learning in iron deficiency were treated with skepticism. The data in early reports were generally anecdotal and inconclusive. The text makes it sound as though the skeptical response to these reports was a stubborn refusal to recognize the obvious.

The *unique* uneven distribution of iron is *not* unique as stated.

Where the reversal of the circadian pattern is mentioned in the text it is appropriate also to cite the two papers that found no evidence of a reversal [1,2]. This issue affects much of the experimental work on iron nutrition and it would be useful to speculate under what conditions reversal might or might not occur. Table C.1 summarizes the conditions from the four groups that have presented experimental data that bears on this issue [1–4]. Admittedly, an activity meter is a reliable way to evaluate the sleep–wake cycle [3,4], but food and water intake, ACTH and corticosterone levels [2], and a voluntary exercise wheel [1] also provide useful information.

The mention of iron deposition in association with neurodegenerative processes seems out of context. Also, I would imagine that the cause and effect relationship that is implied is highly speculative. The abundance of iron in cirrhotic livers and around the tumors of Hodgkin's disease does not mean that the iron caused those diseases.

It seems inappropriate to feature treadmill exercise under the heading of behavioral aspects. In any case, myoglobin is far from being the only factor. The cytochromes and iron sulfur proteins required for the oxidative production of ATP are likely to play an important role, considering the high energy expenditure during muscle exercise [5].

References

1. Edgerton VR, Bryant SL, Gillespie CA, Gardner GW (1972) Iron deficiency and physical performance and activity of rats. J Nutr 102:381–400
2. Dallman PR, Refino CA, Dallman MF (1984) The pituitary-adrenal response to stress in the iron-deficient rat. J Nutr 114:1747–1753
3. Glover J, Jacobs A (1972) Activity pattern in iron-deficient rats. Br Med J 2:627–628
4. Youdim MBH, Yehuda S, Ben-Uriah Y (1981) Iron deficiency-induced circadian rhythm reversal of dopaminergic-mediated behaviors and thermoregulation in rats. Eur J Pharmacol 74:295–301
5. Dallman PR (1986) Biochemical basis for manifestations of iron deficiency. Ann Rev Nutr 6: 13–40

Author's reply to Smart and Dallman: Yehuda (Chapter 4) has discussed the reversal of the normal diurnal rhythms of dopamine-dependent behaviours in iron-deficient rats. The lack of similar observations by Dallman when food and water intake were examined may be due to his use of lighting conditions, as well as the time the animals were kept on an iron-deficient diet. I believe that Dallman used much younger rats than ours. Furthermore he has difficulty in making older rats (48 days old) iron deficient. We are surprised at this, since we have never had such a difficulty. The duration of the iron-deficient diet before the diurnal rhythm is reversed is important. These effects are time-dependent and cannot be observed in the early period of iron deficiency. Because of the reversed rhythms we now usually measure both the behavioural and biochemical changes in the light as well as in the dark periods in which the optimal effects are observed.

Regarding the reversibility of decreased brain iron during iron deficiency in rats of different ages, we have noted an age-dependent phenomenon. The older the animal, the more difficult it is to make them iron deficient as well as to reduce their brain iron. By contrast, rehabilitation of iron deficiency with iron supplementation results in a faster restoration of brain iron in older rats (21 and 48 days old) than in immature animals (10 days old). In the latter we could not restore the brain concentration even after 6 months of supplementation. This agrees with the findings of Dallman.

I accept Smart's point that we should examine dopamine-dependent transmission and dopamine D_2 receptors 3 and 6 months later in these animals before we can be entirely convinced of the irreversibility of iron deficiency in immature rats. Indeed the behavioural studies of Dallman and colleagues showed that the deficit may indeed be reversible even after 6 months of supplementation.

Yip: The unaltered activity of iron-dependent enzymes in the brains of iron-deficient animals is certainly an enigma. Compared with other organs, brain certainly has many physiological exceptions. I cannot help wondering whether the behavioral studies will yield more information than biochemical studies in this case.

Author's reply: The uneven distribution of iron in human, rat and monkey brain regions makes it difficult to state what level of iron is needed in order to be non-iron deficient. It is generally accepted that iron in the brain, particularly in such regions as the globus pallidus and substantia nigra is in excess of the need for the biochemical reactions. However, in our rat studies we have shown a threshold level, as measured in whole brain, which is about 85% of total non-haem iron. If the reduction of brain non-haem iron in iron deficiency exceeds about 15% we do begin to see the behavioural changes in dopamine neurotransmission. We have called this threshold point the "functional pool" of iron. We are fully aware that the threshold "functional pool" may vary from one region of the brain to another.

Although the unaltered activity of iron-dependent enzymes in the brains of iron-deficient rats cannot be explained, this has also been reported in deficiencies of other nutrients such as riboflavin, pyridoxol and copper. However, since iron concentration in some brain regions is excessive, it is possible that with our type of iron deficiency we have not exhausted the threshold level of iron, in which case the iron still available is sufficient to act as a cofactor for iron-dependent enzymes. Indeed we have attempted to produce unphysiological iron deficiency (Hb < 4 g/dl), and even then the activities of iron-dependent enzymes are unchanged.

Felt and Lozoff: In this instructive paper Youdim reviews the available literature concerning developmental, neuropharmacological and neurobiochemical aspects of iron deficiency in the rat model. In this process, he cites his own group's wealth of work exploring the hypothesized role of iron deficiency in central dopaminergic system changes in the rat, and the work of others on rat brain iron content and behavioral changes. As stated in his introductory comments, it is important to remember the developmental age of the animals in each study in any attempt to pull together the information available. Dobbing, in comparing rat and human brain development, observed the following developmental periods: achievement of adult neuronal number (by birth in the rat and by mid-gestation in the human), and the brain growth spurt (the phase of rapid proliferation and myelinization), which continues to about postnatal day 25 (weaning) in the rat and age 2 to 3 years in the human [1]. Thus, in order to discuss the "development" and "rapid growth rate" of rat vs. human brain usefully in Youdim's review, one needs first to know which developmental phase is referred to. If the time of achievement of adult neuronal number is considered, this occurs in the second human trimester and the third rat trimester while the brain growth spurt is primarily postnatal for both species. This framework is crucial to understanding any possible link between human and animal studies of iron deficiency during development and for comparing different animal studies.

The studies reviewed by Youdim vary in design, age of iron-deficiency insult, age of attempt to rehabilitate, and age of testing. Each factor must be kept clearly in mind in interpreting the results. It appears that iron deficiency during the rat brain growth spurt causes an irreversible reduction in brain iron content [2,3], diminished ^{3}H-spiperidol binding at the caudate nucleus [4] and an altered threshold of arousal on passive and active avoidance tasks [3,5]. However, the transfer of learning tasks [6], as well as the majority of Youdim's work on centrally mediated effects of iron deficiency, were performed in *postweaning* rat models. Because the effect of lower iron availability may be quite different for the developing versus the adult brain, it is crucial to define clearly the age of insult and rehabilitation, when discussing these findings. Similar careful atten-tion to timing is necessary to review the information available regarding behavioral changes in animals with iron-deficiency anemia. For instance, while Youdim's group have reported diminished "learning capacity" of postweaning iron-deficient and rehabilitated male rats in the Y maze and the Morris Tank, the work of Weinberg does not. In a series of experiments by Weinberg [3,5] 28-day-old animals who had iron deficiency caused by provision of a low iron diet beginning during late gestation, at birth, or on postnatal day 10, were less responsive (open field), had decreased ambulation, and longer re-entry latencies on shock avoidance. In contrast, 60–65-day-old male but not female rats who had been subjected to iron deficiency during gestation and lactation through day 28, with subsequent iron rehabilitation to the time of testing, made more inter-trial responses on active avoidance learning. No effect of prior iron deficiency was noted for either sex on head dipping or ambulation. In fact, improved performance was noted on passive avoidance testing. These authors hypothe-sized an altered threshold of arousal as the etiology for diminished performance when anemic, and for persistence of some alterations after rehabilitation, rather than a decrease in "learning capacity" or "slower" learning. Similarly, Findlay [7], looked at 100-day-old rats of both sexes, who had been deprived of iron through gestational development and lactation and then placed on a normal iron diet. No effect of prior iron deprivation was observed on number of trials to extinction in a passive avoidance shuttlebox task. However, these animals did have shorter escape latencies and fewer false entries compared with iron-sufficient controls. Thus, in contrast to the results of Youdim with rats made iron deficient in the postweaning period, researchers who have studied behavior in rats who were iron deficient during the brain growth spurt found changes that they attributed to an altered threshold of arousal rather than to altered cognition or learning ability.

Similarly, it is necessary to take great care in any extrapolation of information between studies in rat and human iron deficiency. While there has been the suggestion that iron deficiency in older children is accompanied by cognitive changes that seem to improve with iron treatment, it is less clear that behavioral alterations associated with deficiency in the infant-toddler age group (again, the brain growth spurt in the human) are cognitive or correctable with treatment. The persistence of lower mental and motor test scores after iron treatment in this younger age group is inextricably intertwined with other behavioral changes, at least including altered maternal/child interactions [8]. Thus, it seems premature to state there is a "parallelism" in "iron-deficient learning processes deficits of iron-deficient animals and those observed in children with iron deficiency", even if we had reference 66 to refer to.

Even though in brain iron histochemical localization in iron-deficient rats has not yet been described, the recent work of Hill [9] has extended our knowledge of brain regions with high iron content in the normal rat. While the extrapyramidal areas were found to be high to moderately high, other regions are now known to be "very high": island of Calleja, lateral superficial border of the olfactory tubercle, organum vasculosum of the lamina terminalis, pineal gland, subfornical organ, median eminence and the area postrema. A slow turnover of brain iron was noted by Dallman [10] and thought important to the inability to reverse the diminished brain content seen with iron deficiency during the brain growth spurt, or the maintenance of high levels in specific areas. However, it is difficult to regard slow turnover as an explanation for the *high* accumulation in specific brain areas suggested by Youdim.

References

1. Dobbing J, Sands J (1973) Quantitative growth and development of human brain. Arch Dis Child 48:757–767
2. Dallman PR, Simes MA, Manies EC (1975) Brain iron: persistent deficiency following short term iron deprivation in the young rat. Br J Haematol 31:209–215
3. Weinberg J, Levine S, Dallman PR (1979) Long-term consequences of early iron deficiency in the rat. Pharmacol Biochem Behav 11:631–638
4. Ben-Shachar D, Ashkenazi R, Youdim MBH (1986) Long-term consequences of early iron deficiency on dopaminergic neurotransmission in rats. Int J Dev Neurosci 4:81–88
5. Weinberg J, Dallman PR, Levine S (1980) Iron deficiency during early development in the rat: behavioral and psychological consequences. Pharmacol Biochem Behav 12:493–502
6. Massaro TF, Widmayer P (1981) The effect of iron deficiency on cognitive performance in the rat. Am J Clin Nutr 34:864–870
7. Findlay E, Ng KT, Reid RL, Armstrong SM (1981) The effect of iron deficiency during development on passive avoidance learning in the adult rat. Physiol Behav 27:1089–1096
8. Lozoff B, Brittenham GM (1986) Behavioral aspects of iron deficiency. Prog Hematol XIV:23–53
9. Hill JM (1988) The distribution of iron in the brain. In: Youdim MBH (ed) Brain iron: neurochemical and behavioral aspects. Taylor and Francis, London, pp 1–24

10. Dallman PR, Spirito RA (1977) Brain iron in the rat: extremely slow turnover in normal rats may
    explain long-lasting effects of early iron deficiency. J Nutr 107:1075–1081

Author's reply: I believe that Yehuda and I have often pointed out the limitations of our behavioural studies in iron-deficient rats. We certainly do not wish to suggest that the irreversible deficit in "learning" in iron-deficient postweaning rats is identical or even representative of human studies. What we have stressed is the apparent parallelism with the irreversibility of the iron deficits with continuous iron supplementation. There may be a critical or vulnerable period for irreversibility in the early postnatal rat, and the same may be true for humans.

Finberg: This is a provocative and interesting series of hypotheses, but there is insufficient specific evidence for anything beyond that.

Larkin and Rao: While it is an interesting observation, it is not clear how excessive iron in the substantia nigra and globus pallidus is relevant to iron deficiency and brain function. Furthermore, there is some doubt as to whether Haller Vorden Spatz disease is a discrete entity. Some of these iron depositions have been suggested to be secondary hemorrhage.

Iron deficiency is a systematic disease. Iron is located in various brain subcellular components and about 70% in the myelin fraction. It would not be surprising therefore that meylin in fetal or neonatal animals would be affected by iron deficiency. In fact several recent studies (see Chapter 3) show that iron deficiency affects myelination and the pattern of fatty acids in myelin lipids in neonatal rats. It occurs during a critical growth period and may be partially or completely reversible depending on the time of intervention with iron therapy. Whether or not more subtle changes occur with weanling animals or adults it is not at present clear.

The mechanism for changes in the myelination and the fatty acid pattern (unsaturated to saturated ratio) is not entirely clear and may be multifactorial. However, in view of the iron requirements for fatty acid desaturase it would not be surprising in iron deficiency to find that fatty acid desaturation would be reduced in the brain. The effect of iron deficiency lowering the levels of desaturase enzyme in liver has been shown [1].

The author focuses on iron deficiency as a systemic disease, its potentially deleterious effects on brain function being multifactorial. He clearly recognizes that the behavioral studies showing pathology are based wholly or in part on biochemical alterations. He is clearly sensitive to the relationship of the disparate disciplines of biochemistry, pathology, behavioral sciences and clinical pharmacology; and that each, like one of many blind men feeling an elephant, has some part of the whole truth.

However, it is often unclear whether a general effect of iron deficiency is being discussed or one pertaining to the deficiency during infancy.

Reference

1. Rao GA, Crane RT, Larkin EC (1983) Reduction of hepatic stearoyl-CoA desaturase activity in
   rats fed iron deficient diets. Lipids 18:573–575

Chapter 6

Has Iron Deficiency Been Shown to Cause Altered Behavior in Infants?

Betsy Lozoff

Infancy is an especially important age at which to study behavioral effects of iron deficiency. Animal studies indicate that iron deficiency during early development has more lasting effects than similar deficiency during adulthood; neurotransmitter changes, decreases in brain iron content, and behavioral alterations seem to persist despite treatment when iron deficiency anemia occurs in the infant rat, but not in the adult [1]. In the human, iron deficiency is most prevalent among 6–24-month-old infants, coinciding with the latter part of the brain growth spurt and with the unfolding of fundamental mental and motor processes [2]. In view of the potential clinical significance, a number of recent studies have focused on the behavior and development of iron-deficient infants. This critical review of the several studies addresses two questions, concentrating primarily on the first and touching briefly on the second:

1. Has iron deficiency been proven to cause behavioral alterations in infants?
2. How do the results of studies of iron-deficient infants relate to those in research on other conditions in infancy that are considered to affect behavior and development adversely?

Proving that Iron Deficiency Causes Alterations in Infant Behavior

Establishing a cause–effect relationship between two conditions depends on documenting a reliable association between them, confirming that the supposed cause precedes the supposed effect in time, and proving that the relationship is not spurious, that is, not explained by some other factor [3].

Is Iron Deficiency Associated with Altered Infant Behavior?

Establishing a link between iron deficiency and behavioral alterations in infancy has generally entailed comparisons of iron-deficient and normal infants. Because lack of iron can range from depleted iron stores to iron-deficiency anemia, the degree of iron deficiency has become an important dimension in studies of human infants. The use of multiple iron measures in recent behavioral studies represents an advance over earlier work. Unless specifically indicated, the studies reviewed used at least three measures of iron status in addition to hemoglobin or hematocrit. A few studies have also included hematologic response to iron therapy as a criterion for defining iron deficiency, which is the most definitive of available standards.

Comparisons among studies are also facilitated by the fact that the major outcome measure in ten of them has been performance on the Bayley Scales of Infant Development [4], a standardized test of infant development with three components: Mental Scale, Motor Scale, and Infant Behavior Record. Such a test is best considered a starting point in the search for behavioral effects, since it assesses a variety of functions that also differ with age. A few projects have therefore assessed infant behavior on other more specific cognitive tests or outside the test situation, but there are fewer replicated results. Exact replication of findings is limited due to differences in age of the infants in the different studies, and the timing, duration, or severity of iron deficiency is not necessarily the same. I have omitted details of statistical analyses in reviewing these studies, but only consider those findings that are statistically significant with a probability of 0.05 or less as positive results.

These caveats not withstanding, several studies have compared the developmental test performance of infants with iron deficiency severe enough to cause anemia to that of appropriate non-anemic controls, and each study with careful definition of iron status has found lower developmental test scores in the anemic group. In a study of 6–24-month-old Guatemalan infants, Lozoff et al. found that the mean mental development test score of the 28 infants with iron-deficiency anemia (Hb $\leq$ 10.5 g/dl) was 87, compared to the mean score of 100 among the 40 non-anemic infants (Hb $\geq$ 12 g/dl). A 9–point pretreatment difference in motor scores was also observed [5]. Mental test score deficits were especially marked in older anemic infants (19–24-month-olds), and the pattern in item failure suggested particular difficulty with verbal items [6]. A substantial correlation between the degree of iron deficiency and mental test scores (r= 0.73) was also observed in the older age group [6]. In Walter et al.'s first Chilean investigation [7], the average mental test score of 10 iron-deficient anemic 15-month-olds was 98, 12 points less than the mean score of the 27 infants with Hb levels $>$ 11 g/dl. There was no difference between groups in motor scores. Somewhat similar results were also obtained in a recent study of 145 Asian 21–23-month-olds living in the United Kingdom [8]. Sixty-one children with Hb $<$ 11 g/dl received lower scores on a developmental screening test than children with higher Hb levels. Significant between-group differences were noted in the areas of fine motor and social development.

One study in which iron status was carefully determined focused solely on infants with normal Hb levels but varying degrees of iron lack. Oski et al. [9] examined 38 9–12-month-old infants with Hb levels >11 g/dl. Eighteen infants were iron deficient without anemia, 10 were iron-depleted and 10 were iron-sufficient.* The average mental test score of the infants with iron deficiency was 85 points, 10 points lower than those with iron depletion. However, the scores of the completely iron-replete infants (mean = 91) fell between those of the iron-deficient and iron-depleted babies. Thus, using suitable iron-replete controls, the study did not find a statistically significant test score deficit in the iron-deficient but non-anemic group.

Two studies in which the measures of iron status were more limited did not obtain differences in Bayley test scores. Johnson and McGowan [10] drawing a sample of one-year-old infants from a low income Mexican-American population, found no differences in mental or motor test scores between 25 anemic infants (Hb levels of < 10.5 g/dl) and an equal number of matched non-anemic controls. Iron deficiency was presumed to be the cause of the anemic infants' low hemoglobin levels; however, no measures of iron status were obtained and response to iron treatment was not assessed. Deinard et al. [11], in a study of 9–11-month-old infants, all of whom had hematocrit levels > 34%, did not find cognitive test score differences among either a group of 34 infants with low ferritin levels, a second group of 21 babies with intermediate ferritin values or a third group of 157 babies with higher ferritin values. Because the serum ferritin was the only available measure of iron status, however, infants with iron depletion could not be distinguished from those with iron deficiency.

These studies did not assess whether there was a particular level of anemia at which developmental test performance was adversely affected. None of them found lower developmental test scores in the absence of anemia, but they did not determine whether this was due to some methodologic limitation, such as small sample size or ambiguity in iron status. The lower scores of the infants in the iron-deficient non-anemic group in Oski et al.'s study [9], though not statistically significant, and the observed relationship between degree of iron deficiency and mental scores among older infants in the Guatemalan study [6] suggested that further research was needed to resolve the issue of the *degree* of iron deficiency at which infant behavior and development are altered. A recent study in Costa Rica by Lozoff et al. [12] therefore addressed this issue by enrolling in a single study a relatively large number of infants with varied iron status. The sample consisted of 191 12–23-month-old infants divided into groups ranging from most to least iron-deficient as follows: (1) iron-deficient anemic (n=52); (2) intermediate in hemoglobin level and iron deficient (n=45); (3) non-anemic iron-deficient (n=21); (4) non-anemic iron-depleted (n=38); and (5) non-anemic iron-sufficient (n=35). The data from the anemic infants were further analyzed with respect to actual Hb level, since lower Hb levels indicate more severe iron deficiency once anemia is present. Iron-deficient and iron-depleted conditions were subsequently confirmed by hematologic response to

---

*Iron-deficiency anemia is defined as an Hb level 2 s.d. below reference levels and at least 2 of 3 abnormal iron measures. Iron deficiency without anemia (or iron-deficient erythropoeisis) is defined as 2 of 3 abnormal iron measures and an Hb level within the normal range. Iron depletion refers to depleted iron stores as evidenced by a low serum ferritin. Iron repletion, or iron sufficiency is defined as three normal iron measures and a normal Hb.

iron therapy. The population was generally lower middle class, highly literate, with excellent health care, and free from undernutrition and parasitic disease.

Infants with moderate iron-deficiency anemia (Hb ≤10.0 g/dl) were found to have lower mental and motor test scores than appropriate controls; infants with mild anemia (Hb 10.1–10.5 g/dl) received lower motor scores but not mental scores; and infants with lesser degrees of iron deficiency did not have impairments in developmental test performance. The mean mental test score of the moderately anemic infants was eight points below that of infants with higher Hb levels (> 10.0 g/dl), and the mean motor score of the entire anemic group was ten points below that of infants with Hb > 10.5 g/dl. Mental test scores decreased with age in all groups; the differential decrease observed among older anemic infants in the Guatemalan study was not found [6]. However, anemic infants in all age groups seemed to have trouble with particular motor functions involving balance and coordination.

Similar results were obtained in another study with a strong design, recently completed by Walter and associates in Chile [13]. Infants were studied prospectively from birth as part of a field trial of iron-fortified foods with random assignment of iron fortification or control. Iron measures were obtained at 9 and 12 months and developmental assessments initially performed at 12 months. Not surprisingly, most of the iron deficiency and anemia occurred among the infants who did not receive iron-fortified foods. As in the Costa Rican study, iron status was ultimately confirmed by hematologic response to therapeutic iron, administered after 12 months of age. The developmental assessments at 12 months indicated that the 39 infants with iron-deficiency anemia (Hb < 11.0 g/dl) had significantly lower mental and motor scores than either 127 iron-deficient non-anemic infants or 30 iron-replete controls. The differences were similar to those obtained in Costa Rica: mental scores of the anemic infants averaged 6–7 points lower than those of non-anemic infants, motor scores averaged 9–11 points lower, and test score differences were not observed in the absence of iron-deficiency anemia. An analysis of specific items on the mental scale suggested that the anemic infants had particular difficulty with verbal items, as observed in the study in Guatemala [6]. On the motor test anemic infants had difficulty with items similar to those reported in the recent study in Costa Rica.

Despite the similarity of many results in the most recent studies in Chile and Costa Rica, there are still differences in specific findings about the degree of iron deficiency that is related to altered test scores. For instance, Lozoff et al. found lower motor but not mental scores among infants with mild anemia (Hb 10.1–10.5 g/dl), while Walter et al. found that those with Hb levels between 10.5 and 11.0 g/dl showed an intermediate lowering of both mental and motor developmental test scores. However, the new study in Chile clearly indicates that severity or chronicity of iron-deficiency anemia is important. Those infants who were anemic at both 9 and 12 months had significantly lower developmental test scores than those with anemia of less than 3 months duration (i.e., those who had normal Hb levels at 9 months and anemic levels at 12 months). As would be expected by the pathophysiology of iron deficiency, infants who were anemic at 9 and 12 months of age had lower Hb levels than those whose anemia was not apparent until the 12-month testing.

Significant cognitive or motor deficits have not yet been found among non-anemic infants with varying degrees of iron lack, but it would be premature to conclude that there are no ill effects, given that these are relatively few studies and the behavioral measures are quite gross. Thus, there are still unanswered questions about the relationship between the degree of iron deficiency and the degree of behavioral alterations. It is reasonable to expect that the relationship might also vary according to the influence of other environmental factors. Furthermore, since iron-deficiency anemia develops only after a relatively prolonged period of iron lack, the studies of anemic infants have not determined whether the observed behavioral alterations are linked to anemia per se, or to severe, prolonged iron deficiency. Experimental manipulations, such as transfusion to correct anemia without altering iron deficiency, would enable one to disentangle the effects of anemia from those of iron deficiency. Since these experiments are not appropriate in the human infant, the relative roles of anemia and iron deficiency are likely to remain ambiguous in the foreseeable future.

That lower mental and motor test scores have been observed among iron-deficient anemic infants raises the further question of *why* their scores were lower. Developmental test scores are crude behavioral measures that give little indication of the specific functions involved. Recent investigations have often assumed that disturbances in affect, arousal, or attentiveness were important determinants of anemic infants' poorer developmental test performance [10,14,15]. However, attempts to document such alterations have been hindered by the paucity of standardized measures of non-cognitive behavior in infancy. Several of the studies reviewed here reported assessments of non-cognitive behavior by means of the ratings on the Bayley Infant Behavior Record, but the results are often not directly comparable due to the different analytic methods employed [16]. Other limitations, such as small sample size, restricted measures of iron status, and the absence of either placebo or non-anemic control groups, have already been noted. Nonetheless, a number of behavioral alterations have been observed in those studies that compared iron-deficient infants with normal controls.

In the Guatemalan study [17,18] behavioral disturbances, particularly in affect (based on ratings on the Infant Behavior Record), were evident among the iron-deficient anemic infants. Moreover, these disturbances were closely related to poor developmental test performance. Anemic infants who were unduly fearful, unhappy, tired, tense, and hesitant or withdrawn with the examiner received low mental test scores, whereas anemic infants who were rated normal in affect achieved mental test scores comparable to those of non-anemic controls and normal by US standards. The results of the next study in Costa Rica suggest that abnormal behavior, whether in affect or task orientation, is associated with poor developmental test performance among both anemic and non-anemic infants. However, behaviorally-disturbed anemic infants had the lowest mental and motor scores (93.3 and 97.9 respectively); anemic infants whose behavior was normal and control babies with abnormal behavior received comparable scores (mental means = 99.6, 98.3; motor means = 107.4, 111.3); and the control infants with normal behavior scored highest on both mental and motor tests,

(108.3 and 114.0, respectively). This relationship held even after using structural modeling techniques to consider a number of other influences on test scores, such as family background, neonatal factors, age, sex, growth, and lead levels.

The behavior of mothers and infants was also analyzed by Lozoff and Klein, using videotape recordings during play and developmental testing. In the Guatemalan study, anemic infants and their mothers maintained closer contact during play than non-anemic infants and their mothers [19]. Similar results were obtained in quantitative codings of the motor test of the Costa Rican infants. More of the anemic than comparison infants were wary and hesitant, never becoming engaged in the test (28% vs. 10%, $P=0.01$). The tests of anemic infants were shorter than those of controls (13.0 vs. 15.7 minutes, $P < 0.01$), and fewer different tasks were administered, even though the number of Bayley items actually scored and the number of demonstrations and encouragements were comparable. Other significant differences ($P < 0.05$) were that the anemic infants spent less time at a distance from their mothers and initiated close contact more often. They attended to the tester less often and were less likely to respond to her requests promptly on their own. Their mothers demonstrated the desired motor behaviors and encouraged their children to perform the tasks less frequently [20].

Walter et al. [13], analyzing the Infant Behavior Record in their second study in ways similar to those reported by Lozoff et al. [16,18], found a quite similar pattern of behavioral differences: lower mental scores were noted among anemic infants who were abnormal in affect or task orientation. On individual Infant Behaviour Record ratings, anemic infants were less responsive to the examiner, their mothers, and people in general, were unhappier, were less goal directed, showed shorter spans of attention, vocalized less and moved less. In addition to differences in behavioral ratings, these investigators observed a pattern of cardiac responses to auditory habituation indicative of less advanced attentional processing among anemic infants (DeAndraca et al., personal communication, 1987). In the study by Deinard et al. [11], several behavioral differences between infants with low ferritin values and controls were reported, despite the absence of between-group differences in mental test scores. Only one study, by Johnson and McGowan [10], reported no behavioral differences. On balance, with all but one study noting non-cognitive behavioral differences between anemic and non-anemic infants during developmental testing or play, the results indicate the fruitfulness of examining affect, attention, and activity as well as standard test scores.

In sum, the results of research published to date document an association between iron deficiency severe enough to cause anemia and altered behaviour, including impaired performance on developmental tests in infancy. The five published studies with careful definition of iron status and non-anemic control groups [5,7,8,12,13] found clinically and statistically significant lower mental test scores among anemic infants prior to treatment. Lower motor test scores among anemic infants were also noted in four studies [5,8,12,13]. Thus, although the number of studies is still limited, similar results have been obtained by different investigators working in different countries with different populations. This feature of replicated results is becoming the strongest evidence that iron-deficiency anemia, or some unidentified but closely linked condition, alters infant behavior. However, replication is just a first step in establishing a causal relationship, since the role of "some unidentified but closely linked condition" cannot be eliminated. Iron-deficiency anemia and this other condition might go hand-in-hand, no matter what country or what population was studied.

Does Iron Deficiency Precede Altered Behavior?

Proving a causal connection between iron deficiency and altered behavior among infants depends not only on documenting that the two conditions are reliably related to each other but also on being certain that the infants became iron deficient before differing in behavior rather than vice versa. Investigators have tried to eliminate other factors that adversely affect behavior and development by increasingly stringent entrance criteria: infants who were born prematurely, had complicated births, or had other health problems have been excluded from the studies. However, such entrance criteria cannot guarantee that infants who developed iron-deficiency anemia were previously similar in behavior.

It is also reasonable to ask if pre-existing behavioral differences could account not only for the behavioral findings in the several studies but also for the occurrence of iron deficiency in some infants but not in others. The children must certainly have differed either in the amount of storage iron they accumulated during gestation or in their postnatal intake of dietary iron. Could behavioral factors account for differences in prenatal or postnatal iron balance?

Postnatal behavioral differences could affect feeding, and feeding patterns could relate to iron deficiency. For instance, in the Costa Rican study anemic infants were less likely to have been breast-fed; if breast-fed, they were weaned earlier; and they consumed more unmodified cow milk. These differences in dietary sources of iron provide good physiologic explanation why some infants developed iron-deficiency anemia. However, early weaning and milk consumption could relate to pre-existing behavioral differences. Even slight differences in gestational age or the appropriateness of weight for age, though within the normal full-term range, could conceivably influence behavior.

Although birth weight differences were not statistically significant in any single study, anemic infants in the Guatemalan, Costa Rican and second Chilean studies weighed 150–250 g less than infants with better iron status. These results, consistent in all studies that reported birth weight data, raise the possibility that gestation might have been slightly shorter among babies who became anemic, that there were among them more babies small for gestational age or that the non-anemic babies were unusually large. Analysis of our data indicates that the latter explanation pertains to the Costa Rican data. All such factors related to maturity and size at birth may influence iron balance as well as behavior. Prospective studies that include measures of temperament and behavior in the early postnatal period would be helpful, but the possibility that behavioral factors may subtly influence feeding, iron status, and subsequent development should probably be kept in mind.

Is the Relationship Between Iron Deficiency and Altered Behavior Non-spurious?

Determining that iron deficiency precedes altered behavior is a necessary but not sufficient condition for proving that iron deficiency caused the behavioral changes. A further step in establishing such a cause/effect relationship is to prove that no other factor accounts for the observed association. A strength of most of the recent studies is their inclusion of a therapeutic trial of iron, since improvement with iron treatment could provide convincing evidence that behavioral changes observed among iron-deficient infants were in fact due to iron deficiency and not to some closely associated factor. Until the last two or three years, most studies were designed to detect changes in developmental test performance within 5–11 days of starting iron therapy. This emphasis on short-term treatment effects was guided by two considerations: (1) clinicians, in describing iron-deficient anemic babies as irritable, apathetic, and distractible, have commented that these characteristics seem to disappear within a few days of iron treatment; and (2) it was hoped that early re-testing would allow any behavioral changes, if identified before substantial hematological improvement, to be attributed to brain rather than blood, i.e., to altered central nervous system function rather than to the correction of anemia.

In Oski and Honig's pilot study, published in 1978 [21–23], 24 9–26-month-old iron-deficient anemic infants were randomly assigned to an intramuscular iron or placebo (saline injection) treatment group. A non-anemic control group was not included. One week after treatment, the Bayley mental test scores of anemic infants receiving intramuscular iron showed a significant mean increase of 14 points, while placebo-treated anemic infants had a non-significant mean increase of six points. On the Infant Behavior Record, the treated infants were also rated as more alert and reponsive and better coordinated after one week. These results were interpreted to "support the hypothesis that iron deficiency in infants produces developmental alterations and that these changes are rapidly reversible with iron therapy" [21, p. 21]. However, the findings were equivocal. As Oski and Honig point out, the test/re-test difference in mental test scores between the iron- and placebo-treated groups (14 vs. 6 points) was not statistically significant. Thus, although the increase in the iron-treated group's test scores was significant, the study did not demonstrate a clear effect of iron treatment over and above the effect of repeating the same test within a short period of time. Nonetheless, these results were intriguing and stimulated a number of other investigators to undertake related research.

In the study of 6–24-month-old Guatemalan infants described above, Lozoff et al. [5] compared 28 infants with iron-deficiency anemia with a non-anemic group of 40 infants and assessed the effects of oral iron, the therapy of choice, and of placebo treatment. No changes due to short-term oral iron treatment were noted. Iron-treated anemic infants did not show significantly greater increases in their Bayley mental test scores (+7 points) than either placebo-treated anemic babies (+6 points) or infants in the two non-anemic groups (iron-treated, +6 points; placebo-treated, +5 points). Similarly, neither the motor test performance nor the behavior ratings of iron-treated anemic infants improved more than those of infants in the other groups.

Subsequently, two studies whose pretreatment findings have already been considered found short-term improvements in mental test scores and in ratings of affect and attention among iron-deficient infants [7,9]. One study used oral iron [7] and the other, intramuscular iron [9], but neither included placebo-treated control groups. The first project by Walter et al. [7] in Chile involved 37 15-month-old infants. Ten iron-deficient anemic infants showed a significant increase of 10 points in Bayley mental test scores after 11 days of oral iron therapy, compared to a decrease of one point in the 12 iron-replete control infants. The scores of six iron-deficient infants whose Hb levels were 11 g/dl or higher also increased by 10 points, while those of 9 iron-depleted infants increased by only two points. The anemic infants were more likely to be rated as unhappy during initial developmental testing and to become more cooperative and attentive on re-testing after 11 days. The second study by Oski and colleagues [9], involving infants with normal Hb levels (> 11 g/dl), demonstrated a dramatic increase in the mental scores of the 18 non-anemic iron-deficient infants one week after intramuscular iron. The 22-point increase in their mean scores was unambiguously greater than the 6-point change observed among the 10 iron-depleted and 10 iron-sufficient infants. The iron-deficient infants were also rated as less irritable, more persistent, easier to engage in play, and less solemn after one week of treatment [9,23]. The results of these two studies were interpreted to indicate that the mental developmental test performance and behavior of iron-deficient infants improved rapidly after iron therapy regardless of whether anemia was present or not. Because neither study included a placebo group, however, it is necessary to use caution in accepting this interpretation. It is not the improvements in test scores that are in doubt, (the increases in the iron-deficient groups were both clinically and statistically significant) but the certainty with which these improvements can be attributed to iron therapy. In the absence of a placebo treatment, it cannot be determined whether the increases in test scores were due to iron therapy or to another factor. For instance, if the anemic infants were initially more hesitant or fearful, their scores might improve on re-test due to their increased comfort.

The apparent discrepancies in the results of some of the studies suggested that oral and intramuscular iron might differ in their short-term effects on developmental test scores. The effects of these two modes of treatment were therefore compared in the study of 191 Costa Rican infants by Lozoff et al. [12]. After one week of treatment, the increases in Bayley test scores and hematologic parameters among iron-deficient infants receiving intramuscular iron did not differ from those of iron-deficient infants receiving oral iron. The therapeutic modalities were therefore combined for comparison with placebo treatment. After one week, there was a significant increase in mental test scores regardless of whether the infants were anemic and treated with iron (+6 points) or placebo (+2 points) or non-anemic and treated with iron (+4 points) or placebo (+6 points). Similarly, there was no short-term effect of iron treatment on motor test scores.

One other study has assessed the effects of intramuscular iron. Moffatt and colleagues in Canada (personal communication, 1987) evaluated 34 6–24-month-old infants with iron-deficiency anemia in a double-blind randomized controlled study in which half the children received intramuscular iron and half were given a sham injection. The Bayley Scales were administered before treatment, after

one week and after two months. After one week all infants were given oral iron
for two months. A non-anemic control was not included in the study's design.
Upon re-testing at one week, mental scores increased an average of 4–5 points in
both the iron-treated and placebo groups, and there was no effect of treatment
on motor scores.

The second study by Walter and colleagues in Chile [13] also failed to reveal
rapid improvements in test scores after oral iron therapy. Short-term increases in
test scores were observed regardless of the treatment the infants received or their
iron status prior to treatment. After receiving oral ferrous sulphate or placebo
for 10–12 days, infants in the iron-deficient anemic, iron-deficient non-anemic,
and control groups showed improvement in mental and motor scores, with
increases averaging 4–9 points.

To recapitulate, even though the number of available studies is limited,
consistent results have been obtained in all five that included a short-term
placebo treatment [5,12,13,21, and Moffatt, personal communication].
Together, these studies indicate that increases in test scores observed among
iron-treated anemic infants after one week are not significantly greater than
those among placebo-treated anemic infants; increases in scores were observed
regardless of the treatment the infants received or their iron status prior to
treatment. The results of these studies indicate that an increase in test scores can
be expected if the Bayley Scales are re-administered after a short time period
and that these improvements probably reflect the effect of practice, since they do
not seem due to iron therapy.

The early search for rapid behavioral changes was motivated by an interest in
attributing improvements in behavior and in test scores to improved function of
iron-dependent central nervous system enzymes rather than to the correction of
anemia. Although separating the effects of iron deficiency from those of anemia
is important, a more pertinent question from a clinical perspective is whether or
not iron therapy *completely corrects* any behavioral abnormalities, regardless of
how soon changes might be detectable. Until very recently, none of the infant
studies could address this issue, because none included assessments after a fuller
course of iron therapy.

The recent study in Costa Rica [12] was specifically designed to examine the
effects of a course of treatment commonly used in practice: three months of oral
iron therapy. On the basis of hematologic response to iron therapy, infants who
became iron sufficient by study conclusion were distinguished from those who
did not correct all evidence of iron deficiency. Three months of iron therapy was
sufficient to correct completely the iron deficiency of nine infants in the group of
34 infants initially moderately anemic, even though none of the others remained
anemic. Lower mental test scores were no longer evident among these nine
infants. However, the absence of a post-treatment difference was due *not* to
significant improvements in the mental test scores of the formerly moderately
anemic infants but to the slight but statistically significant decline in mental
scores after three months in the comparison group. A decline in test scores in
disadvantaged populations has been reported in a number of studies, cited in
[12]. Those anemic infants who did not become iron sufficient concluded the
study with mental scores that were still significantly lower (mean = 93.2) than
those of infants with initial Hb levels > 10.0 g/dl, regardless of whether the latter

were iron sufficient after three months (mean = 101.8) or not (mean = 100.2). In contrast to the pattern of mental test score results, previously anemic infants who became iron sufficient by study's end (36% of the mild and moderate groups combined) did show a substantial increase in *motor* test scores, averaging 10 points, while the motor scores of infants with Hb levels > 10.5 g/dl who became iron sufficient remained approximately the same. Previously anemic infants who did not become iron sufficient concluded the study with motor scores (mean = 106.3) that were still substantially lower than those of infants with initial Hb levels > 10.5 g/dl (mean = 114.9). There was laboratory evidence that anemic infants who did not become iron sufficient after three months had more severe and chronic iron deficiency.

Similar results, indicating that the majority of anemic infants do not show improvement after iron therapy, have been obtained in two other studies, one in the United Kingdom [24] and the other in Chile [13]. (The study by Moffatt et al. [personal communication, 1987], despite follow-up after two months, does not address this issue, since all anemic children were treated with iron and there was no non-anemic control group). Aukett et al. [24] in a double-blind randomized study of 17–19-month-old iron-deficient children in the United Kingdom found that 58% of those who showed a distinct hematologic response to two months of therapeutic iron (Hb increase > 2 g/dl) failed to show the rate of development expected for their age. The expected rate of development was defined as the number of new items on a developmental screening test that 50% of average children in this age group would be expected to pass over a 2-month interval. It is important to note, however, that a greater proportion of children showing a marked hematologic response to iron therapy did achieve the expected rate of development than those who were treated with iron but whose increase in Hb level was less than 2 g/dl. The use of placebo treatment for two months is a methodologically strong, though controversial, aspect of this study's design, but the results are difficult to compare to those of other studies for several reasons: the developmental measure was unlike that used in other projects; analyses of mean developmental scores revealed no significant effects of treatment; and the decision to consider an increase in Hb of 2 g/dl or more as indicating effective treatment has no counterpart in other studies and may be an arbitrary cut-off that separated the children in this particular study. The only other study relevant to the question of longer-term iron therapy is the second study by Walter and associates in Chile [13], which is directly comparable in many respects to that in Costa Rica. As in the latter study, the administration of oral iron was carefully supervised and an excellent hematologic response documented. However, in contrast to the results obtained in Costa Rica, even those anemic infants who corrected their hematologic status failed to improve their scores. Thus, no improvements in mental or motor test scores were observed after three months of treatment.

The study by Aukett et al. [24], in conjunction with the one in Costa Rica [12], suggests that iron therapy may favorably effect developmental test scores among some anemic children. These results are the most convincing evidence that some behavioral alterations are correctable with iron therapy. The use of long-term placebo in the United Kingdom study makes it more likely that the increases are in fact due to iron treatment. However, substantial delay in treating iron-deficiency anemia goes against routine pediatric practice and has not been considered in most other studies of infants. The absence of placebo treatment in other studies would be especially problematic if the majority of anemic infants had improved in test scores, since one would not know whether to attribute the improvement to iron or some other factor. This interpretative dilemma is less of an issue, however, because lack of improvement has been the more common finding.

Inasmuch as the follow-up period in the Costa Rican, Chilean, and British studies was only 2–3 months, these studies cannot determine whether ill effects associated with iron-deficiency anemia persist beyond infancy. The lower mental and motor test scores among many of the iron-deficient anemic infants might have responded to a more extended course of iron therapy. It is also possible that these differences might disappear spontaneously, especially because Bayley scores in the second year of life are only moderately correlated with measures of cognitive function in childhood [25,26]. Alternatively, the deficits might persist even if laboratory evidence of iron deficiency had been entirely corrected in all the anemic infants. This outcome would indicate that iron-deficiency anemia in infancy, perhaps of a particular severity or chronicity, has long-lasting ill effects, or that there are persisting effects of some closely-associated but unidentified factor.

To assess these alternatives, two new studies were undertaken in Costa Rica; a trial of 6 months of iron treatment and a follow-up at 5 years of age of the children in the previous cohort. Infants are still being enrolled in the 6-month treatment study, but the follow-up assessments are now complete, and the preliminary results can be briefly summarized [27]. The 5-year-follow-up included a battery of psychoeducational tests, consisting of the Wechsler Preschool and Primary Scales of Intelligence, the Beery Test of Visual-Motor Integration, the Woodcock-Johnson Psychoeducational Assessment, and the Bruininks-Oseretsky Test of Motor Proficiency (a comprehensive motor assessment). All tests were administered in two sessions of 1.5–2 hours each by experienced Costa Rican psychologists who were unaware of the children's iron status in infancy. Approximately 85% of the original cohort was located and agreed to participate in the follow-up assessments.

The approach to analyzing the 5-year data followed from the results of the developmental assessments in infancy. These infant results present one of the dilemmas for analyzing the 5-year data: where should the mildly anemic group go? Our first step was to determine whether the mildly anemic group more closely resembled the moderately anemic group or the groups with better iron status. The mildly anemic group tested significantly higher on every 5-year measure than the moderately anemic group and did not differ from the more iron-sufficient groups. This pattern was found for every single 5-year measure. Therefore, all subsequent analyses compared the children who had had moderate iron-deficiency anemia as infants with the other groups combined. It is important to note at the outset that these children are functioning in the normal range. Thus, the study's stringent entrance criteria had been successful in enrolling a group of normal children. Furthermore, these Costa Rican children are not at a disadvantage when compared with US norms.

The formerly anemic group averaged 8 points lower in Full Scale IQ scores, with an even more marked difference in Performance IQ. They also tested lower in Visual-Motor Integration, but this difference was not significant after controlling for maternal IQ. On the comprehensive motor assessment, the formerly anemic group received scores that averaged 12 points lower than the comparison group, with a marked difference in gross motor performance that remained significant after controlling for maternal IQ. On the Woodcock-Johnson, the formerly anemic children had lower scores overall, with the greatest differences in Quantitative Concepts, Visual Matching and Perceptual Speed; these significant differences all remained after controlling for maternal IQ. These results are preliminary. We are still examining familial and environmental influences.

Even though issues of causality are still unclear, the findings nonetheless indicate that iron-deficiency anemia in infancy is a condition that identifies children who are likely to continue to test lower than their peers in both mental and motor functioning at school entry. It will be important to pursue a longer follow-up of these children to determine the clinical significance of the differences in terms of actual functioning in school.

One other study, though limited, supports the possibility that iron-deficiency anemia in infancy may be associated with lasting ill effects. In a follow-up study of Israeli children treated with iron for anemia in infancy, Palti et al. [28] noted that lower Hb levels at 9 months were associated with lower developmental and IQ test scores obtained as many as 4 years later. Even after controlling for other important factors, such as mother's education, social class, and birth weight, these investigators found a 1.75-point increase in IQ at age 5 with each 1 g/dl increment in Hb level. Upon re-evaluation in second grade, the formerly anemic children were rated by teachers as being significantly lower in learning achievement and lower in positive task orientation than controls [29]. These effects on IQ and learning achievement scores are noteworthy because the infants' anemia had been diagnosed early and treated with iron as part of a health surveillance program. Although iron status was documented only by Hb levels and hematologic response to iron treatment was not confirmed, anemia had been diagnosed and treated as it often is pediatric practice.

In sum, certain studies of iron treatment have noted improvements in test scores, affect, or attention among iron-deficient infants. However, improvements have not been greater in iron-treated than placebo-treated infants after 5–11 days, and after 2–3 months of treatment, the majority of iron-deficient anemic infants continued to show lower mental and motor test scores. The lower test scores still seem to be present at school entry, indicating that children who had iron-deficiency anemia as infants are at risk for persisting developmental disability relative to their peers.

Thus, evidence of improvement with iron treatment and hence strong evidence that iron deficiency *causes* behavioral alterations, has not generally been found. However, such evidence might still be forthcoming if previous studies have failed to measure crucial behavioral dimensions or to treat iron deficiency in the most effective way. Other behavioral dimensions might respond to iron therapy, but they simply have not been measured. Were such a dimension studied, it is conceivable that unequivocal beneficial effects of iron treatment would be demonstrated. It also is possible that iron deficiency has not been treated optimally with respect to behavior and development. If infants were treated for a longer period and both the anemia and the biochemical changes of iron deficiency were completely corrected in all of the anemic ones, behavioral abnormalities might be corrected. Alternatively, iron-deficiency anemia might need to be detected and treated earlier in order to reverse the behavioral ill effects. Once iron-deficiency anemia and its associated behavioral changes have occurred for a certain length of time, iron therapy alone might not correct them, but similar treatment at an earlier time or preventive intervention might be effective. This possibility seems relatively unlikely since several studies have found iron therapy to be ineffective in reversing the behavioral alterations of infants who varied in iron status and in age from 12 to 24 months. However, Oski et al. [9], in the study of 9–12-month-olds who had iron deficiency without anemia, observed a dramatic increase in test scores. Although the increase could not be attributed with confidence to iron therapy due to the absence of a placebo group, the infants were younger than those in other studies, and may have been iron deficient for a short time. A more favorable response is conceivable under these conditions.

A powerful way to establish that the relationship between iron-deficiency anemia and infant behavior is not spurious is to manipulate experimentally infants' iron status. This approach has been applied in only two studies so far: a study by Heyworth and associates in Papua New Guinea [30] and the second study of Walter and associates in Chile [13]. The study in Papua New Guinea used a strong design, which entailed administering intramuscular iron or placebo injections to 2-month-old infants in a double-blind randomized study and assessing attentional processes at one year of age. Interpretation of the results is problematic, however, because virtually all infants were anemic at one year and virtually none were iron deficient, regardless of iron or placebo treatment. In the Chilean study described above [13], the infants were part of a preventive trial of the use of iron-fortified foods. Iron deficiency was thereby prevented in some children and allowed to occur in others who were fed according to the custom of the country. Twenty-six of the 39 infants who developed iron-deficiency anemia were in the unfortified group. Although this study used a strong design, as presented and analyzed, it raises certain other questions. Anemic infants were compared with those with better iron status with little attention to actual supplementation. In any intervention study some families comply with the intervention, and some families who are not receiving the intervention nonetheless manage to have children who are normal in that dimension. For instance, in the Walter et al. study, only some of the unfortified group became anemic and several children in the fortified group became anemic. How did these families differ from those children who had more favorable iron status? Analyzing those who become anemic therefore still does not eliminate the possibility that they differed in some important way. Perhaps a more suitable analysis would have been to compare the entire fortified group with the entire unfortified group. The magnitude of effects that could be detected would be much smaller, but the influence of other factors should be randomly distributed among the two groups.

In the absence of correction with iron therapy or experimental manipulation of iron status, the approach to establish a causal relationship between iron deficiency and altered behavior has been to control for other factors that could explain the relation. As noted above, most of the studies of iron-deficient infants have used careful entrance criteria to eliminate infants who might be at risk for developmental delay for other reasons, such as low birth weight or health problems. However, differences with respect to one nutrient suggest that the intake of calories or other nutrients might have differed. While undernutrition or zinc deficiency might have been a concern in some studies, growth in other studies has been normal. For instance, the growth of the Costa Rican [12] and Chilean [13] babies was at the 50th percentile by US standards, the anemic infants were comparable in size to the other babies, and no infant in the sample had previously been identified for growth failure. While it is impossible to measure all known nutrients, some studies, such as the one in Costa Rica [12], also found no abnormalities in vitamin B_{12}, ascorbic acid, or total protein level. Nonetheless, some other, unidentified nutritional deficiency must still be considered as an explanation for the observed relationship between iron-deficiency anemia and behavioral alterations. In addition, even though none had had major or chronic health problems, the anemic infants may have had more intercurrent illnesses, affecting both iron balance and behavior.

Differences in the caregiving environment could also explain the relationship between iron deficiency and altered behavior. Lozoff and associates in both the Guatemalan [5] and Costa Rican studies [12] paid attention to this possibility by using multiple regression analysis in which potentially intervening or confounding variables were forced into the regression equation before assessing the effect of iron-deficiency anemia. In both studies, iron-deficiency anemia continued to account for a significant part of the variance in developmental scores even after considering all of the other factors. In addition, such factors as stimulation in the home and parental IQ were directly measured in the Costa Rican study, making this study the one in which families were most thoroughly assessed. The families of moderately anemic infants did differ in that they received lower scores on the HOME inventory and the children's mothers had lower IQ scores. However, neither of these factors, when entered into statistical analyses as covariates, eliminated the significant effect of iron-deficiency anemia on lower mental and motor test scores.

Although differences in the family and childrearing environment did not seem to explain the lower test scores in the anemic infants in the Costa Rican study, nonetheless they were relatively disadvantaged among the study population with respect to maternal IQ and HOME scores. Furthermore, differences in infant feeding practices, while providing plausible physiologic explanations for the infants' iron deficiency, point to family differences. Decisions about infant feeding, such as whether or not to breast-feed and when to wean from the breast, are not random. They may be closely correlated with attitudes about childrearing or difficult family circumstances. Statistical control of identified differences in the Costa Rican study may not really control for important differences in the stimulation and nurture the infants received. A large proportion of the variance in scores remained unexplained, and available measures of the microenvironment are simply too crude to dismiss the possibility that family differences may account for the lower scores.

Differences in the caregiving environment could also explain the relationship between iron deficiency and altered behavior. Lozoff and associates in both the maternal education, family income, and number of children were associated with prevalence of iron deficiency [31]. In the Thai study (reported by Ernesto Pollitt last fall in Geneva), the risk of anemia was inversely related to number of electrical appliances in the household.

Environmental disadvantage could relate to lasting developmental disabilities in several ways. Animal studies indicate that understimulation leads to lasting changes in brain and behavior [32]. The restricted behavior of iron-deficient anemic infants could limit the stimulation they receive from caregivers. Alternatively, it is possible that disadvantaged environment becomes important because more limited families cannot provide the extra stimulation that would allow a child to compensate for the effects of iron-deficiency anemia or some other nutritional insult. The above mechanisms might explain why iron treatment does not correct the behavioral alterations. Environmental disadvantage might also contribute to both the iron-deficiency anemia and lasting developmental disability, without any direct connection between iron and development. For instance, if parents of anemic infants are more limited in intellectual functioning or facing more stressful conditions, they might be less aware of, or less able to offer, optimal feeding to their children. Their feeding practices might thus contribute to the children's iron-deficiency anemia. The families' limitations might independently affect the children's development. In any case, poorer developmental outcome in iron deficiency may be inextricably linked to environmental disadvantage.

Relating Research on Iron Deficiency to Research on Other Risk Factors

Research on the behavioral effects of iron deficiency encompasses few studies and a short time span, relative to research on other conditions in infancy that are considered to influence behavior and development adversely. Such other conditions or risk factors include generalized undernutrition, perinatal stress, and increased lead burden. The wisdom and experience gained in these areas warrant review, albeit brief, since the commonality of certain themes seems striking and highly relevant to our own area. Some parallels are sobering, while others are exciting and intriguing.

One of the sobering issues is the attempt to prove cause–effect relationships. If iron treatment in infancy, regardless of timing or duration, fails to correct behavioral alterations, regardless of the dimension studied, this field may be faced with the situation arising in lead studies. Researchers trying to relate lead levels, even in the low range, to developmental outcome have struggled with the problem of proving causality using correlational data [33]. Statistical controls of other factors have been employed to establish that a non-spurious relationship exists, with such approaches being much more elaborate in lead than in iron research so far. Nonetheless, both fields must face that controlling for all intervening or confounding variables is ultimately impossible. The feasibility of experimental manipulation of iron status through prevention means that iron studies, however, may not need to rely solely on correlational data.

In planning, undertaking and interpreting such preventive studies, investigators of iron deficiency may be guided by experience in another condition, generalized undernutrition. Specifically, the experience with food supplementation trials should probably alert us to expect subtle effects or none at all [34]. That experience also indicates that a nutritional intervention alone without environmental enrichment may be ineffective [34,35].

Perhaps the most important issue raised by trying to relate work on iron deficiency to that on other risk factors is to ask if the search for simple cause–effect relationships is outdated and misguided. With the current appreciation of transactional models of child development we should not view nutrition–environment interconnections as methodologic annoyances [36]. Drawing on thinking about perinatal stress [37], perhaps we should expect that infants who may be relatively vulnerable or invulnerable and who may grow up in environments that are relatively facilitative or non-facilitative will respond differently to nutritional insults. An important task is to describe these differences.

Among the intriguing and exciting parallels are the similarities in the specific behavior changes and the postulated chain of events in studies of generalized undernutrition [36] and of iron deficiency. In both conditions, alterations in affect, attention, or activity have been reported, associated with increased body contact with the mother. In each field some investigators have postulated that permanent CNS changes explain the lasting behavioral alterations; others have postulated that the changes in activity, affect or attention lead children to seek and/or receive less stimulation from the caregiving environment, interfering with "the normal acquisition of environmental information" [38], and that this restricted interaction itself has detrimental effects on development. Research on undernutrition may also encourage us to examine additional influences, such as maternal depression and family disorganization and stress [39].

It seems surprising, however, that iron-deficiency anemia, a relatively mild phenomenon of late infancy, is associated with behavioral alterations at school entry like those reported in severe undernutrition, a condition which often occurs earlier in the brain growth spurt and is medically much more serious. Attempting to understand why behavioral alterations are similar in the two conditions might indicate some fundamental properties of early development. Perhaps these behavior patterns are a final common pathway of a variety of brain changes in chronic conditions of infancy and the specific insult is relatively unimportant. Perhaps the common pathway is one of heightened attachment behavior; infants' responses to physiological or emotional stress may involve increased proximity-seeking and lessened activity, regardless of the precipitating problem, whether it be nutritional deficiency, illness, fatigue, or fear [19].

The above observations suggest merely a few ways that relating research on iron deficiency to that on other risk factors may also guide us to new understanding of how early insults affect the developing child.

This critical review of the studies of infant behavior and iron deficiency has pointed to ways in which the causal link between the two phenomena is still weak, although a number of replicated studies now indicate that these are behavioral alterations among iron-deficient anemic infants and a few suggest that differences may last for years. Despite limitations in the ability to attribute causality, the research may have important practical implications. Iron-deficiency anemia, an easily detectable condition, may be a simple and practical way to identify a large group of children at risk for lasting developmental disadvantage relative to peers. Iron deficiency is a preventable problem. Finally and most importantly, preventing iron deficiencies could help foster improved development in disadvantaged infants throughout the world.

Acknowledgments. This work was supported in part by a National Institutes of Health grant R22 HD14122. Critical comments from Abraham Wolf, Edward Nelson, Barbara Felt, and a summer research seminar of Case Western Reserve University students are gratefully acknowledged.

References

1. Lozoff B (1988) Behavioral alterations in iron deficiency. Adv Pediatr 35:331–360
2. Dobbing J (1982) The later development of the brain and its vulnerability. In: Davis JA, Dobbing J (eds) Scientific foundations of pediatrics. University Park, Baltimore, pp 744–759
3. Kenny DA (1979) Correlation and causality. John Wiley, New York
4. Bayley N (1969) Bayley scales of infant development manual. Psychological Corporation, New York
5. Lozoff B, Brittenham GM, Viteri FE et al. (1982) The effects of short-term oral iron therapy on developmental deficits in iron deficient anemic infants. J Pediatr 100:351–357
6. Lozoff B, Brittenham GM, Viteri FE et al. (1982) Developmental deficits in iron-deficient infants: Effects of age and severity of iron lack. J Pediatr 101:948–952
7. Walter T, Kowalskys J, Stekel A (1983) Effect of mild iron deficiency on infant mental development scores. J Pediatr 102:519–522
8. Grindulis H, Scott PH, Belton NR et al. (1986) Combined deficiency of iron and vitamin D in Asian toddlers. Arch Dis Child 61:843–848
9. Oski FA, Honig AS, Helu B et al. (1983) Effect of iron therapy on behavior performance in nonanemic, iron-deficient infants. Pediatrics 71:877–880
10. Johnson DL, McGowan RJ (1983) Anemia and infant behavior. Nutr Behav 1:185–192
11. Deinard A, Gilbert A, Dodds M et al. (1981) Iron deficiency and behavioral deficits. Pediatrics 68:828–833
12. Lozoff B, Brittenham GM, Wolf AW et al. (1987) Iron-deficiency anemia and iron therapy: Effects on infant developmental test performance. Pediatrics 79:981–995
13. Walter T, DeAndraca I, Chadud P et al. (in press) Adverse effect of iron-deficiency anemia on infant psychomotor development. Pediatrics
14. Pollitt E, Greenfield D, Leibel R (1979) Significance of Bayley Scale score changes following iron therapy. II. Infant Behav Dev 2:235–238
15. Honig AS, Oski FA (1979) Reply to Pollitt et al. Infant Behav Dev 2:239–240
16. Wolf AW, Lozoff B (1985) A clinically interpretable method for analyzing the Bayley Infant Behavior Record. J Pediatr Psychol 10:199–214
17. Lozoff B, Brittenham G, Viteri FE et al. (1982) Behavioral abnormalities in infants with iron deficiency anemia. In: Pollitt E, Leibel RL (eds) Iron deficiency: brain biochemistry and behavior. Raven Press, New York, pp 183–194
18. Lozoff B, Wolf AW, Urrutia JJ et al. (1985) Abnormal behavior and low developmental test scores in iron-deficient anemic infants. J Dev Behav Pediatr 6:69–75
19. Lozoff B, Klein NK, Prabucki KM (1986) Iron-deficient anemic infants at play. J Dev Behav Pediatr 7:152–158
20. Lozoff B, Klein N, McClish D, Jimenez E (1989) Motor test behavior of anemic infants (abstr). Soc Res Child Dev 6:150

21. Oski FA, Honig AS (1978) The effects of therapy on the developmental scores of iron-deficient infants. J Pediatr 92:21–25
22. Honig AS, Oski FA (1978) Developmental scores of iron-deficient infants and the effects of therapy. Infant Behav Dev 1:168–176
23. Honig AS, Oski FA (1984) Solemnity: a clinical risk index for iron-deficient infants. Early Child Dev Care 16:69–84
24. Aukett MA, Parks YA, Scott PH et al. (1986) Treatment with iron increases weight gain and psychomotor development. Arch Dis Child 61:849–857
25. Kopp CB, McCall RB (1982) Predicting later mental performance for normal, at-risk, and handicapped infants. Life-Span Dev Behav 4:33–61
26. McCall RB (1979) The development of intellectual functioning in infancy and the prediction of later IQ. In: Osofsky JD (ed) Handbook of infant development. Wiley, New York, pp 707–741
27. Lozoff B, Jimenez E, Wolf A, Klein N (1989) Long-term effect of iron-deficiency anemia in infancy (Abstr). Ped Res 16A:84
28. Palti H, Pevsner B, Adler B (1983) Does anemia in infancy affect achievement on developmental and intelligence tests? Hum Biol 55:189–194
29. Palti H, Meijer A, Adler B (1985) Learning achievement and behavior at school of anemic and non-anemic infants. Early Hum Dev 10:217–223
30. Heywood A, Oppenheimer S, Heywood P, Jolley D (1989) Behavioral effects of iron supplementation in infants in Madang, Papua New Guinea. Am J Clin Nutr [Suppl: International conference on iron deficiency and behavioral development] 50:630–640
31. Life Sciences Research Office (1984) Assessment of the iron nutritional status of the US population based on data collected in the second national health and nutrition examination survey, 1976–1980. Federation of American Societies for Experimental Biology, Bethesda, MD
32. Levitsky DA (ed) (1979) Malnutrition, environment, and behavior. Cornell University Press, Ithaca and London
33. David JM, Svendsgaard DJ (1987) Lead and child development. Nature 329:297–300
34. Sinisterra L (1987) Studies on poverty, human growth and development: The Cali experience. In: Dobbing J (ed) Early nutrition and later achievement. Academic Press, London, pp 208–244
35. Grantham-McGregor S, Schofield W, Powell C (1987) Development of severely malnourished children who received psychosocial stimulation: six-year follow-up. Pediatrics 79:247–254
36. Dobbing J (ed) (1987) Early nutrition and later achievement. Academic Press, London
37. Horowitz FD (1989) Using developmental theory to guide the search for the effects of biological risk factors on the development of children. Am J Clin Nutr [Suppl: International conference on iron deficiency and behavioral development] 50:589–597
38. Levitsky DA (1979) Malnutrition and the hunger to learn. In: Levitsky DA (ed) Malnutrition, environment, and behavior. Cornell University Press, Ithaca and London, pp 161–179
39. Salt P, Galler JR, Ramsey FC (1988) The influence of early malnutrition on subsequent behavioral development. VII. The effects of maternal depressive symptoms. J Dev Behav Pediatrics 9:1–5

Commentary

Smart: This is a very thoughtful and critical review. Lozoff is very aware of methodological deficiences and of alternative interpretations, and she is properly cautious in drawing her conclusions. It has become clear to me that this field of research, more than most, is one in which multiple analysis of the results is possible: shifting from anaemia status to iron deficiency status, employing different cut-off points for anaemia status, etc. I have no strong objection to this; I would probably do the same myself. It could be argued, however, that, strictly, the comparisons to be made and the analyses to be used should be decided in advance of data collection. Where the multiple analysis approach becomes questionable is at the stage of drawing conclusions and there the natural tendency is for selective emphasis, usually of positive results, dwelling upon them and even ignoring the negative findings. It seems to me that Dr Lozoff, through her careful approach, manages to avoid this pitfall. I am not sure that others amongst the reviewers in this volume may not have been over-eager to emphasize positive findings.

The conclusions drawn from the 5-year follow-up studies in Costa Rica are examples of properly cautious conclusions. They prompted me to ask what factors other than iron deficiency might contribute to these effects. Other dietary deficiency, including general undernutrition, and socioeconomic factors came readily to mind, and I was pleased to find as I read further that these are discussed. Apparently, neither has a significant influence. That the children show no evidence of nutritional deficiency other than that of iron, surprises me. Why is there deficiency specifically of iron? The children appear to be receiving enough food, which is of adequate quality except for iron, which is either lacking or, somehow or other, unavailable from the diet.

Lozoff considers the observation that the effects of iron-deficiency anaemia and of severe undernutrition are similar. I would like to make three comments on this. I am ignoring the difference in timing which she suggests, because I do not think that the evidence on timing is good from either field of research. (a) Severe undernutrition probably embodies deficiency of iron as well as that of other nutrients, and so iron deficiency may be a common thread. I must say, however, that I am unconvinced that detected iron deficiency is not often accompanied by other nutritional inadequacy. (b) Lozoff enquires whether the similar behavioural alterations " . . . in the two conditions might indicate some fundamental properties of early development". This might simply reflect that development is progressive and that what is being picked up in both cases are lags in development indicated by lower scores on some global test of infant development such as the Bayley. (c) Nevertheless, I find the suggestion attractive that a common pathway might be one of heightened attachment behaviour regardless of the precipitating problem. This seems to me worthy of further consideration and investigation.

Yip: Both the study of Lozoff in Costa Rica and of Walter in Chile point to a worrisome possibility that adverse developmental outcomes related to iron deficiency may not be reversible with iron treatment. Therefore, the general approach of screening and treatment may not be the optimal solution in managing iron deficiency in early childhood. It appears that prevention is the best alternative.

The fact that both studies have very similar findings increases the chance that these are true adverse effects of iron deficiency rather than the result of selection bias. Lozoff has provided a very detailed discussion on the issues of comparability between iron-deficiency anemia and non-iron-deficiency children which I raised in my Commentaries on Walter's paper. It is obviously an issue that will not be easily resolved, because different nutritional states, such as iron status may reflect different family and environmental factors, and these can also affect behavior or development. The multivariate approach is certainly a major one for resolving the issue. Perhaps the ultimate design, if it is still possible, would be an experimental trial involving non-breast-fed infants in areas with a high prevalence of iron deficiency.

One possible reason why some of the previous studies find developmental scores to be slightly higher among some of the non-anemic iron-deficiency than in the non-iron-deficiency infants may be related to the use of serum ferritin as part of the assignment of iron status. There is increasing evidence that serum ferritin is of limited use in developing countries because of the high rate of infection which causes many children to have values higher than their true iron status. If the non-iron-deficiency "control group" is contaminated with iron-deficient infants who have "falsely elevated" serum ferritin, its developmental score may be reduced. Also it is possible that chronic low-grade infection may adversely affect the developmental assessment. The best way to deal with this potential problem is to measure acute reactants such as C-reactive protein at the time of laboratory assessment of iron status, and only to include children who are free from inflammatory conditions in the study.

It is my feeling that the study power is limited by using Bayley scales to detect changes after iron or placebo treatment. This is because even the iron-deficient anemia group had mean scores within the expected normal range, and hence had limited room for improvement (a ceiling effect). Perhaps a better strategy would be to develop more sensitive and more specific testing procedures based on current knowledge of the "failed" area on a battery of tests. A non-standardized test may not be a major disadvantage when used in an experimental design based on iron vs. placebo.

Parks: The use of long-term placebo in our study [Lozoff's reference 24] was accepted by an ethical committee. These infants would not normally have been identified as anaemic and would probably never have received iron. All were treated at the end of the study. We felt that a placebo-controlled intervention study was vital for answering the questions posed.

Lozoff's 5-year follow-up study in Costa Rica is difficult to interpret. What information is there about the children between the first and second study. Did the children become anaemic again? Did they grow up in comparable environments? Presumably the "effects" leading to the initial anaemia would still be present in the child's environment.

Author's reply: We do not know if they became anemic again, but iron status at age 5 was excellent.

Parks: I agree with Lozoff's criticism of the analysis of data in Walter's 1989 study. Analysis of the original groups (fortified vs. unfortified) removes bias. Analysis comparing those who became anaemic with those who did not does possibly bias the results.

Walter: Lozoff discusses the difficulty of defining iron status and the ways in which several investigators have attempted to solve this. Although using a common outcome measure is useful when making comparisons between studies, this does not prove that the particular measure chosen is adequate. In fact, the use of the Bayley Scale of Infant Development (BSID) has been the single, most criticized aspect of the studies performed in infancy, many of which have used otherwise good experimental design for the exclusion of confounding variables and the definition of iron status. The BSID measurements are currently perhaps the weakest point in research designed to define the effects of iron deficit in infancy. I believe most other experimental problems can be (and have been) dealt with adequately, and thus all efforts should be directed towards the search for better ways of assessing infant development. This is a challenge for psychologists, neurologists, neurophysiologists and neurochemists in this field.

Lozoff, however, makes a strong defence of the results of the well-designed studies thus far, mentioning coincidences that cannot be ignored. With minor differences, all these studies show that iron-deficiency anaemia (and not milder degrees of deficit) adversely affect mental and motor development indices (MDI and PDI respectively). What is more impressive, however, is that the areas where these effects are most noticeable also coincide: verbal-language development and body balance coordination in the movements leading to walking.

These findings should direct future research towards knowledge of the physiology of the acquisition of these skills.

I am always hesitant to attribute mental and motor scores to poorer ratings in the Infant Behaviour Record (IBR). I recognize I have done this myself in a recent paper. The performance of the MDI and PDI is always influenced by the infant's behaviour. The question is whether iron-deficiency anaemia affects MDI and PDI by affecting the IBR. Evidence for this cannot be inferred from any of the research thus far. It is conceivable that the relatively specific areas affected in iron-deficiency anaemia which are mentioned above may be influenced "directly" rather than through behavioural changes. On the other hand, if it is true that anaemic infants show lower developmental scores because of their inadequate behaviour, should we not be studying the IBR more closely? At present we seem to be more concerned in developmental performance. Perhaps we should consider MDI and PDI as a measure of poor behaviour and not vice versa? This again emphasizes the limitations of the BSID for measuring the effect of iron deficit (or any deficit).

The interpretations of the mother–infant interaction videotapes Lozoff describes are also quite interesting. We have performed similar studies of a semi-structured free play situation in our population. However, the quantitation of the studies is far from clear and we tend to regard these studies as "impressions" rather than as hard data. In any event, our impression is that our findings agree with Lozoff's, but we would very much like to be able to come up with a better quantitative measure.

At the same time, in spite of these caveats, I would suggest that the poorer MDI and PDI performance of anaemic infants may not be "mediated" by behavioural inadequacies. Selectivity of the patterns of failure and the extraordinary similarity of our results to those of Lozoff in respect to language and balance-walking cannot be explained by poorer behaviour alone. A more precise method of probing these issues must be used in future studies. Moreover, since in preliminary results Lozoff finds no improvement at 5 years of age, following 10 days or 3 months of iron therapy, could the persistence of disadvantage into the preschool years still be mediated by behaviour?

Studies of iron-deficiency anaemia using the BSID have reached their limit. No more can be asked from or answered with them. Definitely newer tools are urgently needed.

Author's reply: I feel that the Bayley scale, when supplemented with other measures, continues to be useful in this research area. While agreeing that new tools are needed, I would not dismiss the value of the Bayley, since it has consistently identified differences between iron-deficient anemic and non-anemic infants. Nonetheless we still need work on understanding what these differences tell us about the developing child. Objective measures of some dimensions of the IBR, such as affect and attention, would seem most valuable.

Walter: Duration of breast-feeding is a real concern, not only because it affords some protection from iron deficiency, but because it seems to improve scores in the performance of BSIDs when infants are balanced for iron status (see Chapter 7). An alternative explanation is that another nutrient provided by breast milk, and in which early weaned infants are lacking, affects BSID scores.

Separation of infants in whom all measures were corrected from those in whom they were not, may be totally artefactual, in view of what we have learned about the effects of even mild infection. A mild viral infection may influence iron measures several weeks after it has abated. Thus, the requirement for total correction of iron biochemistry is too demanding. It can be explained better if we consider this requisite as separating a group of infants with milder iron deficit from those with more severe deficiences (as is also suggested by Lozoff). Thus, iron therapy may have a favourable effect on those infants with milder anaemia (and presumably iron deficiency of shorter duration). This effect, however, could not be replicated in my own study, which brings up the issue of whether duration and/or severity of iron deficit or age at which anaemia appears affect the reversibility of the alleged effects of iron deficit on behaviour. This must also be a focus of future research.

It would be interesting to know why 15% were lost to follow-up and if all of those located agreed to participate. Unwillingness to participate would become a potent bias.

Author's reply: We lost 6%–7% of the infants between their entry into the study and the end of the 3-month treatment period; and 6%–7% between infancy and 5 years. These are very low attrition rates. Those who dropped out were not more likely to be anemic.

Walter: I cannot understand how maternal IQ may influence these Costa Rican results: presumably it would only do so if the mothers' IQs were distinctly subnormal in the case of infants with poorer performance. If only mean group IQs were different in a covariate or multiple regression analysis, maternal IQ may not be a confounding variable.

Dobbing: Lozoff's admirable analytical discussion of our main question manages to walk the tightrope of what can reasonably be concluded from the best field trial evidence available, without falling to either side into the chasm below of unjustified or over-optimistic conclusion. It is a model of its kind.

Investigating the behavioural effects of early iron deficiency on the development of behaviour indeed has a great deal in common with attempts to delineate those of early general undernutrition and of exposure to minimal environmental lead pollution. Much of the common ground between them stems from the virtual impossibility of disentangling the enormous complexity of other environmental factors which, in real life, inevitably accompany the insult. After a period of hopeless scientific naivety, to which I greatly contributed, the question of the effects of early undernutrition on later human achievement [1] has at last settled down to an acceptance of this environmental complexity and its importance; and this has served to develop a nihilistic attitude in many of us that the reality is too complex to be properly and completely investigated. Such is the multiplicity of confounding and interacting socio-economic, emotional, nutritional, and behavioural factors surrounding the growing infant, including the whole galaxy of environmental disadvantage represented by poverty and the inevitable intercurrent infective and other disease, at a time of the child's extreme sensitivity and vulnerability. I am not alone in believing that the most refined techniques of epidemiological analysis, even when combined with intervention, are inadequate to apportion weights to the various components, if only because of the impossibility of properly measuring most of them, or even enumerating them. Claims to be able to do so should be carefully scrutinized, and not glibly accepted merely because of our desperate need to have an answer. I would give greater emphasis to these difficulties than even Lozoff does.

Early undernutrition, iron lack and exposure to lead are relatively easy to identify, the last two more so than the first, but in each case the probably all-important matter of *duration* of exposure is virtually out of our reach. The outcome measurement of behavioural development is relatively easily made, at least in conventional terms, but it is the confounding collection of factors in the real life environment which is difficult, and puts a large question mark over any interpretation. In addition, any "test" of behaviour or achievement is a measure of *performance,* rather than of a *capacity* to perform: and thus the child's "motivation" to perform, affected by his current state, is a large, and possibly disruptive determinant of the result. The influence of degree of maternal interaction, or of undernutrition, concurrently or in the past, or even the history of breast-feeding or not and for how long, and how supplemented, etc. could matter; to say nothing of levels of affect, attention, activity, etc. If these are lowered they could as well be the *cause* of poorer scores as the scores being caused by iron lack.

In parenthesis, I am not so sure that exposure to lead, short of lead poisoning, does have such a deleterious effect on children's performance. A critical appraisal of the available evidence is not very supportive of that proposition. Indeed if it does, the effect must be perishingly small not to have been easily demonstrated by a series of very careful investigations.

Is a response to iron therapy truly evidence of iron deficiency? That assumes that "normal" is the same as "maximal attainable", and also ignores whether "supranormal" may improve behaviour. Many believe, for example, that maternal iron supplementation in pregnancy, although undoubtedly increasing iron levels in a naturally haemodiluted individual, results in those levels being "supranormal" and is unnecessary.

I was very interested in the finding of clumsiness, since I have long cherished the thought that the differentially very fast rate of growth of the cerebellum might confer increased vulnerability compared to the rest of the brain. Most cerebellar growth occurs closely around birth in the human and we would need to know how long these children had been iron deficient [2].

Whether iron lack came before the behavioural changes or the other way round, is not the whole question. If iron lack is a component of general subnutrition, or related to breast-feeding history, and accompanies suboptimal parental care and emotional support, iron lack could precede, but not be the cause of the behavioural changes.

I very much like the hypothesis of a final common path of effects, with a down-playing of the specificity of the insult.

Surely the final conclusion could be drawn that, whatever fascination we may have with the facts or with the analysis of the mechanism, the important practical matters are (1) *that iron deficiency should be prevented;* and (2) that it should be treated when it occurs?

References

1. Dobbing J (ed) (1987) Early nutrition and later achievement. Academic Press, London
2. Dobbing J, Sands J (1973) The quantitative growth and development of the human brain. Arch Dis Child 48:757–767

Yehuda: In some of the studies reviewed there is a decrease in motor and mental scores, in others there is a decrease only in one variable. What is the theoretical significance of a decrease in both variables versus a decrease in only one of them?

Author's reply: These discrepancies are a puzzle. Given that the same investigators, using similar designs, sometimes do not replicate their own findings, I tend to think the different results are real. The explanation is unknown, but may be important in understanding the behavioral effects of iron-deficiency anemia.

Yehuda: Are there any long-term studies, i.e. of the effect of early iron deficiency on learning and cognition at later ages (age 6 years and up)? Could it be that while no decreases in mental scores are evident now, they may become apparent later in life as a result of this period of iron deficiency? In other words, may a delay in early development have damaging consequences later?

Author's reply: There are no data.

Finberg: The question of causality of long-term effects remains open after thorough review of available data.

Chapter 7

Iron Deficiency and Behaviour in Infancy: A Critical Review

Tomas Walter

In the past decade, at least a dozen studies on the effect of iron deficiency on infant behaviour have been published after the pilot paper from Oski and Honig [1]. Despite extensive research, the issue is far from clear. In this paper I will attempt to comment on some general concepts and will focus on the two most recent studies, pointing out their strengths and difficulties, and finally I will delineate areas for future research.

The working hypothesis is that iron deficiency affects cognition and social-emotional behaviour in infants. It conforms to the classical requirements of a medical hypothesis [2]: it identifies a direct agent, an immediate antecedent of an illness, in this case undernutrition of a particular element; and the disease condition, poorer cognition or development. However oversimplified this may seem, there are three dimensions of complexity: the appropriate definition of iron status at a stage at which haematological development is rapid; the adequate testing of infant cognitive or psychomotor development in order to infer the effect of such a nutritional deficit; and finally, the ability to identify and segregate the multiple intervening factors that may affect both the dependent variable (iron status) and the independent variable (infant behaviour).

In the field of iron metabolism, difficulties in the precise determination of iron status, the measurement of prevalence of iron deficiency, and the scientific basis of experimental data explaining the mechanism whereby iron lack may affect brain function will be discussed by other authors.

Regarding infant behaviour, at issue are the scientific merit and construct validity [3] * of visualizing the interaction between iron and infant development, without clarifying the character of the psychological aspects selected for study and the underlying systems controlling the response [4]. Current understanding of brain function, however, suggests that such a simplistic conceptualization in the iron-behaviour relationship should be considered with scepticism. In infancy, of particular concern are the non-specificity of the behaviours studied (develop-

---

* A construct is an idea which underlies a method of measurement. Examples are "intelligence", "aggression", "learning abilities", and others which could be cited. In this paper infant psychomotor development is the construct, and "validity" refers to the fact that the Bayley Scales of Infant Development may not measure infant development very accurately; and additionally the fact that these scales are poor predictors of future achievement.

mental quotients). Besides the lack of definition of the mechanisms involved, there lies the problem of defining the true magnitude of the functional effects and their biological significance.

Apart from consideration of the iron status, issues such as its adequate representation and measurement, and brain iron concentration and functional relationships, it is worth mentioning that the timing and duration of iron deficit are components of the degree of iron deficiency that may affect behaviour. Timing is a long-standing issue in psychobiology, where it is generally accepted that the vulnerability of the organism is accentuated during periods of rapid growth [5,6]. This notion lies behind the assumption that infancy is a particularly vulnerable period because of the rapid brain growth at this time. This, however, needs precise validation and is discussed in other Chapters. Also, the total iron requirements are very high between the ages of 6–12 months [7], a time at which iron deficiency is usually most prevalent. However, this notion can be oversimplified because it may overlook the remarkable autonomy of the brain in early life which may prevent the manifestation of sequelae following early insult [8–11].

Use of Developmental Scales

Concerning infant behaviour, research has focussed on broad measurements of mental development and learning where the selection of methodology has been guided by practical rather than theoretical considerations [12]. Nevertheless, the merit of the developmental scales has been their apparent usefulness in discriminating between iron-deficient anaemic and non-anaemic infants. Developmental scales, such as the Bayley Scales of Infant Development (BSID) mental and motor development, yield scores that reflect inter-individual differences. However, what is the significance and theoretical meaning of these scores? The items of the BSID, the most popular tool in studying the effect of iron in infancy, were not selected for their ability to explore specific information processes or learning abilities. Most tasks originated from the Gesell Schedule, which included items selected from observational material without any theoretical justification [13]. Thus, at 12 months of age there is no reason to suspect that "pushing a car along" is more important than "pulling a cube". These theories were originated from a selection of goodness-of-fit with evolving age criteria, in longitudinal studies of infants tested with this scale, rather than from theories of mental growth.

Accordingly, the lack of predictive validity of the BSID is not surprising. A recent study [14] reports correlations of 0.23 between tests taken at 3 and 12 months, and 0.16 between 12 and 24 months. The principal component analysis of these data yielded three factors, none accounting for more than 20% of the variance at any of these ages. Thus, the item selection of the Bayley Scales does not form either a strong coherent principal component or a coherent set of factors.

A promising approach in infancy research is the assessment of decrements of attention to unchanged aspects of the environment and recovery of attention in the presence of novelty [15]. The predictive validity of this method and its sensitivity and specificity in screening for developmental disorders are much higher than those of more traditional developmental tests.

The intervening variables interfering with the effects of iron (moderators) or accounting for all or part of them (confounders) may be of a nutritional, health or socio-environmental nature.

In the nutritional aspect, two potential confounders may be zinc deficiency and protein-energy malnutrition. Additionally, lead absorption may be favoured by iron deficit, and lead is known to have serious effects on cognition. Ascorbic acid is a potentially moderating factor because of its important role in dietary non-haem iron absorption. However, even though the concentration of ascorbate in neural tissue is high and is involved as a cofactor in peptide neurotransmitter biosynthesis, evidence suggesting functional effects in cognition is lacking, and thus there is no support for treating it as a potential confounder [16,17].

Epidemiological evidence links iron and zinc deficiency. In particular, diets low in meat, high in phytate and potential interactions between zinc and iron absorption are of particular relevance. However, no studies of the effects of zinc deficiency on infant behaviour have been performed, so that the effect of zinc is only conjectural.

Malnourished infants do not grow, hence their iron requirement decreases, as does the haemoglobin level because of lower metabolic needs. These factors confound iron status. On the other hand, protein-energy malnutrition has extensive effects on cognition that may overshadow any influence of iron status [18,19,20].

Iron deficit enhances absorption of lead and cadmium. Both metals have effects on behaviour that are independent of iron. The effect of subclinical, mildly elevated lead levels may confound the cognitive effects of iron deficit [21–25].

Apart from the fact that iron deficit in tropical areas may be directly caused by blood loss from hookworm infestation, milder illnesses of common and frequent occurrence in childhood, such as upper respiratory infections or gastrointestinal disturbances, may invalidate results of cognitive tests performed during their course.

Finally there are numerous examples of enhancing and damaging effects of social environment and experience on behavioural development [26]. Children with different types of early deprivation have differed in developmental outcome as a function of their social and family environment [27]. These precepts are corroborated by findings from the protein-energy malnutrition and cognitive function literature.

Recent Research

There have been extensive literature reviews on the effects of iron-deficiency anaemia on behaviour [28,29]. The present paper, bearing in mind the previously enunciated general concepts, will discuss the most recent research. Specifically it will discuss the last study reported by Lozoff et al. in Costa Rica [30] and the study by Walter et al. in Chile [31]. Both studies have attempted to avoid defects in research designs that have flawed previous work.

These two studies began almost simultaneously in 1982 and arose as the natural sequel to Lozoff's previous study in Guatemala and our own early study in Chile. The similarities in the results of both protocols give great strength to the conclusions of both Lozoff and ourselves. It is remarkable that these similarities were possible despite the fact that there are important differences in the study design and the research was carried out by two independent investigators in two distant regions.

The study by Walter et al. [31] was initiated by 1983, and performed together with a field trial of fortified infant foods. Briefly, a cohort of healthy, full-term infants from a community clinic in the city of Santiago were recruited to a food-fortification study at 3 months of age and followed to 12 months with monthly clinic check-ups and weekly house calls by a nurse. Complete anthropometric, nutritional, morbidity, and socio-economic data were collected. Those infants spontaneously weaned by 3 months received either an iron-fortified cow's milk or the non-fortified milk normally provided by the clinic at no cost. Those infants who were being breast-fed at 3 months were assigned to one of two groups. The first received a haem-iron-fortified cereal in addition to normal non-milk foods, and the second received no iron fortification. Because the assignment to fortified food products was random, and fortification turned out eventually to be the most potent determinant of the infant's iron status, all other intervening factors were essentially off-set by this design.

Approximately 100 infants were entered in each of the four groups with a 20% attrition during the 9 months of follow-up due mainly to migration. At ages 9 and 12 months venipunctures for a full haematological assessment were performed. At 12 months parents were invited to participate in the psychological study. After informed consent was obtained in accordance with the pertinent institutional review committee, the tests were begun 7–10 days after the 12 month check-up.

Our aims in this study were to provide answers to the following questions:

1. How severe must iron deficiency be to affect behaviour?
2. What was the effect of duration of iron deficiency?
3. What was the effect of short-term iron therapy, before correction of anaemia?
4. What was the reversibility of the changes after a long-term trial (enough to revert anaemia)?
5. What specific areas of mental or motor processes were most affected?
6. Was there an association between developmental deficits and behaviour patterns?

The iron-status assessment at 12 months permitted a preliminary classification based on haemoglobin (Hb), mean corpuscular volume (MCV), and erythrocyte protoporphyrin (FEP), which were readily available. Seven to ten days after this venipuncture the first BSID test was performed. Within each preliminary iron-status group, infants were randomly assigned to ferrous sulphate drops or placebo for 10 days, when BSID tests were again given. At that point all infants received ferrous sulphate 3–5 mg/kg per day in two divided doses for 75 days at the end of which time BSID tests and iron-status assessments were repeated for a third time. All of the BSID tests were administered by the same psychologist who was unaware of the iron status of the child and the therapy assignment, facts which were also unknown to the mother.

The criteria used for classification into three groups (anaemic; non-anaemic iron-deficient (NAID) and iron-sufficient infants, referred to henceforth as "controls", were intended strictly to define anaemic and control subjects with up-to-date measurements, including the therapeutic response, which was considered to be the "gold standard" (Table 7.1). This methodology excluded the majority of infants with intermediate iron status, who fell into the broadly heterogeneous NAID group. The NAID infants were re-classified into grades of severity, depending on their response to the therapeutic trial and measurements of iron status.

Table 7.1.   Classification criteria for iron nutritional status

Control	Haemoglobin > 110 g/l
	Mean corpuscular volume: > 70 fl
	Serum iron/total iron binding capacity: > 10%
	Free erythrocyte protoporphyrin: < 100 µg of zinc protoporphyrin/dl RBC
	Serum ferritin: > 10 µg/l
	Response to iron therapy: Hb < 10 g/l
Anaemic	Haemoglobin: < 110 g/l and two or more abnormal biochemical measures
NAID[a]	Haemoglobin: > 110 g/l
	One or more abnormal biochemical measures or a response to iron therapy: Hb > 10 g/l

[a] NAID = non-anaemic iron-deficient infants.

Complete haematological evaluation was performed in 189 infants at age 9 months, when no BSID tests were done, and in 196 infants at ages 12 and 15 months. The final classification of the infants and mean values for haematological measurements demonstrated that because of the stringent criteria for classification, only 30 control and 39 anaemic subjects were identified (Table 7.2), whereas 127 infants fell in to the NAID group in which the criteria were successful in segregating degrees of severity of iron deficiency as indicated by the progression of iron-status values (Table 7.3).

A total of 576 BSID tests was administered and the results were distributed in a normal fashion. Mean MDI was 102 ± 9 and mean PDI, 98.1 ± 11. There was a significant difference between MDI and PDI in the population as a whole. Both distributions were, however, symmetrical. This population is biassed by design with the selection of healthy infants from a closely followed cohort. We purposely excluded confounding influences in host and environment by following a cohort of infants in an optimal state of health longitudinally, with the exception of iron nutrition, and this iron status was determined randomly by fortified food assignment. The proximity of the score to the US norm, and the symmetry of the BSID distribution are likely consequences of this design, eleminating confounding low performances usually present in disadvantaged populations.

Table 7.2. Iron nutritional status at 12 months (mean + s.d.)

	Control (n=30)	Anaemic (n=39)	NAID[a] (n=127)
Haemoglobin (g/l)	127 ± 8	100 ± 9	121 ± 7
Fe/TIBC (%)[b]	16.7 ± 6.3	6.3 ± 2.9	12.2 ± 0.7
FEP[c]	78 ± 13	195 ± 103	108 ± 33
Serum ferritin[d]	19.8 (12–34)	5.4 (3–9.8)	11.9 (6–24)

[a]NAID = non-anaemic iron-deficient infants.
[b]Fe/TIBC = serum iron/total iron binding capacity.
[c]FEP = free erythrocyte protoporphyrin (μg of ZPP/dl of red blood cells).
[d]Geometric mean and range: 1 s.d.

Table 7.3. Subclassification of non-anaemic iron-deficient infants

	Grade 1[d] (iron-depleted)	Grade 2[e] (non-responder)	Grade 3[f] (responder)
Haemoglobin (g/l)	129 ± 6	123 ± 7	117 ± 5
Fe/TIBC (%)[a]	14.8 ± 3.6	12.3 ± 0.7	11.7 ± 0.5
FEP[b]	81 ± 12	107 ± 30	115 ± 38
Serum ferritin[c] (μg/l)	7.5 (6.7–8.2)	15 (7.7–27)	9 (4.1–20)

[a]Fe/TIBC = Serum iron/total iron binding capacity.
[b]FEP = free erythrocyte protoporphyrin (μg of ZPP/dl of red blood cells).
[c]Geometric mean and range: 1 s.d.
[d]All measures normal except serum ferritin < 10 μg/l.
[e]One or more abnormal measures with a negative response to iron therapy (Hb < 10 g/l)
[f]One or more abnormal measures and a positive response to iron therapy (Hb > 10 g/l).

It is clear that a decrease in haemoglobin affected mental and psychomotor development scores. The performance of the NAID infants as a whole was indistinguishable from the control infants (Fig 7.1). None of the NAID subclassifications was successful in showing differences in performance. Even group 3, i.e. infants who were non-anaemic and responded to the therapeutic trial, and who could therefore be technically defined as anaemic, showed a tendency towards lower scores.

The MDI-PDI difference was present across all iron-status levels. However, this difference between scores was less pronounced in the control group, where mental and motor performances appeared to be better balanced. As iron deficiency increased, motor performances were more affected than mental indices, as seen by the divergence of these mean values. Explanations for this phenomenon remain conjectural.

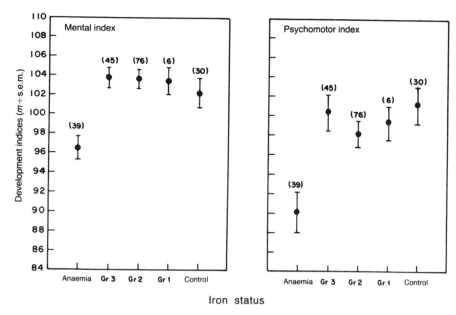

Fig. 7.1. Pretreatment mental and psychomotor development indices (mean ± s.e.m.) according to iron status at 12 months. The NAID are subclassified to: Grade 3, non-anaemic responder; Grade 2, non-anaemic non-responder; and Grade 1, non-anaemic iron-depleted. For definition criteria of anaemics and controls see text. Numbers in parentheses are the number of subjects per data point. The overall ANOVA for MDI (F $_{(4191)}$ = 5.4; P < 0.002) and PDI (F $_{(4191)}$ = 5.4; P < 0.0001). Paired comparisons of anaemic infants versus each and every other group are significant (P < 0.01). Paired comparisons between all non-anaemics are not significant. Only overt anaemia determines significantly lower scores for MDI and PDI.

A sigmoid distribution was found when MDI and PDI were distributed according to Hb levels, the most common indicator of iron status (Fig 7.2). Three groups can be identified: those with Hb < 105 g/l, those with Hb > 110/ g/l and an intermediate group at 105–109 Hb g/l. All are statistically distinct from each other by paired and ANOVA comparisons. Thus, in anaemic infants, Hb concentration was correlated with performance, so that infants with moderate anaemia (Hb 80–104 g/l) had significantly lower scores than those with mild degrees of anaemia (Hb 105–109 g/l). The latter in turn had poorer indices than infants with Hb > 110 g/l, with no graded improvements seen at higher Hb levels.

If the effect of iron deficiency on behaviour is mediated by metabolic processes dependent on the presence of iron, it is understandable that overt anaemia may be necessary to disclose these effects. Siimes et al. [32] reported in an animal model fed graded amounts of iron that tissue-haem proteins were not affected until saturation of transferrin fell significantly. Hb, as well as tissue cytochrome C and myoglobin, decreased steadily thereafter, demonstrating that availability of iron to the erythropoietic marrow is limited concomitantly with other tissues. Changes in iron stores (liver non-haem iron) did not influence Hb level or tissue-haem iron proteins. In humans the stage known as iron-deficient erythropoiesis, when iron availability becomes a limiting factor for Hb synthesis,

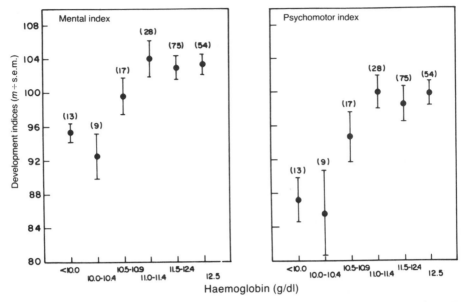

Fig. 7.2. Pretreatment mental and psychomotor development indices (mean ± s.e.m.) at 12 months according to haemoglobin concentration in 0.5 g/dl intervals. Numbers in parentheses indicates number of subjects per data point. ANOVA for Hb < 10.5 (n = 22 MDI: mean ± s.e.m. 94 ± 1.3; PDI: 86 ± 2.5) vs. 10.5–10.9 (n=17 MDI: 99.5 ± 2.1; PDI: 94.6 ± 2.9) vs. > 10.9 (n = 157 MDI: 103.2 ± 0.7; PDI: 99.2 ± 2.9) is highly significant (MDI $F_{(2193)}$ = 6.90; $P\ 10^{-5}$; PDI $F_{(2193)}$ = 8.48; $P\ 10^{-5}$. For each point MDI: $F_{(5190)}$ = 6.9, $P < 0.001$; PDI: F = 8.5, $P < 0.0002$. Paired comparisons between these three groups are significant ($P < 0.05$). Paired comparisons between those groups < 10.5 or ≥ 10.9 are not significant. For each point MDI: $F_{(5190)}$ = 6.9, $P < 0.001$; PDI: F = 8.5, $P < 0.0002$. The intermediate point (Hb 10.5–10.9) is significantly different from both extremes ($P < 0.05$) in MDI and PDI.

corresponds to the moment when Hb concentration begins to decrease, presumably along with other tissue iron proteins. However, the stage of overt anaemia is reached later, only when Hb values fall under 110 g/l for the infants in this study. Anaemia ensues, therefore, after a rather protracted and severe period of iron lack, ensuring significant deficiency of tissue iron proteins. Milder iron deficit may fall short of achieving sufficient tissue depletion to be reflected in behaviour. On the other hand, we must consider that the psychological tests available for this age group may be too crude to identify subtle deficits. These considerations may help explain the absence of cognitive effect seen in the non-anaemic-responder population (subclassification of NAID, Grade 3), which conceivably corresponds to the group of infants with limited Hb synthesis, soon to become anaemic.

To determine the duration of anaemia we studied the effect of iron status at age 9 months on development indices measured at 12 months. The indices were distributed according to the Hb at 9 months, i.e. 3 months before the BSID was performed, and showed a cut-off at 105 g/l (data not shown). To pursue the effect of duration of anaemia further, infants who were anaemic at both 9 and 12 months, i.e. those whose anaemia had a duration of more than 3 months (n=19) were compared with those children who were anaemic at 12, but not at 9

Table 7.4. Effect of duration of anaemia on development indices ($m \pm$ s.e.m.)

	Duration of anaemia		
	< 3 months (n=16)[a]		> 3 months (n=19)[b]
MDI	99.4 ± 2.5	$P < 0.05$	94.1 ± 1.1
PDI	93.7 ± 3.4	$P < 0.05$	86.0 ± 2.6

[a]Infants with Hb < 110g/L at 12 months but > 105g/L at 9 months.
[b]Infants with Hb < 110g/L at 12 months and < 105g/L at 9 months.

months, i.e. those whose anaemia was presumed to be present for less than 3 months (n=16). Of the 39 anaemics at 12 months, only 35 had Hb determined at 9 months. Those infants anaemic for more than 3 months had significantly lower development indices than those anaemic for less than 3 months (Table 7.4). Non-anaemic infants at age 9 months fell mostly into the intermediate Hb range of 105–109 g/l at 12 months where development indices were less severely affected. Thus, infants not anaemic at 9 months tended to have milder anaemia at 12 months. Of the 14 infants in the intermediate Hb group at 12 months, 10 (71%) were not anaemic at 9 months. Of the 21 infants who fell below the intermediate Hb level, only 6 (29%) were not anaemic at 9 months ($P < 0.015$). It is apparent from these results that as anaemia is prolonged, and consequently as it increases in intensity, developmental indices also become more adversely affected.

Summary

In summary, infants whose anaemia had a duration of more than 3 months had significantly inferior scores to anaemic infants whose Hb levels were in the normal range 3 months earlier. Infants without anaemia, but with marginal iron status at 9 months became those who eventually, at 12 months, fell into the intermediate group (Hb 105–109 g/l), having anaemia of shorter duration and lesser severity, associated with milder psychomotor derangements. It is reasonable to assume that if this group of infants (the intermediate anaemic group) were to continue with an iron-deficient diet, their anaemia would increase in duration (and severity) and their psychomotor performance would, hence, deteriorate further. However, since infants with anaemia of longer duration were also more likely to have anaemia of greater severity; these two characteristics of anaemia, duration and severity, could thus not be completely individualized with the current design.

At 12 months infants given 10 days of oral ferrous sulphate were compared with those given placebo. Both groups significantly improved developmental indices in the mental and psychomotor scales to a similar extent, regardless of previous iron status or therapy with iron or placebo, with average improvements of 4.4–8.9 points. After 3 months of therapy, even though anaemia was reversed in all infants and haematological measurements of iron status were completely corrected in 11 of the 39 formerly anaemic infants, no significant improvement was detected between the scores at 12 and 15 months. The control and the NAID infants showed no significant change in their MDI or PDI. Neither paired t comparison within groups (highest $P = 0.18$ for control infants), nor ANOVA of the differences of scores between groups showed significant changes from the baseline BSID scores.

We examined the specific test items involved in the raw scores which, when normalized for age, yield the development index. The MDI scores were encompassed representatively by items 99–117 and the corresponding PDI items were 40–52. Examining the mental scale, the items that required comprehension of language but did not involve a visual demonstration were passed by significantly fewer anaemic infants than control infants. On the BSID, language development at 12 months is best marked by item 106, "vocalization of bi-syllabic words", an item that showed marked differences between anaemic and control infants ($P < 0.01$). The next language item, 113, "says two words (meaningfully)", was passed by too few infants at 12 months to be interpretable, however, at 15 months it became significant ($P = 0.005$). At this age item 117, "shows shoes or other clothing or own toy", also became suggestive ($P < 0.07$). Item 106 continued to show a tendency ($P < 0.07$), partly because at 15 months most infants passed the item (Table 7.5).

Table 7.5. Per cent of infants passing mental scale items at 12 months

Item number	Item description	Infants passing[a]		P
		Anaemic (%)	Control (%)	
99	Pushes car along	56	77	NS
101	Jabbers expressively	92	93	NS
102	Uncovers blue box	31	47	NS
103	Turns pages of book	69	83	NS
104	Pats whistle-doll, in imitation	44	63	NS
106	Imitates words (mama, dada):			
	at 12 months	13	47	< 0.01
	at 15 months	75	100	< 0.07
108	Places 1 peg repeatedly	28	27	NS
113	Says 2 words (meaningfully):			
	at 12 months	0	7	NS
	at 15 months	42	93	< 0.005
117	Shows own shoes, clothing, toy:			
	at 12 months	0	18	NS
	at 15 months	25	60	< 0.07

[a] Analysed by chi-squared of absolute numbers.

In the psychomotor milestones 40–52, it appeared that those items relating to balance in the standing position, and body control (sits from standing, stands alone, and walks alone) were credited by significantly fewer anaemic than control infants. Differences for items 47, "stands up from sitting", and 52, "stands on left foot with help", were not identified at 12 months but became significant at 15 months ($P < 0.05$) (Table 7.6).

Of the 24 items evaluated by the IBR at 12 months, 9 were rated significantly better by control infants compared with their anaemic peers, as shown on responsiveness to the examiner ($P < 0.03$), responsiveness to the mother ($P < 0.0005$), general emotional tone ($P < 0.001$), as well as responsiveness to persons ($P < 0.001$), to vocalizations ($P < 0.05$), and to body motion ($P < 0.002$).

Table 7.6. Per cent of infants passing psychomotor items at 12 months

Item number	Item description	Infants passing[a]		
		Anaemic (%)	Control (%)	P
90	Stepping movements	100	100	NS
41	Pellet: fine prehension (neat pincer)	90	93	NS
42	Walks with help	85	97	NS
43	Sits down from standing	67	97	< 0.01
44	Pat-a-cake: midline skill	82	97	NS
45	Stands alone	64	93	< 0.02
46	Walks alone	38	67	< 0.05
47	Stands up (from sitting)			
	at 12 months	3	7	NS
	at 15 months	42	80	< 0.05
48	Throws ball (forward fling)	59	70	NS
52	Stands on left foot with help			
	at 12 months	0	10	NS
	at 15 months	8	40	< 0.05

[a]Analysed by chi-squared of absolute numbers.

Further analysis of the IBR was performed, associating behaviour items related to "test affect" and "task orientation" as suggested by Wolf and Lozoff [33]. The test-affect combination rated significantly better in the control vs. anaemic groups ($P < 0.04$). Those anaemic infants with abnormal test affect (14/39) commonly had more scores under the mean for MDI ($P < 0.04$) and PDI ($P < 0.04$) whereas control infants showed no differences, probably because very few (3/30) presented an abnormal-affect behaviour pattern. Abnormal task orientation in the anaemic children (12/39) was markedly associated with MDIs under the mean ($P < 0.01$); however, only a marginal tendency was seen for lower PDIs ($P = 0.09$). Control infants showed non-significant associations because only 4 of 30 ranked inappropriate task orientation.

These IBR findings expand our previous experience [34] and that of other investigators. There were no appreciable changes of the IBR after therapy, which correlates with the lack of change in development-index scores. This fact lends support to the hypothesis that the unfavourable behaviour pattern of these infants may be a mediator of the poorer BSID test performances. However if this contention were true, it should probably have affected individual items in a random fashion. In this study item performance failures had a very consistent pattern, with preferences for language in the mental items and body balance and coordination in motor skills. The reason for this selective effect remains obscure. Moreover, these findings coincide quite closely with results from recent research in Costa Rica [30] (Chapter 6) which, with a different study design, show similar selective failure patterns. This agreement is reassuring in that it supports our findings, but it is also worrying because they also fail to show consistent improvement after short- or long-term iron therapy.

These results suggest that:

1. Iron-deficiency anaemia adversely affects psychomotor development. The validity of this inference is threatened because of the self-selection at the food trial entry. However, as is shown below, the effect of anaemia persists after segregating for the duration of breast-feeding, and that disposes of this doubt.

2. There is no influence of iron or placebo more than that expected by a practice effect. Here the question of compliance arises, since the infants were given the medication by the mother with double checking 3 or 4 times in this 10-day interval by the visiting nurse. Our excellent rapport with families that were seen weekly for the previous 9 months assures that compliance was very probably adequate. This was, nevertheless, double-checked by measurement of the quantity of suspension remaining in the bottle, which was changed for a new flask for every child after the 10 day iron-placebo trial, in order to protect the double-blind design. At the end of 10 days of iron therapy it would be difficult to find a discernible effect on iron status due to the latency of the effect of iron on red cell production. On the other hand, the potential confounding of the "regression to the mean" effect could not be easily accounted for.

3. Duration and severity of anaemia had an adverse effect on BSID scores. With the limitation of this retrospective analysis this conclusion remains quite strong, however, although the confounding effect of breast-feeding duration was not looked at. Additionally, severity and duration of anaemia could not be segregated in this design.

The most important issue is the validity of these conclusions. Statistically significant differences in scores of the BSID between the anaemics and non-anaemics, both at 12 and 15 months, do not mean they are developmentally different. For the mental index the absolute differences were small (5.5–6 points). At issue is the functional significance of this difference. However the changes in the psychomotor index are greater (10.5–11.5 points) and more likely to be of functional importance.

At age 12 months the infants were randomized between treatment with ferrous sulphate or placebo. However, these infants had been the subjects of two previous interventions, one that was random (iron-fortified foods or non-fortified products) and one that was not random, whether they were on breast milk as the exclusive source of milk – "breast milk group" (BF) – or were receiving more than 50% of their estimated energy requirements from sources other than breast-milk – "early weaned group" (EW) – at the time of the fortification assignment.

At this point, let us describe the experimental setting in more detail. All the infants in this study were obtained from the same clinic, at the same time and with the same criteria, and were treated in a standardized fashion. The study was carried out over a perod of 2.5 years and the infants were assigned to a food product (with or without iron fortification) in an alternate fashion, according to order of recruitment to the study. The non-random stratification applied was the breast-feeding history, over which the investigators had no influence whatsoever. However, once the infant became part of the study, efforts to maintain or reinstitute breast-feeding were routinely carried out by the staff caring for these babies, as will be appreciated by the duration of breast-feeding in the EW infants. It is also important to note that the food products normally handed out by the National Food Supplementation Program, to which all these infants belonged, are not iron fortified. Thus, we were in fact not experimentally removing a benefit but rather experimentally adding a well-recognized potential need.

The fortification randomization assignment determined to some extent the iron status of the infant at age 12 months. Iron fortification was more efficient in the EW group because milk is consumed in large and fairly predictable quantities throughout the first year of life. Thus, only 2/37 (5%) of infants in the EW fortified group became anaemic, whereas 10/56 (18%) of the BF fortified group had a Hb < 110 g/l at 12 months (Table 7.7).

Table 7.7. Fortification assignment in breast-fed and early-weaned infants according to iron status

	Anaemic		NAID[a]		Controls	
	+Fe	−Fe	+Fe	−Fe	+Fe	−Fe
Breast-fed (n=104)	10	8	34	34	12	6
Early-weaned (n=92)	2	19	26	33	9	3

[a]NAID = non-anaemic iron-deficient infants.

The distribution of treatment with iron or placebo was fairly even, except for a larger number of EW anaemic infants getting iron compared with placebo.

To interpret the result of the iron-placebo therapy trial adequately, it is important to evaluate the influence of breast-feeding history on the performance of the BSID.

Infants in the BF group received breast milk as the exclusive source of milk for an average (+ s.d.) of 275 ± 78 days and non-exclusively for 334 ± 55 days. Infants in the EW group had breast milk exclusively for 74 ± 61 days. By definition, no infant in this group was exclusively breast-fed for more than 90 days; however, most continued to be breast-fed at least once a day for 171 ± 120 days. Thus, even though the differences between the duration of breast-feeding in the BF and EW groups are large and highly significant, all the infants in this study had more than 60 days of breast-feeding, and even in the EW group some were breast-fed, although not exclusively, for as long as 9 or 10 months.

When the development scores were examined at 12 months, there was an appreciable difference between the BF and EW, favouring the BF group. However, the difference in MDI (Table 7.8) and PDI (Table 7.9) between the infant iron status groups, showing that anaemic infants have a poorer performance than all non-anaemic infants, persists unaltered. Thus, even though the BF infants have better scores overall than the EW group, this effect is overcome by a persisting effect of iron status.

The next step was to examine the performance of the infants after 10 days of iron or placebo. Infants were analysed as EW and BF, each segregated according to iron status (six groups). After 10 days all six groups improved their performance significantly both in MDI and PDI (paired t test). The analysis of whether some infants improved their scores more than others failed to show differences (ANOVA), showing that neither breast-feeding nor iron status, or iron vs. placebo, have an influence on developmental indices that cannot be explained as a practice effect (data not shown).

Finally, stepwise multiple regression analysis was executed with MDI or PDI as dependent variables, including duration of breast-feeding and all the other intervening variables together. Haemoglobin and iron status group were the most powerful factors, and when forcing Hb in first, all other variables lost significance when 0.12 was the limit-of-significance cut-off to enter the stepwise equation.

Table 7.8. Mean mental development index scores in breast-fed and early-weaned infants according to iron status.

	Breast-fed	Early-weaned
Anaemic	98.2 (n=19)	95.1 (n=17)
NAID[a]	105.9 (n=68)	100.9 (n=57)
Control	102.3 (n=17)	99.7 (n=11)
Weighted mean	103.8	99.7
ANOVA	< 0.05	< 0.05

[a]NAID = non-anaemic iron-deficient infants.

Table 7.9. Mean psychomotor development index scores in breast-fed and early-weaned infants according to iron status.

	Breast-fed	Early-weaned
Anaemic	92.1 (n=19)	87.3 (n=17)
NAID[a]	100.3 (n=18)	97.1 (n=57)
Controls	102.6 (n=17)	98.8 (n=11)
Weighted mean	99.1	95.4
ANOVA	< 0.0002	< 0.01

[a]NAID = non-anaemic iron-deficient infants.

The study in Costa Rica by Lozoff et al. was aimed at: determining differences in the effects of oral compared with intramuscular iron on behaviour, to answer inconsistencies posed by previous research; investigating the effects of varying degrees of iron deficit; and exploring the effect of short- and long-term iron therapy on the reversal of the effects of iron deficiency on behaviour.

For the first question, the design was a double-blind randomized iron (oral and intramuscular) supplementation or placebo trial. Since the infants were selected in a cross-sectional survey from a community, and not from a prospective follow-up as was the study by Walter et al., numerous criteria for exclusion were applied to exclude confounders. Even though these were carefully searched for and quite comprehensive, it cannot be assumed that infants in each group had similar backgrounds. However, after exhaustive analysis only age turned out to select (older) infants who were less anaemic. Anaemia was defined as Hb < 105 g/l and serum ferritin < 12 ng/l, % saturation of transferrin < 10 and/or free erythrocyte protoporphyrin > 100 μg/dl RBC. This group was broken down further into mild anaemia (101–105 g/l) and moderate anaemia (< 101 g/l). The iron-sufficient infants required a Hb greater than 120 g/l with other measures in the normal range. As in the study by Walter, iron therapy confirmed the iron deficit. However response to iron was not used as a *post-facto* criterion for classification.

The BSID was used for the assessment of Mental and Motor Development as well as the Infant Behaviour Record.

Regardless of iron therapy or placebo, short-term oral or intramuscular, all infants significantly improved their scores. This is a similar result to that of Walter et al. except that here a haematological assessment was performed to ensure that haemoglobins had risen in the iron-treated anaemics compared with those given placebo.

The remaining 3 months of iron therapy performed without a placebo-treated group, strictly necessary to establish internal validity (an objection also applying to the study by Walter), was studied for potential confounders, and it was found that non-anaemic infants were significantly older than anaemic infants. Nothing is known, however, about the previous iron status of these older infants. The natural history of nutritional iron-deficiency anaemia is that when it is present at 6–12 months of age, it tends to disappear later because of decreased requirements and a more varied diet. Therefore this potential confounder cannot be elucidated. Nevertheless, Lozoff introduced this age factor into all further analysis in an attempt to dissipate statistical bias. Anaemic infants who became iron sufficient (all measures in the normal range) were analysed separately. This group was generally less severely affected, and thus required less therapy time for complete haematological rehabilitation. After 3 months of therapy 9 completely corrected anaemic infants were compared with infants with initial Hb > 100 g/l. The former infants initially scored significantly lower in the MDI. However this difference was no longer present after 3 months. This was due, disappointingly, to a fall in the non-anaemic's MDI, not to a real rise in the anaemics. This underscores the importance of controlling for age, since age is a plausible explanation for this finding. Anaemic infants who did not reach iron sufficiency at the end of the therapeutic trial persisted with a MDI significantly under that of infants with Hb > 100 g/l initially. This could be due to severity or chronicity, an effect demonstrated in Walter's study. However, the design precludes a firm conclusion.

Regarding PDI, those infants who initially had an Hb > 105 g/l and became iron replete were compared with those who had Hb < 105 g/l. The iron-repleted anaemic infants improved their scores by an average of 10 points, thereby reaching the level of the non-anaemic infants. Though the increase was statistically significant, the final PDI of the two groups was not different. Limitations of study design (i.e. lack of a placebo-anaemic group) precludes discrimination between "practice" or "real iron" effect.

Conclusions

The two studies presented here in detail, along with previous work, show an association between iron deficiency and suboptimal behaviour in infancy, expressed as lower scores on tests of psychomotor development. The first problem that arises in the interpretation of results is the common association of anaemia with adverse health, environment and nutrition. However, these studies using randomized designs and longitudinal follow-up appear to show consistent and coinciding effects that cannot be easily ignored. Issues of internal validity can be dismissed with optimal research design, a task easier said than done, because the form in which iron-deficiency anaemia appears in the community is difficult to segregate from intervening variables. A more crucial issue, and where there is ample room for improvement, is that of construct validity. The BSID's popularity no longer serves as an excuse for its use in this context.

We agree that better methods of probing mental processes in infancy must be used in any future protocol in this area of research. The visual habituation paradigm described by Lewis et al. [35] is an interesting alternative.

However, other neurophysiological measures to search for subtle maturational effects of iron lack should also be incorporated into this line of research in the next generation of studies. Sleep–wakefulness cycle studies seem warranted, based on the patterns of sleep inversion found in experimental animals. Measurements of myelination of peripheral and central nervous system pathways and synaptic activity found altered in the parietal cortex on the rat, with methods such as brain-stem evoked potential, are non-invasive and need to be further evaluated. Even findings in factorial analysis of EEG have already been described [36]. The sleep-wakefulness cycle, found to be inverted in iron-deficient experimental animals, has also a well described maturational sequence in the first 2 years of life and could be explored. Newer techniques of positron emission tomography could be designed to search for intracerebral metabolic defects.

Nevertheless, the Bayley Scales are the only tool that has been looked at extensively, and such coincidences as have been found by independent investigators working in distant regions and with different study designs cannot be ignored. The BSID, therefore, has become the standard measurement with which all future research in the effect of iron deficiency in infancy must be compared, until a better tool becomes available.

In summary, we should now move to a third generation of studies on the effect of iron deficit on infant brain function and eventually attempt to clarify the intimate mechanisms whereby they may affect behaviour.

References

1. Oski FA, Honig AS (1978) The effects of therapy on the developmental score of iron-deficient infants. J Pediatr 92:21–25
2. Engel GL (1979) The biomedical model: a procrustean bed? Man and Medicine 4:257–275
3. Cook TD, Campbell DT (1979) Quasi-experimentation. Design and analysis issues for field settings. Houghton Mifflin, Boston.
4. Tucker DM, Sandstead H (1984) Nutrition and brain function: theoretical models. In: Brozek J, Schurch B (eds) Malnutrition and behavior: critical assessment of key issues. Nestlé Foundation publication series, vol 4. Nestlé Foundation, Lausanne, Switzerland, pp 348–357

5. Lozoff B, Brittenham GM (1985) Behavioral aspects of iron deficiency. Prog Hematol 14:23–53
6. Gottlieb G (1983) The psychobiological approach to developmental issue. In: Mussen P (ed) Handbook of child psychology, vol 2, Infancy and developmental psychobiology, 4th edn, Haith MM, Campos J (eds) Wiley, New York
7. Stekel A (1984) Iron requirements in infancy and childhood. In: Stekel A (ed) Iron nutrition in infancy and childhood. Nestlé workshop series, vol 4. Raven Press, New York, pp 1–7
8. Gollin ES (ed) (1981) Developmental plasticity. Behavioral and biological aspects of variations in development. Academic Press, San Francisco
9. Horowitz F (1989) Using developmental theory to guide the search for the effects of biological risk factors on the development of children. Am J Clin Nutr (Suppl) (in press)
10. McCall RB (1981) Nature–nurture and the two realms of development: a proposed integration with respect to mental development. Child Dev 52:1–12
11. Waddington CH (1971) Concepts of development. In: Tobach E, Aronson LR, Shaw E (eds) Biopsychology of development. Academic Press, New York, pp 17–23
12. Walter T (1989) Infancy: mental and motor development. Am J Clin Nutr [Suppl] (in press)
13. Goodman JF (1989) Infant intelligence: do we, can we, should we assess it. In: Reynolds CR, Kamphaus R (eds) Handbook of psychological and educational assessment. Guildford, New York (in press)
14. Lewis M, Jaskir J, Enright MK (1986) The development of mental abilities in infancy. Intelligence 10:321–354
15. Fagan JF III (1988) Screening infants for later mental retardation: from theory to practice. In: Vietze PM, Vaughan HG (eds) Early identification of infants with developmental disabilities. Grune & Stratton, Philadelphia, pp 253–265
16. Beaton G (1989) Comments on the paper by Hallberg L: "Search for nutritional confounding factors in the relationship between iron deficiency and brain function". Am J Clin Nutr [Suppl] (in press)
17. Scrimshaw N (1989) Comments on the paper by Hallberg L: "Search for nutritional confounding factors in the relationship between iron deficiency and brain function". Am J Clin Nutr [Suppl] (in press)
18. Pollit E, Thompson C (1977) Protein-calorie malnutrition and behavior: a view from psychology. In: Wurtman RJ, Wurtman JJ (eds) Nutrition and the brain, vol 2, Control of feeding behavior and biology of the brain in protein-calorie malnutrition. Plenum Press, New York, pp 261–306
19. Galler J (ed) (1984) Nutrition and behavior. In: Alfin-Slater R, Kritchevsky D (eds) Human nutrition: a comprehensive treatise. Plenum Press, New York
20. Brozek J, Schurch B (eds) (1984) Malnutrition and behavior: critical assessment of key issues. Nestlé Foundation publication series, vol 4. Nestlé Foundation, Lausanne, Switzerland
21. Schroeder SR, Hawk B, Otto D, Mushak P, Hicks RE (1985) Separating the effect of lead and social factors on IQ. Environmental Res 38:144–154
22. Ernhart CB, Landa B, Wolf AB (1985) Subclinical lead level and developmental deficit: re-analysis of data. J Learning Disabil 18:475–479
23. Fulton M, Thomson G, Hunter R, Raab G, Larn D, Hepburn W (1987) Influence of blood lead on the ability and attainment of children in Edinburgh. Lancet i:1221–1226
24. Needleman HL, Gunnoe C, Leviton A, Reed R, Peresie H, Maher C, Barrett P (1979) Deficits in psychologic and classroom performance of children with elevated dentine lead levels. N Engl J Med 300:689–695
25. Lansdown R, Yule W, Urbanowocz M, Hunter J (1986) The relationship between blood lead concentrations, intelligence, attainment and behaviour in a school population: the second London study. Internat Arch Occupational Environ Health 57:225–235
26. McKinney JD (1986) Reflections on the concept of risk for developmental retardation: a summary. In: Farran DC, McKinney JD (eds) Risk in intellectual and psychosocial development. Academic Press, New York, pp 121–124
27. Werner E (1986) A longitudinal study of perinatal risk. In: Farran DC, McKinney JD (eds) Risk in intellectual and psychosocial development. Academic Press, New York, pp 3–27
28. Leibel RL, Greenfield DB, Pollitt E (1979) Iron deficiency: behavior and brain biochemistry. In: Wininck M (ed) Nutrition: pre and postnatal development. Plenum Press, New York, pp 383–439

29. Lozoff B, Brittenham GM (1985) Behavioral aspects of iron deficiency. Prog Hematol 14:23–25
30. Lozoff B, Brittenham GM, Wolf AW, et al. (1987) Iron deficiency anemia and iron therapy. Effects on infant developmental test performance. Pediatrics 79:981–995
31. Walter T, DeAndraca I, Chadud P, Perales CG (1989) Iron deficiency anemia: adverse effects on infant psychomotor development. Pediatrics 84:7–17
32. Siimes MA, Refine C, Dallman PR (1980) Manifestations of iron deficiency at various levels of dietary iron intake. Am J Clin Nutr 33:570–574
33. Wolf AW, Lozoff B (1985) A clinically interpretable method for analysing the Bayley Infant Behavior Record. J Pediatr Psychol 10:199–214
34. Walter T, Kovalsky J, Stekel A (1983) Effect of mild iron deficiency on infant mental development scores. J Pediatr 102:519–522
35. Lewis M, Goldberg S, Campbell H (1969) A developmental study of learning within the first three years of life: response decrement to a redundant signal. In: Hale GA, Lewis M (eds) Monographs of the society for research in child development, 34 (9 Serial No. 133)
36. Tucker DM, Swenson RA, Sandstead HH (1983) Neuropsychological effects of iron deficiency. In: Dreosti IE (ed) Neurobiology of the trace elements, vol 1. Humana Press, Clifton, NJ

Commentary

Lozoff and Felt: Walter and our group have been working in this research area for the last 9 years or so, with studies that are remarkably similar in a number of respects. Despite the many similarities, there are some real issues for discussion.

One relates to the way in which the most recent Chilean study has been analyzed and presented [1]. Although starting with a very powerful study design, one of a randomized preventive intervention, the analyses compare children who developed iron-deficiency anemia with those who did not. The children who developed iron-deficiency anemia do not bear a one-to-one correspondence with the intervention. That is, some children who received iron fortification became anemic and many children who were not fortified nonetheless failed to develop iron-deficiency anemia. Thus, even though randomization of fortification probably did produce groups that were similar with regard to intervening or confounding variables, those who became anemic may have differed in background in very important ways.

The inter-relations between lead and iron are important, but it is also pertinent that in the sole behavioral study of iron-deficient infants that actually measured lead levels [1], lead levels were low and did not explain the lower test scores.

There is a study of zinc-deficient monkeys in which behavioral abnormalities have been documented [2]. In addition, there are clinical descriptions of abnormal behavior in human zinc deficiency syndromes.

The logic that unfavorable behavior does not mediate poor test performance is thin. Language items are certainly highly dependent on the infant's sociability and thus could be easily affected by abnormally fearful, unhappy, or hesitant behavior. Fearfulness, hesitance, or tension could also interfere with smooth motor coordination.

Concerning the three conclusions from the analysis of the results (p144), the first statement can be made only if it is proven that the infants who developed iron-deficiency anemia differed in no other respect from the infants who did not. No analysis to date seems to have addressed this question except in relation to breast-feeding. In the third statement, it is not clear why the data on duration and severity of anemia are considered to be retrospective.

Some might consider that randomization by alternation is less than optimal, since it is relatively easy to break the code.

We are curious why hemoglobin was entered first in the regression analysis. In our own work we have used the more conservative approach of forcing in all the background variables first to see if there was an effect of iron-deficiency anemia even after allowing all of the other factors to account for their portion of the variance [3,4].

As Walter considers the limitation of our own study in which there were no long-term placebo-treated anemic infants, he notes that it is impossible to discriminate between a practice effect and a real effect of iron treatment. If a practice effect were the explanation, why would it only have been observed among those infants who became iron sufficient and not noted among the majority of the anemic infants?

References

1. Walter T, DeAndraca I, Chadud P, Perales CG (1989) Iron deficiency anemia: adverse effects on infant psychomotor development. Pediatrics 84:7–17
2. Golub MS, Gershwin ME, Hurley LS, Hendrickx AG, Saito WY (1985) Studies of marginal zinc deprivation in rhesus monkeys: infant behavior. Am J Clin Nutr 42:1229–1239
3. Lozoff B, Brittenham GM, Wolf AW, et al. (1987) Iron deficiency anemia and iron therapy: effects on infant developmental test performance. Pediatrics 79:981–995
4. Lozoff B, Brittenham GM, Viteri FE, Wolf AW, Urrutia JJ (1982) Developmental deficits in iron-deficient infants: effects of age and severity of iron lack: J Pediatr 101:948–952

Author's reply: Lozoff and Felt point out that some of the anaemic infants did, in fact, come from the fortified groups as is seen in Table 7.7. Even when the biological reasons for this are clear (infants who consumed less than the recommended amounts of fortified foods or whose requirements exceeded the iron absorbed from them), other reasons for the failure of fortification cannot be excluded. However, even when issues of compliance and morbidity are accounted for, a small percentage of infants on a fortified diet will become anaemic. There is no satisfactory explanation for this at present.

Parks: There is now much evidence that duration of anaemia is important in determining the effect on development. We need to assess if there is a "critical age" (duration) at which anaemia should be sought out.

Iron therapy corrected the iron status in only 11 of the 39 anaemic infants. This fits well with data from Lozoff et al. [1] and ourselves [2]. This may imply that treatment is required for longer than 2–3 months to have a significant effect on developmental progress of the group as a whole.

References

1. Lozoff B, Brittenham GM, Wolf AW, et al. (1987) Iron deficiency anemia and iron therapy. Effects on infant developmental test performance. Pediatrics 79:981–995
2. Arkett MA, Parks YA, Scott PH, et al. (1986) Treatment with iron increases weight gain and psychomotor development. Arch Dis Child 61:849–857

Author's reply: The question of a "critical age" is indeed critical. New studies should be designed to determine whether anaemia (or iron deficiency without anaemia) may affect development or other functions at different ages. The time between 6 and 12 months is the one likely to yield the most important results.

The duration of iron therapy is one of the factors which may account for the lack of improvement of most anaemic infants after treatment. New studies should introduce longer therapy periods before re-testing.

Smart: This paper is principally an account of Walter and his colleagues' monumental study in Chile, together with broader consideration of some of the issues involved in this area of research. Having now read a number of reviews of the field, it was interesting to read about a very recent study [his reference 3] in some detail. To some extent I am confirmed in my impression (see my commentary on Lozoff) that this is an area which lends itself to multiple analysis of the results with the ensuing pitfall of selective citation and emphasis of findings. (I do not put myself above this tendency, I merely comment upon it.) For instance, in this investigation the emphasis is very firmly on the relationship between iron status, determined haematologically, and infant development, in spite of the fact that there was a quite complex, factorial, experimental design. Indeed, this generated eight "treatment" groups, yet there is very little analysis presented on the effects of the treatments.

The 400 infants entering the study appear to reduce to less than 200, which gives a rate of attrition far in excess of 20%.

Author's reply: I sympathize with Smart's concern about the multiple complexities of field studies of this nature. All of us working in the field are striving towards designs less influenced by environmental factors. Any suggestion would be welcome!

The effect of therapy is only briefly mentioned because of the negative results. Studies of longer iron treatment must be performed to evaluate infants with complete correction of iron status, and eventually long-term follow-up, over years, will be necessary to see whether there is recovery of performance to the level of the non-anaemic "control" group.

Iron deficiency did not determine increased morbidity, nor vice versa. Therefore we cannot correlate morbidity with developmental index. Nonetheless, morbidity in our population was infrequent and mild, resulting in infants with excellent nutritional status. Mean weight/age, height/age and weight/height was within 2% of the 50th centile of the National Center for Health Statistics tables.

The reason for there being only 200 infants in the analysis is that funding only became available half way through the field study.

Yip: Concern about the lack of specific construct on instruments as IQ test or Bayley scales for studying the effect of iron deficiency is valid. What about the development of, or focus on methods that can measure behaviors such as irritability and pica that have been empirically observed among infants with severe iron-deficiency anemia by clinicians? Even though this approach does not provide a better construct, it is built upon more specific clinical observations.

I think the best example of a confounder in the study of iron and infant behavior is the socio-economic factor or social environment. Children of low socio-economic status are more likely to have iron deficiency because of less resource for adequate nutrition. They also are more likely to receive less stimulation, which may result in lower IQ or Bayley scores. Therefore, if socio-economic status were not controlled between iron-deficient and non-iron-deficient infants, a bias can potentially occur.

Another potential confounder is recent or current illness affecting both iron metabolism as well as behavior test performance.

One general issue that warrants future attention is comparability of the environment between iron-deficiency anemic and the non-iron-deficient groups. Since the placebo and iron treatment did not demonstrate a "treatment effect" to prove that iron deficiency was the likely reason for the observed behavioral deficit, it is necessary to demonstrate the assumption that the anemic group and the non-iron-deficient group had the same environment except for their iron status. However, this was not part of the design *a priori*. Even though the general family, socio-economic, and feeding background are similar among the study groups, I could not help wondering whether those infants who developed iron-deficiency anemia were on the edges of the population. Perhaps there were other aspects of their family and health which may also be different? For future studies more detailed accounts of the environment will be needed to control for potential bias when using the multivariate approach.

Dallman: The review as a whole is helpful and interesting. Despite considerable duplication with Parks and Wharton and with Lozoff, it is useful having the benefit of different perspectives.

A small 5 point difference in score may not have much significance in the assessment of an individual but must be more meaningful in comparing groups if it is a statistically significant difference. Using hemoglobin as an analogy, a 1 g/dl difference may have no demonstrable effect in an individual but if there is a change of that magnitude in a population, it indicates a major change in distribution and a considerable alteration in the number of very low values. Note that the major decline in anemia described by Vazquez-Seoane et al. [cited by Yip, his reference 7] was only associated with a 0.7 g/dl rise in mean hemoglobin concentration, a change that would be of doubtful significance in an individual.

It would be interesting to compare the Bayley data of the early-weaned fortified and the early-weaned unfortified groups since these groups were truly randomized. Any evidence of a difference between these two groups, in frequency distribution of Bayley scores, for example, would provide the strongest available evidence of a cause and effect relationship between iron nutrition and Bayley score.

Author's reply: When the BSID data from the early-weaned fortified and unfortified infants are compared, no significant differences are to be found, even when the anaemic ones are excluded. The reason seems to be that once anaemia is excluded, Bayley scores do not correlate with further improvements of iron status or haemoglobin, as can be seen in Figs 7.1. and 7.2.

Larkin and Rao: The author's question "what is the significance and theoretical meaning of these numbers?" focusses on a very important issue. I think that part of the answer depends on knowing the sensitivity and specificity of these tests in light of the prevalence of iron deficiency in the population examined.

Since zinc deficiency is referred to by the author, it is of note in animal experiments that zinc deficiency has been shown to modify brain lipid composition in suckling rats. It has been suggested that altered cholesterol/phospholipid ratio observed in marginally zinc-deficient animals may adversely affect membrane-dependent processes. The effects of iron deficiency in brain lipids of suckling rats is the subject of Chapter 3. The effects of combined zinc and iron deficiencies on brain lipids has yet to be studied. As appears to be the case in iron deficiency, infant behavior may be affected by zinc deficiencies. The effects may be amplified or quite different with combined deficiencies.

The author is right on target with, " . . . I believe that harder data should be also searched for having as a basis the neurochemical and structural experimental data existent to date . . .".

Dobbing: You refer to "the structural basis of functional competence". For me this is a fine concept, but has no tangible reality, except for well-defined motor and sensory, etc. pathways. What is the physical basis of intellect, or cognition?

I do not think that *"extensive* effects on cognition" have been shown to be due to protein-energy malnutrition. Neither am I sure that lead has serious effects on cognition. Do you mean lead poisoning, or exposure to minimal amounts, short of poisoning?

Was the elimination of intervening factors demonstrated, or assumed? That is, was similarity of environmental factors (family or selective nutrition, etc.) checked in the two groups, or was it assumed that the whole population was homogeneous except for the supplements?

Author's reply: The elimination of intervening factors was performed for demographic, socio-economic and nutritional data available after 12 months of prospective follow-up. Multiple regression analysis and ANOVA (chi-squared for non-parametric measures) showed that mothers' education was significantly *better* in the anaemic group, that there were more male infants, and that fortification assignment determined prevalence of anaemia. No other variables were significant.

Breast-feeding had an influence on the developmental test performance, but it was swamped by anaemia as seen in Tables 7.8. and 7.9.

Yehuda: I am an outsider to the field of assessing infants' behaviour, but I have some knowledge of psychology. In these pages the author severely criticizes the Bayley Scales of Infant Development (BSID). His main points are that (a) the

BSID lack theoretical basis and background, and that (b) they lack predictive validity. He then suggests adopting Horwitz's approach to behavioural science theory.

In general, I share the author's criticism of the BSID. I am less impressed by his claim that they lack theoretical background. It is generally agreed, among psychologists, that there is no single intelligence test which is soundly based on theory. I read Horowitz's paper [1] very carefully. Unfortunately, I do not share this author's enthusiastic approach, mainly because I believe that she is wrong. Emotion and motivation are, in my opinion, *more* universal than motor development, language acquisition and cognitive function. Emotion and motivation are apparent in infant behaviour much earlier than other behaviours, are mediated by more "primitive" areas of the brain, and are less dependent on culture. Moreover, the study that the author cites as constituting a "promising approach" is on "habituation", one of the most universal kinds of learning.

At any rate, at this age range (first years of life) what we can measure is only "sensory-motor alertness".

However, the discussion of the BSID leaves me puzzled. If the BSID are so inadequate, I cannot understand why the author has used them in his own research, and calculates complex statistical analyses on the basis of the BSID, at the same time asking "what is the significant and theoretical meaning of these numbers?"

I believe that the author has presented a very good piece of research. Now his task is to explain why he used the BSID, and why the results are important.

Reference

1. Horowitz FD (1989) Using developmental theory to guide the search for the effects of biological risk factors on the development of children. Am J Clin Nutr [Suppl] 50:589–597

Chapter 8

Iron Deficiency and the Brain: Clinical Significance of Behavioural Changes

Yvonne A. Parks and Brian Wharton

Introduction

It has long been stated that in adults iron-deficiency anaemia is associated with fatigue, weakness and lack of ability to concentrate, but this has not been documented in controlled studies. Iron-deficient children are reported to be irritable, apathetic, distractable and anorexic. There is now a large number of observation and intervention studies showing that iron deficiency has an adverse effect on brain function in children. Changes occur in both cognitive and non-cognitive abilities, and any adverse effect on one may have a secondary effect on the other. For instance a child with a cognitive deficit may become frustrated and exhibit abnormal behaviour patterns or, on the other hand, poor concentration may lead to poor learning.

The mechanisms for these changes involve a number of biochemical pathways in which iron is essential. Most research has centred on the effects on the neurotransmitters dopamine and serotonin, and on dopamine D_2 receptors (see Chapters 4 and 5).

Infancy is a particularly important time as during the first 2 years brain growth and development is at its maximum. Iron deficiency is most prevalent between 6 and 24 months and if it does have an adverse effect on these developmental processes then this may be of long-term significance.

At every consultation the clinician assesses not only the physical condition of the child but also the developmental progress. Any common condition that might adversely affect development will therefore be of great importance. It may be that for each individual child the effect on development is small but for the population as a whole the effect may be significant.

For the clinician there are therefore several important issues:

1. How might iron deficiency affect behaviour?
2. What degree of iron deficiency affects behaviour?
3. Does iron therapy reverse any change in behaviour?
4. Are there any long-term effects on behaviour?
5. What are the implications for the clinician?

How Might Iron Deficiency Affect Behaviour?

The majority of the iron in the body is in haemoglobin. Iron is also important in various haem-containing enzymes in the mitochondria involved in oxidative metabolism (cytochromes, myoglobin, catalase, peroxidase) [1]. There are also iron-dependent enzymes involving non-haem iron such as flavoproteins and sulphur-containing proteins [1]. Iron acts as a cofactor for some enzymes important in the metabolism of catecholamines [1]. Within the brain, iron is present in highest concentration in the extrapyramidal regions (globus pallidus, substantia nigra, putamen, red nucleus, thalamus and caudate nucleus) [2].

Brain iron accumulates during childhood, being only 10% of adult levels at birth [3]. This low concentration of brain iron during infancy may explain why the brain of the young child is vulnerable to iron deficiency. In the experimental rat iron deficiency early in life (10 days old) leads to a permanent deficit in brain iron which persists despite iron supplementation [4]. The rat is most frequently used as a model for iron deficiency. Nutritionally iron-deficient rats have pathophysiological and haematological characteristics similar to those in humans [2].

The majority of recent research in this field has focussed on the effect of iron deficiency on the neurotransmitters dopamine, noradrenaline and serotonin. Dopamine is the major neurotransmitter of the extrapyramidal system. Pharmacological agents that alter dopaminergic activity also cause behavioural changes, e.g. D-amphetamine, apomorphine [2]. Early studies suggested that in iron deficiency there may be alteration in the enzymes involved in the metabolism of these neurotransmitters [5–8].

Monoamine oxidases (MAOs) are involved in the catabolism of catecholamines and their activity was found to be reduced in iron-deficient rats [5], and in platelets taken from iron-deficient humans [6]. Symes et al. [5] found MAO activity reduced to 60% of control levels in iron-deficient rats. Following iron supplementation the levels of MAOs quickly returned to normal.

Noradrenaline acts as a neurotransmitter at sympathetic nerve terminals and is metabolized by MAOs. If MAO activity is reduced an increased amount of noradrenaline is excreted in the urine. Voorhess et al. [7] demonstrated such an increase in iron-deficient children, and showed a quick response to iron with noradrenaline levels returning to normal. The levels of noradrenaline did not vary directly with haemoglobin, serum iron or the serum iron saturation. Children with anaemia due to other causes, e.g. thalassaemia, did not have elevated levels of noradrenaline, suggesting that iron deficiency per se rather than anaemia was responsible.

Another iron-dependent enzyme, aldehyde oxidase, may be reduced in the brains of iron-deficient rats [8]. This enzyme is involved in the degradation of serotonin which is therefore increased in the same tissue. Levels of the enzyme and serotonin return to normal with iron therapy. Youdim et al. [9,10] failed to confirm these findings and were not able to show any effect of iron deficiency on MAO, tyrosine, tryptophan hydroxylase or succinic dehydrogenase. Despite these findings iron-deficient rats exhibited behaviour suggestive of altered serotonin and dopamine activity, i.e. a decrease in motor activity and a decrease in stereotypic movements. The probable site of this alteration in dopaminergic activity is the dopamine D_2 receptor site [2]. In iron-deficient rats the D_2 binding sites estimated by [^{3}H]spiroperidol binding are decreased to about half of the control number. In the adult rat D_2 receptor sites are restored by iron therapy.

In the rat postnatal deposition of iron in the brain parallels the development of the D_2 receptor, reaching a maximum concentration at 4–5 weeks after birth [2]. This therefore coincides with the period of maximum growth, development and differentiation of the brain. Rats with a mean age of 10, 28 and 48 days made iron deficient all show a decrease in D_2 receptor sites and brain iron. The youngest rats were most susceptible to iron deficiency taking only 2 weeks to become iron deficient compared with 7 weeks for the older rats. Iron supplementation returned the D_2 receptors and brain iron to normal within 3 weeks in the rats aged 28 and 48 days. The youngest rats showed a continued deficit of brain iron and D_2 receptors despite iron supplementation. Of greatest interest to the clinician was the finding that these young rats also had a significant deficit in learning capacity as assessed by maze tests [2]. How these findings relate to those found in children is as yet unclear.

Studies with neurotoxins that selectively cause a lesion of dopaminergic neurons suggest that dopamine and possibly noradrenaline have important roles in learning and cognition [11]. Youdim and Ben-Shachar [2] have shown that the reduction in the numbers of D_2 receptors correlates negatively with the increase in errors and decreased learning of maze patterns.

Biochemical studies show, therefore, not only which neurotransmitter system is effected by iron deficiency but also a probable site for its action. The most important finding is that in the youngest rats the effects of iron deficiency, biochemical and behavioural, may be irreversible.

In the clinical situation infants aged between 6 and 24 months are the most vulnerable, and also most likely to become iron deficient.

What Degree of Iron Deficiency Affects Behaviour?

Iron Status

It is essential when assessing the relationship between iron deficiency and development to define the measurements used to quantify iron status. In addition to haemoglobin most authors measure serum ferritin, transferrin saturation, free erythrocyte protoporphyrin (FEP) and mean cell volume (MCV). A classification commonly used is shown in Table 8.1. Many studies involve only small numbers of infants, and subdividing the groups further by iron status leads to very small study groups from which conclusions must be carefully drawn. The standard for defining iron deficiency is the response to iron [12] in an infant free from infection and some studies use this in addition to the other measures.

Table 8.1.   Classification of iron status: taken from Oski et al. [23]

	Laboratory parameters				
	Ferritin (mg/l)	Saturation (%)	FEP (mg/dl)	MCV (fl)	HB (g/dl)
Iron-sufficient	$\geqslant 12$	$\geqslant 10$	$\leqslant 100$	$\geqslant 70$	$\geqslant 11$
Iron-depleted non-anaemic	< 12	$\geqslant 10$	$\leqslant 100$	$\geqslant 70$	$\geqslant 11$
Iron-deficient non-anaemic	< 12	< 10	< 100	$\geqslant 70$	$\geqslant 11$
Iron-deficient anaemic	< 12	< 10	< 100	< 70	< 11

Behavioural Tests

The majority of studies reviewed use the Bayley Scales of Infant Development
[13] which are designed to assess children aged 3–30 months. This test is well
standardized and widely used in the USA. It has three components: mental
scale, motor scale and infant behaviour record. The mental scale (Mental
Developmental Index – MDI) is designed to assess sensory-perceptual activities,
discriminations, and the ability to respond to these; the early acquisition of
"object constancy" and memory, learning and problem-solving ability; vocalizations and the beginnings of verbal communication. The motor scale (Psychomotor Developmental Index – PDI) provides a measure of gross and fine motor
coordination and motor skills. These two scales are scored with a norm of 100
and standard deviation of 16.

The Infant Behaviour Record (IBR) consists of 30 items assessing general
behaviour areas including affect, task orientation and motor coordination, also
modes of sensory interest and other miscellaneous measures (judgement of
adequacy of the test, evaluation of the child, assessment of play and object
attachment).

In the UK studies have used either the Denver Developmental Screening Test
[14] or the Sheridan Gardner Developmental Sequence [15]. Each assesses four
main areas of psychomotor development, but they do not include any behavioural assessment. The Denver Developmental Screening Test is suitable to be
administered by a non-psychologist, it has good test-retest reliability and has
been validated against the Bayley Scales.

Cognitive Function

There is now an increasing body of evidence that iron deficiency sufficient to
cause anaemia is associated with lower developmental test scores (Tables 8.2 and
8.3). In Guatemala, Lozoff et al. [16] assessed both mental (MDI) and motor
(PDI) skills in infants aged 6–24 months. Twenty-eight iron-deficient anaemic
infants (Hb $\leqslant$ 10.5 g/dl) were compared with 40 control infants (Hb > 12 g/dl).
The anaemic infants also had at least two other abnormal measures of iron status
(Table 8.1). The iron-deficient anaemic infants scored significantly less well on
both MDI and PDI (MDI 86 vs. 100 ($P < 0.0025$): PDI 86 vs. 94. ($P < 0.05$). In

this study many possible confounding variables were taken into account e.g. parental education, sex, birth weight and weight for length, but none had a significant effect on the overall results. In addition there was no evidence that those infants with mild malnutrition (weight less than 90% of ideal weight for length) had lower scores.

This study used a very wide age range, which is not ideal if using the Bayley scales, as at different ages differing abilities are being tested. This makes comparisons between the infants less reliable. Age-matched controls or a narrow age range would give a stronger study design.

Table 8.2. Association of iron-deficiency anaemia with "poorer" psychomotor development

Study	Main conclusions	Reservations about study design
Lozoff et al. [16]	Anaemic infants (Hb ≤ 10.5 g/dl) scored less well for both MDI & PDI	Wide age range used (6–24 months)
Walter et al. [17]	Anaemic infants (Hb 8.5–11 g/dl) scored less well for MDI only	Small numbers used (10 anaemic, 12 controls)
Grindulis et al. [18].	Anaemic infants (Hb < 11 g/dl) scored less well for fine motor and social skills	Investigation not specifically designed for this question therefore developmental test used, although blind, was not rigorous
Lozoff et al. [21]	Anaemic infants (Hb ≤ 10 g/dl) scored less well for MDI	Varying definition of anaemia
	Anaemic infants (Hb ≤ 10.5 g/dl) scored less well for PDI	(Hb ≤ 10 g/dl or Hb ≤ 10.5 g/dl)

Table 8.3. Association of iron deficiency, in the absence of anaemia, with developmental progress

Study	Main conclusions	Reservations about study design
Deinard et al. [22]	Iron-depleted infants did not score significantly lower than controls	Haematocrit used to define anaemia rather than haemoglobin
Oski et al. [23]	Iron-deficient infants did not score significantly lower than iron-depleted or iron-sufficient infants	Small numbers used (iron-deficient 18 : controls 20)
Lozoff et al. [21]	Iron-deficient infants did not score significantly lower than controls	

Similar observations have been made in two studies using a narrow age range. Walter et al. [17] in Chile studied infants aged 15 months. Ten iron-deficient anaemic infants had a MDI of 98 compared with 12 controls whose MDI was 108 (P 0.0025). No differences in PDI scores were found. Grindulis et al. [18] in the UK used the Sheridan Developmental Sequence to assess infants aged 21–23 months. Fifty-five iron-deficient anaemic infants had significantly lower scores for fine motor (20.6 vs. 21.5) and social (20.6 vs. 21.4) skills, than 79 non-anaemic controls ($P < 0.05$).

In contrast, a study of older children (18–60 months) failed to show any difference in developmental score between iron-deficient anaemic children and controls [19]. The three studies of children aged less than 24 months all show a strong association between iron-deficiency anaemia and poorer developmental progress. It must be noted that the infants had a mean score well within the normal range for the developmental tests.

The age at which an infant becomes anaemic appears to be important in determining the effect on development. This may well reflect the duration of the iron deficiency. Lozoff et al. [20] re-analysed their data by looking at developmental scores in three age groups, 6–12 months, 13–18 months and 19–24 months. Anaemic infants in each group scored lower than controls for motor scores, with no age effect. In contrast the MDI scores showed a significant decrease with age in the anaemic infants. Those anaemic infants aged over 18 months had a significantly lower MDI (73.4) than the younger infants. These infants were also significantly lighter (9.5 kg vs. 10.7 kg) and thinner (arm circumference 14.6 cm vs. 15.4 cm) than controls ($P < 0.05$) [20]. These older infants were generally less well nourished and had lived in an "underprivileged" environment for longer than the younger infants. Poorer developmental progress may be secondary to this underprivileged environment as well as to the iron deficiency.

The degree of iron deficiency was also important in determining the effect on development, i.e. iron-replete MDI 120.7, iron-depleted MDI 91.6, iron-deficient non-anaemic MDI 82 and iron-deficient anaemic MDI 73.4. No such relationship between PDI and degree of iron deficiency was found [20].

In an effort to define the exact level of iron deficiency that was important Lozoff et al. [21] completed a comprehensive community-based project involving 191 children in Costa Rica aged 12–23 months. Within this group 52 infants had iron-deficiency anaemia (Hb $\leq$ 10.5 g/dl) and 139 infants had Hb > 10.6 g/dl). Results of developmental tests were analysed in terms of actual haemoglobin concentration. In evaluating the MDI data in increments of 0.5 g/dl haemoglobin the score for infants with haemoglobin 10.2–10.5 g/dl were similar to those with haemoglobin $\geq$ 10.5 g/dl. Only infants with haemoglobin $\leq$ 10 g/dl had significantly lower MDI scores (96.6 vs. 104.6) ($P < 0.0002$). In evaluating the PDI in relation to haemoglobin those infants with haemoglobin 10.1–10.5 g/dl were not significantly different from those with haemoglobin < 10 g/dl. As a group infants with a haemoglobin of $\leq$ 10.5 g/dl had significantly lower PDI score (103 vs. 113) then those with a haemoglobin of > 10.5 g/dl ($P < 0.001$). This correlation between developmental score and degree of iron deficiency is what one would expect.

Analysis of the items failed by the anaemic children in both Guatemala [16] and Costa Rica [21] showed that they were the items thought to be predictive of IQ at 3 years. Items failed included showing shoes, putting a peg in a peg board, naming one object. These are all initial threshold items in important graded sequences of the Bayley Scales that require language comprehension, verbal expression and fine motor coordination. Although the anaemic infants failed more of these items the difference was not significant.

Further work has focussed on infants with iron deficiency in the absence of anaemia. Deinard et al. [22] studied infants aged 11–13 months with a haematocrit > 34% and did not show any difference in developmental score between those with low ferritin, intermediate ferritin or high ferritin. This study is limited by the use of haemotocrit rather than haemoglobin and by using only a single measure of iron status. Oski et al. [23] assessed infants aged 9–12 months with haemoglobin > 11 g/dl. Infants were defined as iron sufficient, iron depleted or iron deficient (Table 8.1). The iron-deficient infants had a mean MDI of 84.6 compared with 94.6 for the iron-depleted infants and 91 for the iron-sufficient controls. There were therefore no significant differences between these infants' developmental scores. Most recently Lozoff et al. [21] in their community-based study have shown that iron-deficient and iron-depleted non-anaemic infants did not score any lower than iron-replete controls. Hence there is no evidence that mild iron deficiency in the absence of anaemia (Hb > 11 g/dl) has a significant effect on developmental scores.

Non-cognitive Function

Deficits in cognitive function may have their origin in alteration of non-cognitive behaviour patterns. Anaemic infants are said to be "irritable" and to demonstrate a "lack of interest in their surroundings" [24]. These characteristics disappear within a few days of starting iron therapy. Walter et al. [17] found that the iron-deficient anaemic infants were more unhappy than control infants, but all other measures of behaviour were within the normal range. Deinard et al. (22) found infants with low ferritin to be more fearful, less visually and auditorily attentive, more vocal and less likely to mouth toys.

In Guatamala Lozoff et al. [25] assessed IBR and videoed part of each assessment. For 4 of the 16 items on the IBR scale the anaemic infants scored significantly differently from controls. They were more withdrawn and hesitant, fearful, tense and less reactive to visual stimuli. They also seemed to show a decrease in bodily activity and a lack of persistence but these differences were not statistically significant.

These data have been further analysed and a summary score for the IBR generated [26]. This score assesses affect and task orientation. A significantly greater number of anaemic infants have abnormal affective behaviour but showed no abnormality in task orientation. Abnormal affective behaviour was closely related to poor mental test scores in iron-deficient anaemic infants, in all age groups. The anaemic infants who scored low in affect scored only 66 for MDI compared with an MDI of 97 for those whose affective score was normal. A few infants with severe anaemia (Hb < 9 g/dl) showed pervasive behavioural disturbances and had low MDI and PDI scores.

This may suggest that abnormality in non-cognitive behaviour has a significant effect on the performance of cognitive tests. The severity of the iron deficiency appears to be of importance in determining the changes in general behaviour.

There is therefore agreement that iron deficiency sufficient to cause a haemoglobin of < 10.5 g/dl in the second year of life does significantly reduce developmental progress. Infants with haemoglobin 10.5–11 g/dl also show a significant but less marked reduction in developmental progress. Mild iron deficiency in the absence of anaemia (Hb > 11 g/dl) does not appear to alter developmental progress. The duration of the iron deficiency is also important in determining the effect on development.

Does Iron Therapy Reverse Any Changes in Behaviour?

Short-Term Effects on Cognitive Function (Table 8.4)

Oski and Honig's [27] original study on the effect of iron therapy on development assessed the response to intramuscular iron over 5–10 days. Twenty-four infants aged 9–24 months with iron-deficiency anaemia were allocated to receive iron or placebo. After 1 week the treated infants showed a significant increase in MDI of 14 points ($P < 0.01$), whereas the placebo group had only increased by 6 points. However the difference between the two test-retest scores (14 vs. 6) did not in itself reach statistical significance. Also no non-anaemic control group was included in the study. Despite this, the general impression was that iron therapy did improve developmental test scores.

Table 8.4. Immediate effects of iron therapy on development

Study	Main conclusions	Reservations about study design
Oski and Honig [27]	Anaemic infants: significant response to treatment with a 14 point increase in MDI	Test–retest scores not significantly different (anaemic + 14 : controls + 6) No placebo group
Lozoff et al. [16]	Anaemic infants: no greater response to treatment than placebo or control infants	Wide age range (6–24 months)
Walter et al. [17]	Anaemic infants: significant response to treatment with a 10 point increase in MDI	No placebo group. Small numbers used (anaemic 11, iron-deficient 15, controls 12)
	Iron-deficient non-anaemic infants: no greater response to treatment than controls	
Oski et al. [23]	Iron-deficient non-anaemic infants: significant response to treatment with a 22 point increase in MDI	No placebo group

Lozoff et al. [16] designed a study with these criticisms in mind. Twenty-eight iron-deficient anaemic infants were compared with 40 controls (age range 6–24 months). Within each group infants received oral iron or placebo. Developmental score did not significantly increase with treatment or placebo in either group after 6–8 days.

In contrast, Walter et al. [17] studied a group of infants aged 15 months, 10 with iron-deficiency anaemia and 12 iron-sufficient controls. All infants were treated with oral iron. The iron-deficient anaemic infants had a significant increase in MDI (98–108) whereas the iron-sufficient infants showed no change in score (113–112) ($P < 0.0025$). The difference in the test-retest scores between the two groups was significant. In the same study a group of infants with iron deficiency without anaemia were also treated. As a group they did not show a significant increase in score, but those with evidence of iron deficiency by two or more biochemical measures did show a significant increase in score (108–118). One other study of iron-deficient non-anaemic infants was completed by Oski et al. [23] in which the response to iron was compared in 18 iron-deficient non-anaemic infants, 10 iron-depleted infants and 10 iron-sufficient infants. The iron-deficient non-anaemic infants showed a 22 point increase in MDI compared with a 6 point increase for the other two groups ($P < 0.01$). A test-retest change in score of 10 points would be accepted as within the normal range. Fourteen of the 18 iron-deficient non-anaemic infants achieved more than a 10 point increase in score compared with only 4 of the 20 controls ($P < 0.01$).

These two studies therefore suggest that correction of iron deficiency, even in the absence of anaemia, does improve test performance. Neither study included a placebo group, so the response to iron needs to be accepted only with this in mind, and it may be that the iron-deficient child responds to retesting in a different way to non-iron-deficient children.

Most authors have used oral iron but Oski et al. used intramuscular iron [3, 27]. Over the short study periods intramuscular iron may be more bioavailable and this could explain the large change in score found by Oski [3,27]. In fact Lozoff et al. [21] have compared oral and intramuscular iron given over 1 week in the Costa Rica study. On retesting there was no difference in change of score whether having intramuscular iron, oral iron or placebo.

It is interesting to note than in Oski's study [23] there was no apparent difference between the groups before treatment, but following treatment the iron-deficient infants' scores increased significantly. It could be that the infants, whether iron-deficient or not, were underachieving before treatment, perhaps reflecting other (non-nutritional) aspects of environmental deprivation. Iron therapy corrected just one environmental factor. This response to iron therapy suggests that infants even with only mild iron deficiency will benefit. This means that many more children may need to be identified than those with just a haemoglobin less than 11 g/dl. This had implications for any programme to identify children who would benefit from iron therapy. Such a programme would have to include other indices of iron status, e.g. ferritin free erythrocyte protoporphyrin, mean cell volume.

Short-Term Effects on Non-cognitive Function

As mentioned before, these changes in cognitive function may have their origin in changes in non-cognitive behaviour. In Oski and Honig's [27] original study the Infant Behaviour Record (IBR) of the Bayley scale was assessed. The items reactivity, attention span, gross motor movements and fine motor coordination was analysed. Iron therapy led to a significant improvement in reactivity, gross muscle movement and fine motor coordination. Attention span did not show any real change with treatment. Although there were changes in this general behaviour they were not sufficient to explain the overall increase in developmental score. In contrast, Walter et al. [17] found that improvements in MDI coincided with improvements in IBR items of cooperativeness and attention span. Lozoff et al. [25] showed that following 1 week of iron therapy there was a significant improvement in responsiveness to the examiner and in body tension, but overall changes in IBR with iron were no greater than with placebo. This correlated with the small changes in MDI shown by this group in response to iron. Analysis of summary scores for affect and task orientation have shown a correlation between increase in affect score and MDI [26]. Honig and Oski [28] have reported that iron-deficient infants become less solemn following iron therapy. Those whose solemnity ratings improved increased their MDI score by 30 points. In this study there was no placebo group but in Lozoff's study even placebo-treated infants whose affect score improved showed an increase in MDI score [26].

These improvements in general behaviour may help to explain the brisk response in developmental score following iron therapy. It may be that the iron-deficient infants are more cautious at first testing than the controls. On retesting, these infants may be much more relaxed and therefore perform better. It is obviously difficult to separate the cognitive and non-cognitive changes.

Long-Term Effects of Treatment on Cognitive Function

If some of the immediate changes in development following iron therapy are due to changes in general behaviour, what is the response to a prolonged course of iron?

In Birmingham we completed a double-blind randomized intervention study to determine the effect on psychomotor development of oral iron given for 2 months [29]. Immigrant infants, mainly from the Indian subcontinent, aged 17–19 months with haemoglobin 8–11 g/dl were enrolled, 48 received oral iron and 49 placebo. All infants were born in Birmingham, 85% had parents who originated from the Indian subcontinent. The placebo used was vitamin C, and the iron preparation was combined with vitamin C. Psychomotor development was assessed using the Denver Developmental Screening Test. Overall there was only a weak relationship between the improvement in developmental score and the rise in haemoglobin ($P = 0.08$). Three distinct effects however were seen (Table 8.5). The average rate of development expected (six new skills) was achieved by 31% of the treated infants but by only 12% of the untreated infants ($P < 0.05$). This rate of development was achieved by 37% of those infants whose haemoglobin rose by at least 2 g/dl and by only 16% whose haemoglobin rose by less than 2 g/dl ($P < 0.05$). The average rate of development was achieved by 42% of the effectively treated infants and by only 13% of those who did not receive iron and whose haemoglobin did not rise by 2 g/dl ($P < 0.02$). It must be noted that 58% of the effectively treated infants failed to achieve the six new skills.

Somewhat similar trends were found by Lozoff et al. in Costa Rica examining the effects of 3 months of oral iron therapy [21]. On the basis of haematological response to iron therapy infants who became iron sufficient by the end of the study were distinguished from those who did not correct all evidence of iron deficiency. Only 26% of the moderately anaemic infants fulfilled these criteria. These infants no longer had significantly lower mental score, but this was due to a decline in mental scores in the control group and not to an increase in the study group. In this same group the motor scores did substantially increase by a mean of 10 points compared to controls that did not change.

Table 8.5. Birmingham intervention study (from Aukett et al. [29])

Method of trial analysis	Number of new skills achieved in 2 months[a]	
	Less than 6	6 or more
Empirical trial		
Treated	33	15 (31%)
Untreated	43	6 (12%) $P < 0.05$
Explanatory trial A		
Rise in Hb > 2 g/dl	17	10 (37%)
Rise in Hb < 2 g/dl	59	11 (16%) $P < 0.05$
Explanatory trial B		
Effectively treated[b]	14	10 (42%)
Not effectively treated[c]	41	6 (13%) $P < 0.02$

[a]Denver developmental test.
[b]Received iron and Hb rose by more than 2 g/dl.
[c]Did not receive iron and Hb did not rise by more than 2 g/dl.

These two studies are complementary and suggest that if iron-deficiency anaemia is effectively treated, then developmental test performance can be improved in a proportion of infants. More recently Walter et al. (see Chapter 7) have failed to demonstrate such a response in performance with 3 months of iron therapy in infants aged 12 months. It is unlikely that iron deficiency is the only culprit in the slower development of these children but it is at least easily identified and treated.

Are There Any Long-Term Effects on Behaviour?

There is now some evidence that iron deficiency may have irreversible effects. As mentioned earlier, studies in young rats (aged 10 days) have shown that a permanent deficit in brain iron and even dopamine D_2 receptors can result from iron deficiency [2]. These rats exhibit behavioural changes and decreased learning ability [2].

A follow-up study from Israel showed that those infants with low haemoglobins at 9 months had lower developmental and IQ scores up to 4 years later [30]. There appeared to be a trend in that for each 1 g/dl increment in haemoglobin there was a 1.75 point increase in IQ at age 5 years. These findings occurred even when the anaemia had been treated at time of diagnosis.

These findings of the long-term effects of iron deficiency although not fully documented, are of potentially great importance. To examine this area further it is necessary to look at the work on the effects of iron deficiency in older children.

Two studies by Pollit et al. [31,32] suggest that older children (3–6-year-olds) with iron deficiency perform less well in psychological testing than controls. In a study in the USA 15 iron-deficient children performed less well on the Standford-Binet Intelligence Scale and on measures of attention, conceptual learning and short-term recall than 15 normal controls [31]. The main area of difficulty appeared to be inattention to tasks rather than in conceptual learning. Following on from this a further study of more severely iron-deficient children was performed in Guatemala [32]. Twenty-five iron-deficient anaemic children were compared with 25 non-anaemic controls. All received iron for 11 to 12 weeks. Tests of discrimination learning and oddity learning were performed pre- and post-treatment. Before treatment the anaemic children performed significantly less well in both tests. The differences between the iron-deficient and control children were eliminated following treatment. This suggests that the effects of iron deficiency are not restricted to attention but may also involve higher cognitive processes such as conceptual learning.

Similar trends are also shown in older children. Soemantri et al. [33] in Java assessed school-age children (mean age 10.8 years). Seventy-eight children (Hb ≤ 11 g/dl) were compared with 41 iron-replete controls. Children in each group received either iron or placebo for 3 months. Before treatment the non-anaemic children had significantly higher achievement scores and their scores did not change with treatment. The iron-deficient children showed a significant increase in score with treatment, but their final scores were still lower than the non-anaemic controls. This latter finding is worrying, as the iron deficiency had been fully reversed by treatment. It may be that this reflects on the long-term effect of chronic iron deficiency, but it should be noted that there was no difference in IQ between the two groups.

In Egypt, Pollitt et al. (34) selected a group of 28 iron-deficient anaemic and 40 iron-replete children mean age 9.5 years. Children received either iron or placebo for 4 months. The efficiency of the non-anaemic children before treatment was significantly better than that of the iron-deficient children. Following treatment the iron-deficient children showed a significant rise in efficiency that did not occur in the placebo group. At the end of the study there were no significant differences between the groups, in contrast to those found by Soemantri et al.

It appears then that in both infants and older children the main area of deficit in iron deficiency is in attentional processes, but that there is also some evidence that cognitive processes may also be affected. In the young child this will present as poor developmental progress whereas in the older child it may present with poor school performance and possibly behaviour problems.

What Are the Implications for the Clinician?

Iron deficiency is common in both advantaged and disadvantaged populations [35]. Most research has focussed on disadvantaged populations, but even in more affluent populations 5%–10% of infants are anaemic. Most surveys employ only an estimation of haemoglobin which will obviously underestimate the incidence of iron deficiency. In large surveys iron-deficiency anaemia has been found in 5%–30% of children screened and iron deficiency in up to 55% of children [3,29,35–38].

Definitions of anaemia vary as can be seen from the studies reviewed earlier. First, the statistical definition (mean plus or minus 2 standard deviations) can be used, and this usually results in a cut-off haemoglobin of 11 g/dl [38, 39]. Alternatively, the positive response to a therapeutic trial of iron may be used (a rise in haemoglobin of ≥ 1 g/dl) [12]. Other authors use a cut-off haemoglobin concentration of 10.5 g/dl or even 10 g/dl [16,21,27]. A cut-off haemoglobin of 11 g/dl will pick up the majority of infants with iron deficiency of a degree that may be adversely affecting developmental progress.

There is now evidence that improved infant feeding practices will lead to a reduction in iron deficiency. Breast milk, although having only a low iron content (0.1–1.2 mg/l), provies sufficient iron for the infant under 6 months as bioavailability is high [40]. Once weaning begins then iron-fortified formula milk should be advised. Early introduction of whole cows' milk can lead to an increase in the incidence of iron deficiency [41,42]. Sadowitz and Oski [41] found in a group of 280 infants that 66 infants had whole cows' milk in the diet before the age of 6 months. Of these 66 infants 62% had evidence of iron deficiency compared with only 21% of those infants in whom introduction was delayed. In another study 68 infants were fed whole cows' milk from 6 months and 94 were fed infant formula [42]. At follow-up, when 1-year-old the infants fed on whole cows' milk had a higher incidence of anaemia (24% vs. 11%). There is therefore good evidence that mothers should be advised to withhold whole cows' milk until after the child's first birthday.

In America the WIC Program was initiated to improve the nutritional status of pregnant women, lactating women and children under 5 years who were at risk for nutritionally related health problems. Follow-up data have now been analysed to assess the contribution that this programme has made in limiting the occurrence of iron deficiency in young children [43]. Enrolment into this programme resulted in a significant decrease in iron deficiency throughout infancy. At age 18–23 months only 23% of infants in the programme were anaemic (haematocrit < 36%) compared with 43% of infants who were not in the programme.

In Israel supplementation between 3 and 12 months of age reduced the occurrence of anaemia [44]. Compliance was variable and those infants who received iron for 7–9 months had higher haemoglobin than those who had iron for only 1–3 months. The supplemented population had a mean haemoglobin 0.3 g/dl higher than that of non-supplemented infants. Anaemia (Hb < 11 g/dl) occurred in 38% of control infants and in only 18% of supplemented infants ($P < 0.01$). These iron supplements were given free of charge and a full discussion with the mothers about the supplementation was provided. Despite this, only 26% complied for the full period of 9 months. Although supplementation was effective, iron-fortified foods would probably be more readily accepted by parents.

The clinician is therefore able to approach the problem in two ways. First, improvement in the infant diet should lead to a reduction in iron deficiency within a population. Second, a screening programme to pick up iron-deficient anaemic toddlers could be attempted checking haemoglobin at about 15 months. Other indices of iron status could also be assessed. The anaemic infants would need iron therapy for at least 2–3 months and a re-check of iron status at completion.

Conclusions

Iron-deficiency anaemia remains a common nutritional disorder worldwide. It has adverse effects on behaviour both cognitive and non-cognitive. Within the central nervous system the dopaminergic pathways are involved, in particular the dopamine D_2 receptors. The very young experimental animal is particularly vulnerable to these biochemcal and behavioural effects, which may be irreversible.

In infants the degree and duration of iron deficiency are important in determining the final effect on developmental progress. A haemoglobin of less than 10.5 g/dl, in the second year of life, is definitely associated with lower developmental scores, which, in a proportion of cases, improve with iron therapy. Those infants with iron deficiency and a haemoglobin between 10.5 and 11 g/dl also have lower-than-average developmental scores and may respond to iron therapy.

There is debate as to whether changes in developmental test score following a week of iron therapy are due to real changes in cognitive function or, as is more likely, due to changes in performance. Over the longer term, effective treatment of iron-deficiency anaemia is associated with changes in cognitive function, but less than half the infants respond.

For the clinician the most worrying findings are those of long-term follow-up studies, where anaemic infants showed changes in behaviour up to 7 years after the anaemic episode.

The problem of iron deficiency can be tackled on two fronts.

1. *Health Education.* Infant feeding practices should be improved with advice to parents on withholding cows' milk until the age of 1 year. Adequately fortified infant formula should be available for the weanling as should other fortified foods. Parents should also receive advice of a balanced and iron-sufficient diet for the older infant.

2. *Screening.* A programme is needed first to estimate the prevalance of iron deficiency in the UK and then to hunt out and treat the iron deficient toddlers. This could become part of the routine child health programme. A haemoglobin check at 9 months, coinciding with a routine attendance at a child health clinic

could identify children with a haemoglobin less than 11 g/dl. These children should receive iron therapy for 3 months.

Iron deficiency is an important factor in the slower development of children living in underprivileged circumstances and it is one that can be easily identified and treated.

References

1. Dallman PR (1986) Biochemical basis for the manifestations of iron deficiency. Ann Rev Nutr 6:13–40
2. Youdim MBH, Ben-Shachar D (1987) Minimal brain damage induced by early iron deficiency: modified dopaminergic neurotransmission. Isr J Med Sci 23:19–25
3. Pollitt E, Leibel RL (1976) Iron deficiency and behavior. J Pediatr 88:372–381
4. Dallman PR, Siimes MA, Maines EC (1975) Brain iron: persistent deficiency following short-term iron deprivation in the young rat. Br J Haematol 31:209–215
5. Symes AL, Missala K, Sourkes TL (1971) Iron and riboflavin dependent metabolism of a monoamine in the rat in vivo. Science 174:153–155
6. Youdim MBH, Grahame-Smith DG, Woods HF (1975) Some properties of human platelet monoamine oxidase in iron deficient anaemia. Clin Sci Mol Med 50:479–485
7. Voorhess ML, Stuart MJ, Stockman JA, Oski FA (1975) Iron deficiency anaemia and increased urinary norepinephrine excretion. J Pediatr 86:542–547
8. Mackler B, Person R, Miller LR, Inamdar AR, Finch CA (1978) Iron deficiency in the rat: biochemical studies of brain metabolism. Pediatr Res 12:217–220
9. Youdim MBH, Green AR (1977) Biogenic monoamine metabolism and functional activity in iron deficient rats: behavioral correlates. In: Porter R, Fitzsimmons W (eds) Iron metabolism, Ciba Foundation Symposium 51. Elsevier North-Holland, Inc. New York, pp 201–226
10. Youdim MBH, Green AR, Bloomfield MR, Mitchel BD, Heal D, Grahame-Smith DG (1980) The effects of iron deficiency on brain biogenic monoamine biochemistry and function in rats. Neuropharmacology 19:259–267
11. Mason ST, Wood C, Angel A (1983) Brain noradrenaline and varieties of alteration learning. Brain Behav Res 9:119–127
12. Dallman PR, Reeves JD, Driggers DA, Lo EYT (1981) Diagnosis of iron deficiency: the limitations of laboratory tests in predicting response to iron treatment in 1-year-old infants. J Pediatr 98:376–381
13. Bayley N (1969) Bayley scales of infant development manual. Psychological Corporation, New York.
14. Frankenburg WK, Dodds JB, Fandal AW (1973) Denver developmental screening test: manual workbook for nursing and paramedical personnel. University of Colorado Medical Center, Colorado
15. Sheridan M (1978) Children's developmental progress. NFER, Windsor, pp 1–55
16. Lozoff B, Brittenham GM, Viteri FE, Wolf AW, Urrutia JJ (1982) The effects of short term oral iron therapy on developmental deficits in iron deficient anaemic infants. J Pediatr 100:351–357
17. Walter T, Kavalskys J, Stekel A (1983) Effect of mild iron deficiency on infant mental developmental scores. J Pediatr 102:519–522
18. Grindulis H, Scott PH, Belton NR, Wharton BA (1986) Combined deficiency of iron and vitamin D in Asian toddlers. Arch Dis Child 61:843–848
19. Deinard AS, List A, Lindgren B, Hunt JV, Chang P (1986) Cognitive deficits in iron deficient and iron deficient anaemic children. J Pediatr 108:681–689
20. Lozoff B, Brittenham GM, Viteri FE, Wolf AW, Urrutia JJ (1982) Developmental deficits in iron deficient infants: effects of age and severity of iron lack. J Pediatr 101:948–952
21. Lozoff B, Brittenham GM, Wolf AW, et al. (1987) Iron deficiency anaemia and iron therapy. Effects on infant developmental test performance. Pediatrics 79:981–995

22. Deinard A, Gilbert A, Dodds M, Egeland B (1981) Iron deficiency and behavioral deficits. Pediatrics 68:828–832
23. Oski FA, Honig AS, Helu B, Howanitz P (1983) Effect of iron therapy on behaviour performance in nonanaemic, iron deficient infants. Pediatrics 71:877–880
24. Oski FA (1979) The non haematologic manifestations of iron deficiency. Am J Dis Child 133:315–322
25. Lozoff B, Brittenham G, Viteri FE, Urrutia JJ (1982) Behavioral abnormalities in infants with iron deficiency anaemia. In: Pollitt E, Leibel RL (eds) Iron deficiency: brain biochemistry and behavior. Raven Press, New York, pp 183–194
26. Lozoff B, Wolf AW, Urrutia JJ, Viteri FE (1985) Abnormal behavior and low developmental test scores in iron deficient anaemic infants. J Dev Behav Pediatr 6:69–75
27. Oski FA, Honig AS (1978) The effects of therapy on the developmental scores of iron deficient infants. J Pediatr 92:21–25
28. Honig AS, Oski FA (1984) Solemnity: a clinical risk index for iron deficient infants. Early Child Dev Care 16:69–84
29. Aukett MA, Parks YA, Scott PH, Wharton BA (1986) Treatment with iron increases weight gain and psychomotor development. Arch Dis Child 61:849–857
30. Palti H, Pevsner B, Adler B, (1983) Does anaemia in infancy affect achievement on developmental and intelligence tests? Hum Biol 55:189–194
31. Pollitt E, Leibel RL, Greenfield DB (1983) Iron deficiency and cognitive test performance in pre-school children. Nutr Behav 1:137–146
32. Pollitt E, Saco-Pollitt C, Leibel RL, Viteri FE (1986) Iron deficiency and behavioral development in infants and pre-school children. Am J Clin Nutr 43:555–565
33. Soemantri AG, Pollitt E, Kim I (1985) Iron deficiency anaemia and educational achievement. Am J Clin Nutr 42:1221–1228
34. Pollitt E, Soemantri AG, Yunis F, Scrimshaw NS (1985) Cognitive effects of iron deficiency anaemia. Lancet i:158
35. Oski FA (1985) Iron deficiency–facts and fallacies. Pediatr Clin North Am 32:493–497
36. World Health Organisation (1975) Control of nutritional anaemia with special reference to iron deficiency. WHO Tech Rep Serv No 580
37. Ehrhardt P (1986) Iron deficiency in young Bradford children from different ethnic groups. Br Med J 292:90–93
38. World Health Organisation (1972) Nutritional anaemia. WHO Tech Rep Serv No 503
39. Dallman PR, Siimes MA (1979) Percentile curves for hemoglobin and red cell volume in infancy and childhood. J Pediatr 94:26–31
40. Saarinen UM, Siimes MA, Dallman PR (1977) Iron absorption in infants: high bioavailability of breast milk iron as indicated by the extrinsic tag method of iron absorption and by the concentration of serum ferritin. J Pediatr 91: 36–41
41. Sadowitz PD, Oski F (1983) Iron status and infant feeding practices in an urban ambulatory center. Pediatrics 72:33–36
42. Tunnessen WW, Oski FA (1987) Consequences of starting whole cow milk at 6 months of age. J Pediatr 111:813–816
43. Miller V, Swaney S, Deinard A (1985) Impact of the WIC Program on the iron status of infants. Pediatrics 75:100–105
44. Palti H, Adler B, Hurvitz J, Tamir D, Freier S (1987) Use of iron supplements in infancy: a field trial. Bull WHO 65:87–94

Commentary

Lozoff and Felt: This chapter makes some very helpful observations and distinctions. For example, reminding us that the relationship between cognitive deficit and abnormal behavior can go in both directions is especially timely. The example the authors give is a telling one: "a child with a cognitive deficit may become frustrated and exhibit abnormal behavior patterns or, on the other hand, poor concentration may lead to poor learning". The possibility that the direction of effects may go both ways probably cannot be emphasized enough. Of similar utility is the comment that the magnitude of adverse developmental effects may be small for an individual child but, if found in an entire population, could have major clinical significance. The paper is also important in its emphasis on the need not only for prevention but also for systematic screening. Some countries excel in one component but not the other and the need for both should probably be emphasized.

Parks and Wharton are thoughtful in pointing out the limitations of a number of the infant studies that have already been published. Perhaps because of the care with which the studies' limitations are described, it is surprising that the studies' conclusions are sometimes accepted so uncritically. For instance, the statement that anemic infants who are over 18 months of age may be at particular risk for lower developmental test scores is based on our own Guatemalan data [1], a result which has not been investigated by other workers and which was not replicated in our second study, in Costa Rica [2]. One also might question the conclusion that iron therapy improves developmental test scores, when the majority of infants in all studies to date failed to show such improvement.

Several other specific questions and comments will simply be listed.

Our use of a wide age range in infant studies is seen as a limitation by Parks and Wharton. We would submit that a wide age range is either a liability or essential, depending on the purpose of the study. If one goal of a study is to see if different ages are affected differently by iron deficiency, then including infants who vary in age is a must.

In the Birmingham study we have been curious about the choice of 2 g/dl as the criterion for a significant hematologic response to iron. Although admittedly arbitrary, hematologic studies have often used 1 g/dl as the criterion for therapeutic response [3].

The studies of older children are not critically reviewed by others in this symposium. It might be unwise to include them, unless they are to be questioned with the same thoroughness that the infant studies are.

References

1. Lozoff B, Brittenham GM, Viteri FE, Wolf AW, Urrutia JJ (1982) Developmental deficits in iron-deficient infants: effects of age and severity of lack. J Pediatr 101:948–952
2. Lozoff B, Brittenham GM, Wolf AW et al. (1987) Iron deficiency anemia and iron therapy: effects on infant developmental test performance. Pediatrics 79:981–995
3. Reeves JD, Driggers DA, Lo EYT, Dallman PR (1981) Screening for iron deficiency anemia in one-year-old infants: hemoglobin alone or hemoglobin and mean corpuscular volume as predictors of response to iron treatment. J Pediatr 98:894–898

Author's reply: See my reply to Walter (Commentary, Chapter 7).

Walter: The Hb cut-off of 11 g/dl is used up to the age of 6 years. A more appropriate range could have been used with what we now know of normal hemoglobins in childhood. Yip offers a nice exercise in this book.

At this time this is the only study to involve a long-term placebo group. Currently, ethical constraints would preclude such protocol. As a matter of fact, this withholding of therapy for 2 months stands on weak ground when other investigators are having a hard time obtaining consent from their institutions to hold off therapy for 7 to 10 days!.

Author's reply: I agree that in older children a cut-off Hb of 11 g/dl is not ideal. Regarding ethical permission: these infants would have gone undetected if we had not performed the study and therefore it was deemed acceptable by an ethical committee.

Walter: To use response to therapy as the indication of iron-deficiency anaemia is a strength in this design. However the use of 2 g/dl is unorthodox and not explained. Only the most severely anaemic could have sustained such a rise in such a short trial with an average dose of less than 3 mg/kg per day of iron. Moreover compliance is a concern when even after "chasing" more than 15% of the study infants eventually did not return for follow-up.

Author's reply: The rise of 2 g/dl in haemoglobin was what we expected after 2 months on regular iron, if the treatment was taken regularly. It also takes into account the test-retest variability of the Hb estimation. The loss of 13 infants (12%) reflects the high mobility of the urban population studied. Others lost may have failed to understand the full details as much of the work was done via an interpreter.

Walter: Many comments can be made regarding the use of the Denver Developmental scale. Why was the 50th percentile pass rate used? Is 18 to 20 months a "narrow" age range when testing development at this age? What was the impact of the one month difference in age at the outset? In which areas of the DDST did the infants tend to fail? Was there a pattern? Did severity of anaemia have an effect on DDST achievement? This is indirectly answered if we assume that only the most severely anaemic were able to raise their haemoglobins by 2 g/dl.

Author's reply: The average performance of the DDST was taken as it represented the developmental level of a "normal" population. There was no effect of age at outset on the developmental score. There was no pattern to the "failures" in the DDST, but in both groups the maximum increase in score was in language. We did not document a direct relationship between severity of anaemia and DDST score.

Smart: It seems to me a point of some importance to consider how a child comes to be iron-deficiency anaemic. Is it constitutional, through disease or as a result of dietary deficiency, which might occur through inadequate intake or low bioavailability. If low intake is the culprit, then it seems to me quite likely that the child will be deficient in other nutrients as well. Hence the possibility should be entertained in non-supplementation studies that effects apparently due to iron deficiency might owe something to other deficiencies, including general under-nutrition, as well. I think that I would go further than the authors' statement that "The standard for defining iron deficiency is the response to iron" to say that the standard for attributing short-term behavioural effects to iron deficiency is the response to iron.

Author's reply: During the first year the infant relies mostly on the iron stores available at birth. These obviously can be affected by events during the antenatal and perinatal periods. During infancy weight gain trebles but less iron is accumulated i.e. the iron/body mass ratio falls [1]. Iron deficiency can occur in otherwise well, rapidly growing children. Children living in the same environment may consume very different diets with differences in the amount of meat eaten and the mixtures of vegetables eaten. Bioavailability of iron is greatly enhanced by presence of vitamin C in a meal.

Reference

1. Wharton BA (1989) Iron nutrition in childhood: the interplay of genes, development and environment. Acta Paed Scand [Suppl] (in press)

Smart: The authors conclude that long-term treatment of iron deficiency " . . . is associated with *real* changes in cognitive function", but that improvements in developmental scores resulting from short-term therapy are " . . . more likely due to changes in *performance*" (my italics in each case). It seems to me that both could be due to changes in performance. The problem of how far performance, which is what we measure, reflects cognitive ability, which is a quality intrinsic to the subject, is an extremely difficult one and one that behavioural scientists working with laboratory animals have long been aware of. One approach is to measure level of performance in different ways in a variety of circumstances and, if these measures are highly correlated, they are probably a fair reflection of ability. Another attitude is to say that performance is what the subject actually does and that is what matters to him or her, so why agonize whether or not it reflects real cognitive ability.

Yehuda: "Iron Status"; a note should be made here that the major factor is the level of iron in the *tissues,* particularly in the brain. Depletion of brain iron may occur after a depletion of iron in the liver, which is the site of the body's iron storage. While haematological variables are used to examine iron status, Youdim and I found that rats whose haemoglobin levels are not reduced may behave like iron-deficient rats, due to a reduction in the brain iron level [1]. Very recently, we observed (unpublished data) a case in which the haemoglobin level was very significantly reduced, while the animal behaved normally, due to sufficiently high levels of iron in the tissues. We have been told that such conditions may occur in children. A word of caution should be inserted here, therefore, to the effect that one should not rely solely on haematological variables.

Author's reply: A very important point. Infants with thalassaemia and sickle cell disease who are anaemic but not iron-deficient do not show any developmental abnormality.

Dallman: As mentioned later in the paper, the biochemical mechanisms for behavioral changes in children are really not known. The animal data simply suggest a few of the factors that may eventually prove to be important.

The long-term changes in behavior seem to suggest that prevention deserves more attention than detection and treatment. In view of the findings of more severe manifestations with greater duration of deficiency, might not 9 or 12 months of age be a better time than 15 months for a hemoglobin check?

Yip: The statement on the low concentration of brain iron during infancy may explain why the brain of younger children is vulnerable to iron deficiency, and suggests that a certain level of brain iron is needed to be non-iron-deficient. Are animal studies able to provide evidence of a critical brain iron level?

Parks and Wharton say that the cut-off hemoglobin of 11 g/dl will pick up the majority of infants with iron deficiency. The experience in the US is that this cut-off will pick up less than half of the children with iron deficiency as defined by low serum ferritin, low transferrin saturation, and elevated erythrocyte pro-toporphyrin.

Author's reply: (1) There is no evidence so far for a "critical" level of brain iron. (2) We do not yet have data on a population basis in the UK. When we have these we will be able to determine more accurately the appropriate tests to use.

Chapter 9

Prevention of Iron-Deficiency Anemia: Iron Fortification of Infant Foods

Howard A. Pearson

Fortification is defined as the addition of a nutrient to a food in excess of that which is naturally present. When the natural diet of a defined population does not contain sufficient amounts of the nutrient to prevent deficiency; and studies of that population corroborate a significant prevalence of deficiency, fortification may be indicated. Whenever possible, the food vehicle selected for fortification should be consumed almost exclusively by the population at risk for deficiency. However, fortification should not be harmful, but if there are detrimental effects, these should not be serious nor should they affect very many persons in the target population.

The fortification with iron of infant cereals and milk formulas over the past 25 years has very closely conformed to these objectives. The case for routine iron fortification of foods, primarily consumed by older populations, is somewhat less compelling.

Iron Requirements of Infancy

The iron requirements of the infant can be summarized succinctly. The term infant is born with a body iron content of approximately 75 mg/kg. Most of this (about three quarters) is represented by hemoglobin iron contained in the circulating red blood cells. The red cell volume of the newborn is proportionately high, reflecting the erythropoietic response to the low levels of oxygen that obtain in utero. At the moment of birth, if all goes well, the PaO_2 (partial pressure of arterial oxygen) of the newborn rapidly rises from about 45 mm Hg (6 kPa) (torr) to 95 mm Hg (12.7 kPa). The hypoxic drive to erythropoiesis is abruptly shut off and red cell synthesis ceases. For the next 2 months, there is a linear decrease in the hemoglobin level that is designated the "physiological anemia" of infancy.

As the hemoglobin falls from an average of 16.5 g/dl to 11.0 g/dl, iron from the catabolized hemoglobin accumulates in the reticuloendothelial stores. This is reflected by a sharp increase in the level of serum ferritin in the first months of life. Levels of serum ferritin correlate well with body iron stores [1].

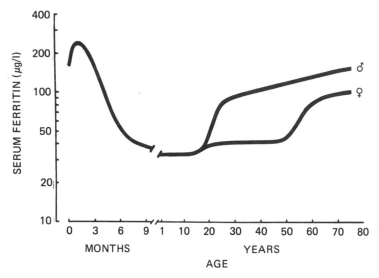

Fig. 9.1.   Mean serum ferritin values through life. (From Worwood [1]).

When physiological anemia reaches its nadir at 6–8 weeks of age, red cell synthesis again resumes. The movement of iron into the stores is reversed. Storage iron is utilized for hemoglobin synthesis for the increasing red cell mass of the rapidly growing infant. This utilization of iron stores is mirrored by a fall of the level of serum ferritin (Fig 9.1).

At about 6 months of age when the transplacental iron endowment is exhausted, the infant becomes dependent on dietary iron for maintenance of normal erythropoiesis. If insufficient iron is absorbed from the diet during the second 6 months of life, iron depletion and ultimately iron deficiency will inevitably ensue reflected in a drop of serum ferritin level below 10 µg/l. During the first year of life, because of the rapid rate of growth, "iron requirements in proportion to iron intake exceed those of any other period of life" [2]. The premature or small birth weight infant has an iron requirement that is greater and begins earlier than that of the term infant.

Iron requirement has three components. First, the amount of iron that must be absorbed from the diet to balance a small, but finite, iron loss. This occurs chiefly through desquamation of epithelial cells from the gastrointestinal tract and skin. Iron loss has been estimated at about 0.03 mg/kg per day [3]. This is probably a high value. No more recent experimental data are available, but by extrapolation to more secure studies in adults, and correcting on the basis of body surface area, a figure of 0.02 mg/kg per day may be more appropriate.

The second component of daily requirements during infancy is imposed by growth. During the first year of life the total red cell and hemoglobin mass approximately triples and 3.4 mg of iron is utilized for every gram of hemoglobin synthesized. To these requirements additional iron is necessary to assure maintenance of iron stores. This is estimated at 0.2–0.5 mg/day. These also increase linearly with growth.

Table 9.1. Estimated requirement (mg/day) of iron absorption from the diet

Age	0–6 months	6–12 months	12–24 months
Growth	0.25	0.53	0.29
Losses	0.2	0.2	0.4
Stores	–	0.2	0.1
Total			
	0.45	0.93	0.79

Table 9.1 depicts the estimated daily requirements for iron as calculated by Stekel [4]. Based on weight gain in normal term infants, similar calculations and conclusions were made by Shulman [5]. It can be estimated that a total of 150 mg of iron must be absorbed during the first year of life to maintain normal iron balance and hemoglobin synthesis.

Studies by Sturgeon showed that daily administration of 1.0 mg/kg of iron was associated with higher hemoglobin levels than lesser amounts of supplemental iron [6].

Content of Iron in Infant Food

For much of the first year of life, the usual food of the infant is milk, either human or cow. Cook and Bothwell have presented a useful description of the overlapping periods of dietary iron related to feeding practices, at least in the USA [7]. For the initial 3 months the infant's diet consists chiefly of milk. At about 3 months of age, cereals are usually added. After 6 months of age, mixed foods, eggs and meat are gradually introduced.

Human Milk

After the first few days of lactation human milk contains 0.2–0.4 mg/l of iron [8,9]. This iron content is usually believed to be virtually independent of the maternal iron status [10, 11].

High bioavailability of iron in breast milk has been demonstrated. Isotopic and balance studies as well as derived values from calculations based upon serial serum ferritin determinations indicate a 40%–50% absorption of the iron of breast milk [12]. By utilizing the transplacental iron endowment and the iron absorbed from the diet, the breast-fed infant is able to maintain iron sufficiency for about 6 months.

Cows' Milk: Non-fortified Infant Formulas

Although the iron content of unfortified cows' milk is comparable to that of human milk, only about 10% of the 0.2–0.4 mg/l of unfortified cows' milk is absorbed [13]. A diet consisting predominantly of milk will not, by any measure, meet the dietary requirements for iron during infancy.

In addition, there is evidence that consumption of whole cows' milk, particularly in large amounts, is often associated with gastrointestinal blood loss that can further compromise the precarious iron status of infancy [14].

Prevalence of Iron Deficiency Anemia in Infants

On a global scale, iron lack is the most common single nutrient deficiency of humans. This is usually a consequence of inadequate dietary intake. Poor absorption is occasionally operative. In some areas of the world blood is lost as a consequence of intestinal parasites, especially hookworm infestation.

Regardless of the criteria used for the diagnosis of iron-deficiency anemia of infancy, its prevalence in Third World countries in Asia and Latin America is high and has been estimated between 20% and 70% [15].

In the USA in the 1970s, the NHANES II (Second National Health and Nutrition Examination Survey) study indicated that the prevalence of probable infantile iron deficiency was 7%. It was higher in blacks than in other ethnic groups [16]. It has long been acknowledged that iron deficiency is more frequent in children from low socio-economic backgrounds. However, in the early 1970s, even children seen in private pediatric practice were shown to have a prevalence of iron-deficiency anemia of 5% [17].

Fortification of Cows' Milk Formulas

Iron deficiency is common in infancy. The major food of the infant during the first 6 months of life is milk. These two facts not surprisingly have led to attempts to improve iron nutrition by fortification of cows' milk formulas. The spectacular success of fortification of milk with vitamin D that led to the virtual eradication of rickets in the USA during the 1930s doubtless served as a model and goal for iron fortification of milk.

In the late 1940s a trial of fortification of a cows' milk formula was conducted by adding ferrous sulfate to dry powdered infant formulas in an amount of 12 mg per reconstituted quart (1.13 liter) to assess its acceptability and lack of side effects [18], and iron fortified liquid formulas were introduced.

Through the middle of the 20th century, most infant formula preparations utilized evaporated cows' milk, water and carbohydrates. The evaporated milk industry rejected iron fortification for commercial reasons. The major consumer use of evaporated milk at the time was not for infant feeding but for adding to coffee. Iron-fortified evaporated milk when added to coffee imparted an unappetizing green color.

Studies in the USA and elsewhere have demonstrated higher hemoglobin performances in term infants who received iron-fortified compared to those receiving non-iron-fortified cows' milk formulas [19–21]. It has also been demonstrated that the iron needs of the premature infant can be met with iron-fortified formulas [22].

In Europe most formulas are supplemented using 6 mg/liter. This amount appears to be effective in preventing iron deficiency probably because of increased absorption of the lesser amount of iron.

Fortification of Cereal Preparations

Iron-fortified infant cereals are an additional or alternative vehicle for meeting the iron requirements of infancy. In the USA infant cereals were initially fortified with iron salts, notably iron pyrophosphate, a form that has extremely low bioavailability [23]. Poor absorption has been suggested as the reason that the use of infant cereals appeared to have little effect on reducing iron deficiency in the 1950s and 60s [3].

The iron compound currently favored for fortification of infant cereals is designated small-particle electrolytic iron with particles that are less than 45 μm in diameter. This form has reasonable bioavailability and when included in the infant's diet can be shown to prevent iron deficiency [24].

Industry attention to issues of bioavailability of iron has been reflected in an increased use of a highly bioavailable form of iron for fortification of infant foods between 1972 and 1982 [25].

Epidemiological Effects of Iron Fortification of Infant Food in the US

Beneficial effects of iron-fortified formulas and cereal have also been suggested by epidemiologic observations that have demonstrated a marked reduction in the prevalence of iron deficiency in high-risk infant populations. In 1972 the US Department of Agriculture implemented a special food program for women, infants and children that was given the acronym WIC. WIC provided supplemental food for low income pregnant women, and for their infants and children. Because of the acknowledged high prevalence of iron deficiency in infants from low socio-economic families, iron-fortified milk formulas as well as iron-fortified cereals were given as standard infant food supplements.

Studies of socio-economically and ethnically comparable groups of children before and after the introduction of the WIC program indicate that it has had a markedly beneficial effect on iron nutrition. In 1971, before implementation of the WIC program in New Haven, CT, moderate and severe anemia (< 9.8 g/dl) was present in 23% of 9–36 months old black and Hispanic children from an inner city, economically deprived community [26]. Study of a comparable group of children from the same community in 1984 showed a significantly higher mean hemoglobin and a virtual elimination of significant anemia. Only 1% of the 1984 cohort had hemoglobin levels < 9.8 g/dl [27]. (See Fig. 9.2.)

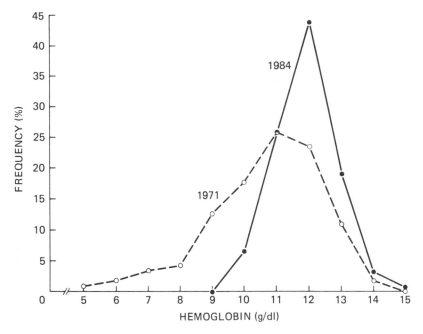

Fig. 9.2. Distribution of hemoglobin values in 258 infants in 1971 and 324 infants in 1984. All subjects were studied between 9 and 36 months of age. (From Vasquez-Seoane [27]).

Although this was not a controlled study, the striking improvement in iron nutrition was considered to be, at least in part, a result of the introduction of the iron nutritional prophylaxis directed at the high-risk infant population by the WIC program. Similar results and conclusions have been described from other American cities and from the country at large [28]. (See Chapter 2.)

There have been few studies of prophylaxis on iron-deficiency anemia in underdeveloped countries. Stekel utilized an acidified iron-fortified cow's milk preparation for Chilean infants and showed improvement of iron nutrition and hematologic performance [4]*.

Possible Adverse Effects of Iron Fortification of Infant Foods

There are two theoretical ways that iron fortification of food could be detrimental. First, long-term absorption of increased amounts of iron could lead to parenchymal deposition of increased amounts of iron and this could ultimately

---

*This was done in part because acidic milk is sour. Thus it was less likely to be consumed by older members of the family, ensuring its use by the infant.

cause tissue damage (hemosiderosis). It is very unlikely that the relatively small amounts of iron that are used in ordinary food fortification could result in enough absorption of iron to produce tissue damage in normal individuals. There are, however, a few situations where iron absorption is considerably increased and iron-induced tissue damage might be accelerated by food fortification.

The first of these is hereditary hemochromatosis, a relatively rare inherited disease characterized by markedly increased iron absorption. It has a frequency estimated between 1:1000 and 1:5000 in the American population [30]. However, there is considerable ethnic variability in gene frequency. Males with hemochromatosis develop symptoms of parenchymal iron damage (bronze diabetes) in middle age. Females develop it later. Hallberg [29] believes that it is doubtful that the number of hemochromatosis homozygotes who would develop overt disease would be increased by "moderate" iron fortification of food. It is very unlikely that the use of infant cereals and milk foods for less than 1–2 years would have an appreciable effect on the total lifelong iron burden of the patient with hemochromatosis.

Heterozygotes for the hemochromatosis gene are much more common than homozygotes. However, the hemochromatosis heterozygote has minimally increased iron absorption and does not develop increased iron stores [30, 31].

Severe congenital hemolytic anemias are also associated with increased absorption of dietary iron. When the treatment of hemolytic anemia requires regular blood transfusions, exemplified by thalassemia major, the amount of transfusional iron delivered to the tissue is large, each 200 ml of red cells (RBCs) contains more than 200 mg of iron. In this situation, the contribution of dietary iron to body iron burden is relatively small. Iron absorption is also affected by the level of hemoglobin and degree of marrow erythroid activity. Modern transfusion programs for thalassemia major (hypertransfusion) are designed to maintain a near normal level of hemoglobin (> 9.0 g/dl). At this level, iron absorption is not greatly increased in thalassemia patients maintained on hypertransfusion [32].

A subset of patients with homozygous ß thalassemia does not require regular transfusions (thalassemia intermedia). Their hemoglobin levels average 6.5–9.0 g/dl and this is maintained by intense erythropoeitic activity. Patients often develop hemosiderosis in adult life owing to increased absorption of dietary iron and may require chelation therapy [33]. Such patients have been advised to take tea with their meals to reduce iron absorption [34].

Patients with sickle cell anemia also absorb increased amounts of iron. However, increased body iron stores as reflected in increased levels of serum ferritin are only seen in patients who have been transfused [35].

From a practical point of view, it should be stressed that when hemosiderosis develops in non-transfused patients with chronic anemia, it can almost always be attributed to non-indicated, injudicious long-term administration of medicinal iron rather than dietary iron.

Iron and Host Resistance

Iron is essential for growth and the replication of a variety of microorganisms. In order to obtain the element from their surrounding medium many iron-trapping systems involving organisms have evolved siderophores. These are phenolates or hydroymates that have the capacity to act as chelating agents that are nearly specific for iron [36]. The concentrations of iron in various biological fluids (plasma, milk, gastrointestinal secretions) far exceed the minimal requirements for bacterial growth. However, specific iron-binding proteins such as transferrin, lactoferrin and gastroferrin are also present in these fluids. The binding of iron to these proteins is so tight that the actual concentration of free iron is very small.

A body of experimental evidence shows that low levels of available iron inhibit the growth of microorganisms. Sera from a variety of mammals are bacteriostatic and much of this appears to be a consequence of unsaturated transferrin. Bacteriostasis can be reversed by the addition of iron to the serum. This phenomenon in vitro is largely the basis for the theory of "nutritional immunity" [37] which holds that the unavailability of iron in body fluids due to the presence of iron-binding proteins is an important defense mechanism against microbiological invaders.

There is some evidence that the extreme hyperferremia and reticuloendothelial blockade associated with parenteral administration of iron-dextran may predispose to serious bacterial infections. Barry and Reeve described a probable cause/effect association betwen iron-dextran administration to premature infants and gram-negative neonatal sepsis [38].

Confirmation of any causal association of bacterial infections and ordinary oral doses of medicinal iron or consumption of iron-fortified food is non-existent. In fact, several, albeit poorly controlled, studies suggest the contrary [19,39,40].

Only small increases in serum iron levels are expected in infants receiving iron-fortified formulas and cereals. Mellhorn and Gross measured serial levels of serum iron in four groups of premature infants between 1 and 16 weeks of age [41]. Ten to 20 mg of elemental iron (ferrous sulfate) were given to two groups of infants, beginning at 2–4 weeks of age. Serum iron levels did not differ significantly before 6 weeks of age whether iron was given or not. After 6 weeks of age, significantly higher serum iron levels were found in the groups receiving iron medication, but no level was considered "high", nor were transferrin saturations markedly increased.

In the past 10 years, the use of iron-fortified formulas has progressively increased so that now they constitute more than 50% of the cows' milk formulas employed in the USA. One would have anticipated that such as increased usage would have resulted in evidence of infections if there were a detrimental effect.

A non-infective, clearly pathological effect of iron supplementation infant feeding has been described. In the early 1970s a new hemolytic syndrome was increasingly recognized in the premature nurseries of America. Otherwise thriving infants developed a hemolytic syndrome at 4–8 weeks of age, characterized by lower than expected hemoglobin levels and reticulocytosis. Its other features included pretibial edema, thrombocytosis and poikilocytic red cell morphology. The prevalence of the syndrome varied markedly among various American institutions suggesting that local differences in management might be involved.

Ultimately this hemolytic syndrome was shown to be a consequence of interactions between three factors: vitamin E, iron, and polyunsaturated fatty acids (PUFA). The pathogenesis of the syndrome was elucidated as follows [42]. When the diet of the premature infant contains a high proportion of PUFA, the RBC membrane lipid component also assumes a high proportion of PUFA that makes it susceptible to oxidant damage. Oxidant damage of the abnormal RBC membrane lipid can be prevented by vitamin E. In the face of the relatively low levels of vitamin E which are characteristic of the premature infant, the membrane lipid can be damaged by ionic iron. In the absence of iron-induced oxidation, significant hemolysis does not occur despite the abnormal membrane.

The various cows' milk formulas of the 1970s differed considerably in their fatty acid composition. Some brands had relatively high PUFA in relationship to vitamin E (PUFA/E ratio). Significant hemolysis was almost totally restricted to iron-fortified formulas having high PUFA/E. The same formulas without iron fortification were not associated with hemolysis. Other formulas with lower PUFA/E, whether iron fortified or not, were not associated with hemolysis. Almost as soon as these relationships were defined, changes in formulations were made that lowered PUFA and increased vitamin E content.

None of the presently marketed American commercial formulas cause this hemolytic syndrome. Most neonatologists, however, do not begin iron supplementation until 4–6 weeks of postnatal age in very small premature infants.

Summary and Conclusions

The diet of the infant usually contains insufficient iron to meet the relatively high requirements imposed by active growth during the first 1–2 years of life.

Iron deficiency and iron-deficiency anemia are common in infants in both Third World and developed countries.

Iron fortification of infant foods and cereals provides sufficient iron to prevent most instances of iron-deficiency anemia of infancy. Small scale and very large studies have proved its effectiveness.

Although iron fortification of infant foods might theoretically be detrimental in states associated with increased iron absorption, it is unlikely that they would significantly accelerate tissue iron overload and damage because of the short time that they are used. Iron-induced hemolysis of infancy can be prevented by increasing the vitamin E content and decreasing the PUFA content of cows' milk formulas.

References

1. Worwood M (1982) Ferritin in human tissues and serum. Clin Haematol 28:27–50
2. Committee on Iron Deficiency Council on Foods and Nutrition. AMA (1968) Iron deficiency in the United States. JAMA 203:61
3. Smith NJ, Rios E (1974) Iron metabolism in infancy and childhood. Adv Pediatr 21:
4. Stekel A (1984) Prevention of iron deficiency. In: Stekel A (ed) Iron nutrition in infancy and childhood. Raven Press, New York, pp 179–92
5. Schulman I (1961) Iron requirements in infancy. JAMA 175:118–120
6. Sturgeon P (1958) Studies of iron requirements in infants and children. In: Iron in clinical medicine. Wallerstein RO, Mettier SR (eds) Berkeley University of California Press, p 183
7. Cook JD, Bothwell TH (1984) Availability of iron from infant foods. In: Stekel A (ed) Iron nutrition in infancy and childhood. Raven Press, New York, pp 119–143
8. Fransson GB, Lonnerdal B (1980) Iron in human milk. J Pediatr 96:380–438
9. Picciano MF, Guthrie HA (1976) Copper, iron and zinc contents of mature human milk. Am J Clin Nutr 29:242–254
10. Vaughan LA, Weber CW, Kimberling SR (1979) Longitudinal changes in the mineral content of human milk. Am J Clin Nutr 32:2301–2306
11. Lonnerdal B (1984) Iron and breast-milk. In: Stekel A (ed) Iron nutrition in infancy and childhood. Raven Press, New York, pp 95–111
12. McMillan JA, Landaw SA, Oski FA (1976) Iron sufficiency in breast-fed infants and availability of iron from human milk. Pediatrics 58:686–691
13. Schultz J, Smith NJ (1958) A quantitative study of the absorption of food iron in infants and children. Am J Dis Child 95:109–119
14. Wilson JF, Hiner DC, Lahey ME (1972) Milk induced gastrointestinal bleeding in infants with hypochromic, microcytic anemia. Am J Dis Child 124:18–32
15. Florentino RF, Guirriec RM (1984) Prevalence of nutritional anemia in infancy and childhood with emphasis on developing countries. In: Stekel A (ed) Iron nutrition in infancy and childhood. Raven Press, New York, pp 61–72
16. Expert Scientific Working Group (1985) Summary of a report on assessment of the iron nutrition status of the United States population. Am J Clin Nutr 42:1318–1330
17. Fuerth JH (1971) Incidence of anemia in full term infants seen in private practice. J Pediatr 79:562–565
18. Sehring D. Personal communication
19. Marsh A, Long H, Steirwalt E (1959) Comparative hematological response to iron fortification of a milk formula for infants. Pediatrics 24:404–412
20. Andelman MB, Serered BR (1966) Utilization of dietary iron by term infants. A study of 1048 infants from a low socioeconomic population. Am J Dis Child 111:45–55
21. Saarinen UM (1978) Need for iron supplementation in infants on prolonged breast-feeding. J Pediatr 93:177–182
22. Gorton MK, Cross ER (1964) Iron metabolism in premature infants. II. Prevention of iron deficiency. J Pediatr 64:509
23. Cook JD, Minnick V, Moore CV, et al. (1973) Absorption of fortification iron in bread. Am J Clin Nutr 26:861–872
24. Rios E, Hunter RE, Cook JD, et al. (1975) The absorption of iron as supplements in infant cereals and infant formulas. Pediatrics 55:686
25. Rees JM, Minsen ER, Merrill JE (1985) Iron fortification of infant foods: a decade of change. Clin Pediatr 24:707–710
26. Katzman R, Novack A, Pearson HA (1972) Nutritional anemia in an inner-city community: relationship to age and ethnic group. JAMA 222:670–673
27. Vasquez-Seoane P, Windom R, Pearson HA (1985) Disappearance of iron-deficiency anemia in a high-risk infant population given supplemental iron. N Eng J Med 313:1239–1240
28. Miller V, Sevaney S, Deinard A (1985) Impact of the WIC program on the iron status of infants. Pediatrics 75:100–105
29. Hallberg L (1982) Iron nutrition and food iron fortification. Semin Hematol 19:31–41
30. Finch CA, Huebers H (1982) Perspectives in iron metabolism. New Engl J Med 306:1520–1528

31. Cartwright GE, Edwards CQ, Kravitz K, et al. (1979) Hereditary hemochromatosis. Phenotypic expression of the disease. N Engl J Med 301:175–179
32. Erlandson ME, Walden B, Stern G, et al. (1962) Studies on congenital hemolytic syndromes. IV Gastrointestinal absorption of iron. Blood 19:359–366
33. Pearson HA and Benz EJ (1984) The thalassemias. In: Miller DM (ed) Blood diseases of infancy and childhood. CV Mosby, St Louis, p 455
34. DeAlarcon D, Donovan ME (1979) Iron absorption in the thalassemia syndromes and its inhibition with tea. N Engl J Med 300:5–8
35. O'Brien RT (1978) Body iron burden in sickle cell anemia. J Pediatr 92:579–585
36. Lankford CE (1973) Bacterial assimilation of iron. Crit Rev Microbiol 2:274–287
37. Weinberg ED (1984) Iron withholding: a defense against infection and neoplasia. Physiol Rev 64:65–102
38. Barry DMJ, Reeve AW (1977) Increased instance of gram negative neonatal sepsis with intramuscular iron administration. Pediatrics 60:908–912
39. Burman D (1972) Hemoglobin levels in normal infants aged 3–24 months and the effect of iron. Arch Dis Child 47:261–267
40. Shaw R, Robertson WO (1963) Anemia among hospitalized infants. Ohio Med J 60:45–52
41. Melhorn DK, Gross S (1971) Vitamin E dependent anemia in the premature infant. J Pediatr 79:569–580
42. Williams ME, Shott RJ, O'Neal PL, Oski FA (1975) Role of dietary iron and fat on vitamin E deficiency of infancy. N Engl J Med 292:887–891

Commentary

Lozoff and Felt: This chapter provides a useful review of iron physiology in infancy and a convincing demonstration of the need for supplemental iron in the infant diet. Two important questions are raised by this paper: (1) Why would a condition that has deleterious effects be so widespread in human populations? (2) What are the special problems of preventing iron-deficiency anemia among infants in developing countries?

The question of why a deleterious condition would be widespread in human populations arises from an evolutionary perspective, since one generally assumes that a diet adequate for a given species has evolved. There are at least three ways in which the widespread nature of iron deficiency could be compatible with this perspective: (a) if iron deficiency is a relatively recent condition, (b) if the ill effects of iron deficiency are transient, or (c) if there are benefits that compensate for the deleterious effects.

There has been some speculation on each of these points. With regard to the possibly recent arrival of iron deficiency, both archeologic studies and research with contemporary hunters and gatherers indicate that hunter-gatherers had less iron-deficiency anemia than agricultural populations [1]. With the advent of agriculture about 10 000 years ago, human diets became heavily dependent on single cereals or grains. With this dependency, it is likely that iron deficiency became more widespread. With respect to the possibility that the ill effects of iron deficiency are either transient or not very important, one could say that the cognitive and affective alterations implicated so far might not limit function in subsistence economies without dependence on education or the kind of academic achievement that is currently more important. Certainly the ill effects described in children are unlikely to interfere with later reproductive function, even though severe iron deficiency during pregnancy is associated with adverse fetal outcome [2]. However, any limitations in activity or energy are likely to be functionally important in subsistence economies that require hard physical labor. With respect to a possible benefit of iron deficiency that might counterbalance deleterious effects, the most likely candidate is serious infection. Although disputed, some workers have noted that certain diseases, such as malaria, get worse after iron treatment, especially if given parenterally [3,4]. One could imagine a potential benefit of iron deficiency prior to the advent of effective therapeutic agents. If this were the case, then iron-deficiency anemia might have served a protective function similar to that of the hemoglobinopathies with regard to malaria. What is the current status of such speculations?

The second important issue raised by this paper relates to the challenge of preventing iron-deficiency anemia in developing countries. The story of the use of iron-fortified formulas and cereals in the US dramatically demonstrates that infant iron deficiency can be prevented. However, there are serious and well-known difficulties in implementing these solutions in developing countries. The use of iron-fortification of cereals is also, perhaps, problematic partly because their efficacy in preventing iron deficiency is less well-established and partly because there may be some logistic difficulties in finding ways to fortify cereals that can withstand heat and humidity without discoloration or spoilage of the food. Because iron deficiency is such a problem in developing countries where these constraints apply, we may still have a long way to go before we have identified effective ways of preventing the problem in the populations that are most at risk.

References

1. Eaten SB, Konner M (1985) Paleolithic nutrition: a consideration of its nature and current implications. N Eng J Med 312:283–289
2. Murphy JF, O'Riorden J, Newcombe RG, Coles EC, Pearson JF (1986) Relation of haemoglobin levels in first and second trimesters to outcome of pregnancy. Lancet i:992–994
3. Pollack S (1983) Annotation: malaria and iron. Brit J Haematol 53:181–183
4. Oppenheimer SJ, Macfarlane SBJ, Moody JB, Bunari O, Hendrickse RG (1986) Effect of iron prophylaxis on morbidity due to infectious disease: report on clinical studies on Papua New Guinea. Trans R Soc Trop Med Hyg 89:596–602

Author's reply: The putative protective effects of iron deficiency on various infections are far from clear.

The static effects of various body fluids on microbial growth are acknowledged. However, extrapolation of the principle to clinical disease is tenuous.

Delayed hypersensitivity is blunted in iron deficiency. The "reactivation" of tuberculosis and malaria when malnourished individuals receive nutritional rehabilitation, including iron, may more reflect a host response than an effect on the infectious process.

The case of a protective effect of hemoglobinopathies is strong, based upon in vivo, in vitro and epidemiologic evidence. This is not the case with iron deficiency and malaria.

Larkin and Rao: The author makes a strong case for mild iron fortification of infant foods. The enormous morbidity and mortality in infants with iron deficiency weighs against any potential adverse affects of iron overloading. In addition, efficacious chelator therapy is now available which can obviate even a slight increase in iron load.

When considering the possible adverse effects of iron fortification of infant foods, while it is improbable that the amounts of fortified iron mentioned could result in long-term problems in normal children and infants, with regard to hemochromatosis, two things are worth noting:

1. Studies with HLA typing show a higher incidence of this disease than previously thought [1,2,3].

2. The amount of total iron in the body is less important than the amount in parenchymal cells. "For example, the patient with HLA-related disease and selective parenchymal loading may have cardiac failure with 0.2 mg to 0.4 mg of iron per kilogram, the patient with thalassemia with combined macrophage, parenchymal loading is considered to be in jeopardy with about 1 mg per kilogram, and the patient with pure erythrocyte aplasia and predominantly macrophage loading may have 2 mg per kilogram" [4].

In the section on iron and host resistance, the author notes the prevalence of iron deficiency in Asia and Latin America. In view of the controversy surrounding iron and susceptibility to infectious disease, some information concerning iron's effects on malaria and trypanosomiasis might be in order if that information is available [5].

References

1. Bassett ML, Halliday JW, Powell LW (1984) Genetic hemochromatosis. Semin Liver Dis 4:217–227
2. Beaumont C, Simon M, Fauchet R, et al. (1979) Serum ferritin as a possible marker of the hemochromatosis allele. N Engl J Med 301:169–174
3. Dadone MM, Kushner JP, Edwards C, et al. (1982) Hereditary hemochromatosis. Analysis of laboratory expression of the disease by genotype in 18 pedigrees. Am J Clin Pathol 78:196–207
4. Finch CA, Huebers H (1982) Perspectives in iron metabolism. N Engl J Med 306:1520–1528
5. Hegenauer J, Saltman P (1985) Iron and susceptibility to infectious disease. Science 188:1038–1039

Smart: I would have been grateful for Pearson's definition of iron-deficiency anaemia. He could either give his own definition or refer to that in the paper by Parks and Wharton. I should also be interested to know how such definitions (labels) are arrived at; perhaps through centuries of clinical practice?

The issue of "bioavailability" is mentioned in several places. This is obviously a topic of crucial importance and deserves further discussion.

Author's reply: Absorption of iron: bioavailability of food iron. In the average diet of the American adult there are approximately 6–7 mg iron per 1000 k cal (4200 kJ) of food that is consumed. However, only a small proportion of this dietary iron is absorbed.

Dietary iron occurs in two general chemical forms: (1) Heme iron, predominantly from animal proteins, is relatively well absorbed (20%–40%). Its absorption is largely unaffected by other constituents of the diet. (2) Non-heme (ionic) iron, by contrast, is relatively poorly absorbed and in the usual diet it is the preponderant form of iron. Its poor absorption is related to other dietary constituents, such as phytates and phosphates. Absorption of the iron in grain and vegetables is 5% or less. However, the low absorption can be enhanced by ascorbic acid, perhaps because this maintains ionic iron in the reduced (divalent) form.

A number of factors affect the absorption of dietary iron. Some of them might be designated as "extrinsic". These include the form of iron presented to the intestine (heme vs. non-heme), the amount of iron (larger amounts are proportionally less absorbed), the presence of dietary enhancers of absorption (ascorbic acid), and inhibitors (phosphates). In the individual, host factors also modulate iron absorption, either increasing (anemia, increased erythropoiesis, decreased body stores), or decreasing it (polycythemia, pancreatic enzymes, etc.).

The bioavailability of iron in a specific food was originally measured by biosynthetically incorporating radio-iron into specific foods. However, valid studies of bioavailability can be realized by merely adding radio-heme or ionic iron to foods.

Walter: A historical control is of no value in attributing improvement of iron status to WIC. Many other iron sources may have become available, or other causes of anaemia may have decreased. Lead poisoning is a plausible example of the latter. See Chapter 2.

On the other hand, decrease of haemoglobin under a certain level is a poor means of demonstrating improvement of iron status in a community.

The citation of the totally untenable work of Barry and Reeve (Pearson's ref. 38) is rightly cautious, in the hope that new studies may disprove (or confirm) this association. Thus far, in 2-month-old infants Oppenheimer in Papua New Guinea has not shown immediate untoward effects. There are also Finnish and American investigators that have given intramuscular iron-dextran to newborns without consequences to immediate health.

Parks: The WIC Program suggests that iron fortification of infant foods reduces the prevalence of anaemia. Are the two groups of children (1971 and 1984) really comparable? Surely there will have been many changes in basic diet and environment over these 13 years.

Subject Index